THE PAINTER RAs

THE PAINTER RAs

A guide to the painter members of the Royal Academy of Arts with examples of their work

Dennis Toff

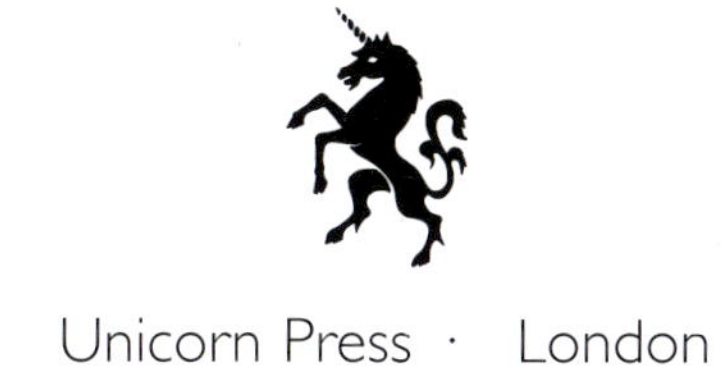

Unicorn Press · London

Unicorn Press
76 Great Suffolk Street
London
SE1 0BL

email: unicornpress@btinternet.com
www.unicornpress.org

First published by Unicorn Press 2008

ISBN 978 1 906509 00 2

Designed by Karen Wilks
Printed by Saxon Print Group, Norwich

Front cover: Philip Sutton RA in his studio

to Jacqueline for her patience and help

A photograph is a meeting place where the interests of the photographer, the photographed, the viewer and those who are using photographs are often contradictory.
John Berger

In making a portrait the photographer must forge a harmony between the aspirations of the sitter, who wishes to look his or her 'best', and the expectations of the viewer who seeks the 'identity' of the subject.
Dennis Toff

What started as a personal project, photographing a few artists whose work I admire, developed into a major undertaking when I realised that no single painting or series of images had been produced which attempted to include all of a current membership or group of Painter RAs since George Dance's drawings of 1793.

The public, 150,000 of whom visit the Summer Exhibition at Burlington House each year, tend to know about only a few of the Painter Members whose works they view and admire. Together with their colleague Sculptor and Architect Members and the permanent staff, the holders of this honour are responsible for managing this unique, independent and non-publically funded Gallery and School and guiding it into the future.

Currently there are 116 Royal Academicians of whom 39 are Senior and of the rest 40 are Painters, 22 Sculptors and 15 Architects. I attempted to photograph all 63 of the Painters (including Seniors) but perhaps inevitably there were a few who could not be included. My sincere thanks to the 58 who are represented here, not only for allowing me into their studios and making their time available but also, for their warm, friendly participation and help. They have made my efforts both enjoyable and educational.

My thanks also to the staff of the Academy, in particular, Tessa Abineri, Assistant to the President, and Nick Savage and his Collections Department without whose help contact with many of the Members would have been difficult if not impossible.

Dennis Toff
April 2008

The Royal Academy of Arts was founded in 1768 by a group of leading artists under the patronage of George III with 40 Members and 20 Associates very much in control of their own destiny and receiving no State funds.The Academy was first housed in Pall Mall, then moved to Somerset House and later shared premises with the National Gallery in Trafalgar Square before moving to Burlington House in 1867. The first President, Sir Joshua Reynolds, established it as a school to train artists in drawing, painting, sculpture and architecture and as a public institution to represent the interests of artists.

• Academicians are nominated and elected by existing Royal Academicians into one of the original categories of membership ie, painters, sculptors, architects and printmakers. All elected members are invited to donate a representative work to the Academy's Collection.

• There are 80 RAs (excluding Seniors) of whom there must be at least 14 Sculptors, 12 Architects and 8 Printmakers. Vacancies arise ether on the death of an RA or as they reach the age of 75 and become Senior Academicians. Although there are currently now 20 women RAs, when Laura Knight was elected in 1936, she was the first since the original 2 foundation members, Angelica Kauffman and Mary Moser.

• The Academy is self-governing with the President re-elected each year, usually unopposed, though unable to serve for more than 10 consecutive years. The Schools are the responsibility of the Keeper, who serves for 3 years.

• The Treasurer is elected for 5 years. The Council comprises the President and 13 other RAs, all members being eligible to sit for 2 to 4 years by rotation. The varying activities of the Academy come under a variety of Committees of Members aided by Senior members of the RA staff.

• The establishment of the Royal Academy gave its members the opportunity to exhibit and sell their work at the Summer Exhibition. Each Member can submit 6 works and members of the public also submit work from which a selection is made by Council Members. Approximately 9,000 works are submitted each year from which about 1,200 are chosen.

• In 2008 The Royal Academy will become a Company Limited by Guarantee so that its Directors – the RAs – are no longer personally liable for any potential losses. As a consequence, Council Members are now Directors of the RA and Trustees of the RA as a charity. In order to conform to charity law regulations, they now need to be more accountable and transparent in their actions and must take notice of outside advice.

NORMAN ACKROYD CBE RA

Treshnish Islands – Hebrides
Etching
Courtesy of the artist
56 x 46 cm

Born 26th March 1938
Leeds, Yorkshire

Norman Ackroyd studied at Leeds College of Art 1956-61 and the Royal College of Art 1961-64 and was made Senior Fellow of the College in 2000. From 1965-93 he taught Printmaking at the Central College of Art and Design and Central St Martins and was made CBE in 2007. Norman Ackroyd is one of Britain's best known contemporary printmakers. His work includes etching, monotype, watercolour and oil. His work is seen in a large number of commissions in public and commercial spaces and the books that he publishes at regular intervals.

To aid him in representing the mood and shifting light of the British landscape, to which he is dedicated, he has developed a method of working on his plates directly, painting the acid as if it were watercolour, giving him the freedom to take his inks, plates and acid treatments to sometimes remote locations. Lately these have focused on the islands of the West Coast of Ireland but also include his fascination with the material evidence of the remains and legends of the early Christian Saints and the images left by the eroding coastline and its wildlife.

Norman Ackroyd lives and works in London.
www.normanackroyd.com

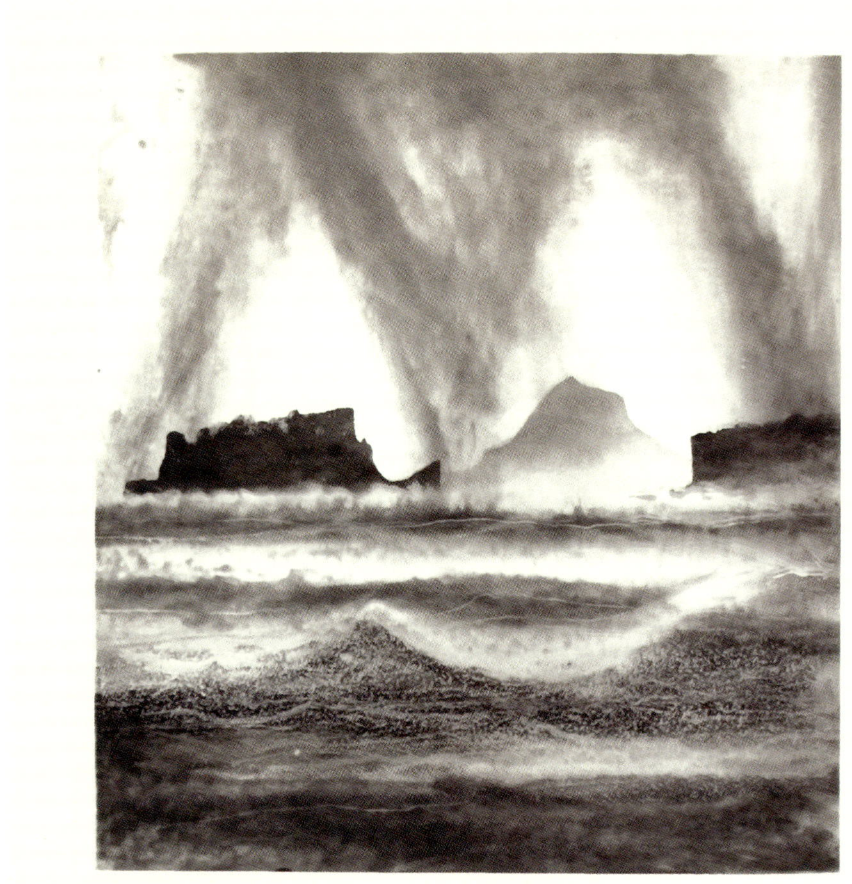

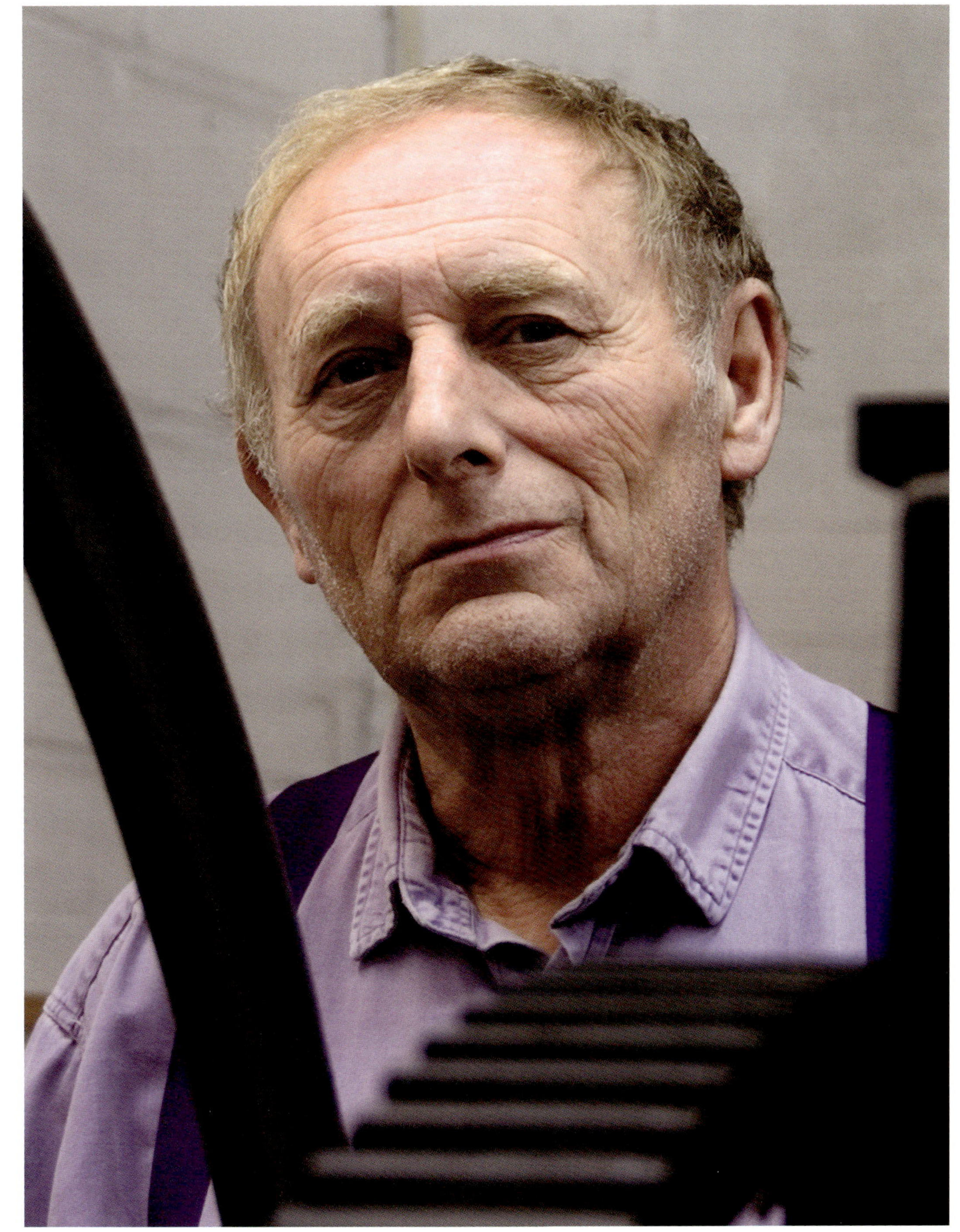

DIANA ARMFIELD RA

Elected ARA 1st June 1989
Elected RA 26th June 1991

Geraniums on the Easel
Oil on panel
Courtesy of Browse & Darby
35 x 20 cm

Born 11th June 1920
Ringwood, Hampshire

Diana Armfield studied at the Slade School of Fine Art and the Central School of Arts & Crafts. She taught for many years at Byam Shaw School of Art and was Artist in Residence at Claremont Art School, Perth, Australia in 1985 and Jackson, Wyoming, USA in 1989. Diana believes that by painting what she enjoys experiencing, she is able to transmit and share with others the lasting importance and beauty of her chosen subject matter.

Diana is married to Bernard Dunstan RA; they are the only husband/wife painters in the current RA membership and have been described as 'quintessentially English artists'. When recently asked how they have survived as a creative couple Diana replied *'You can't be married to someone for over 50 years and compete with each other'*. In addition to their very apparent closeness, their secret may be that they do try not to tread on each other's toes.

Diana Armfield and Bernard Dunstan live and work in London and Wales and make painting trips abroad.

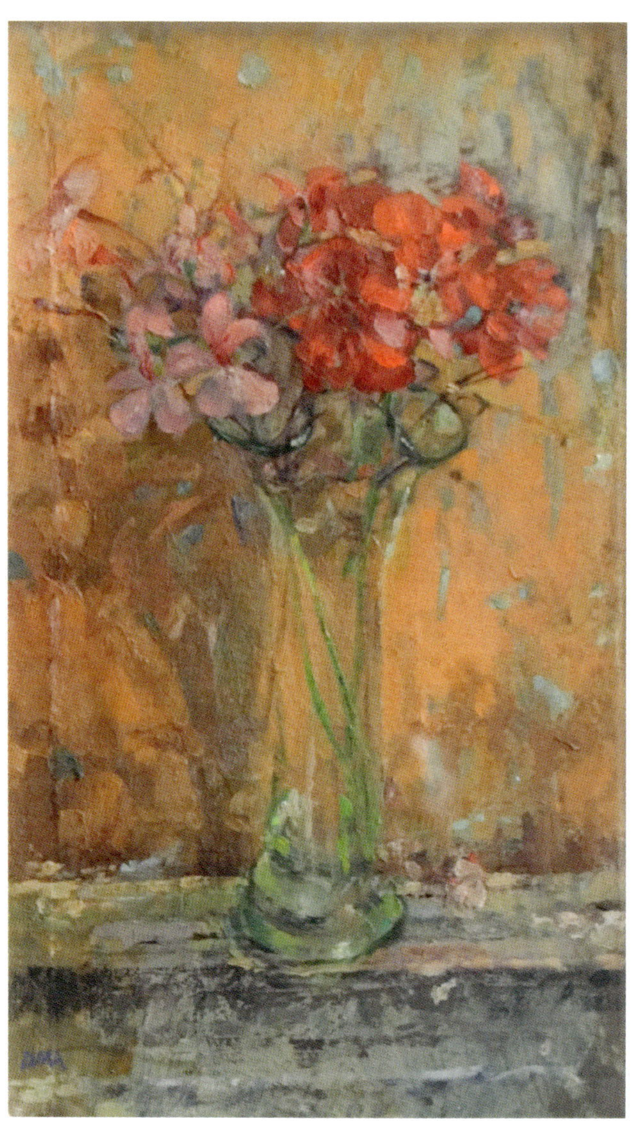

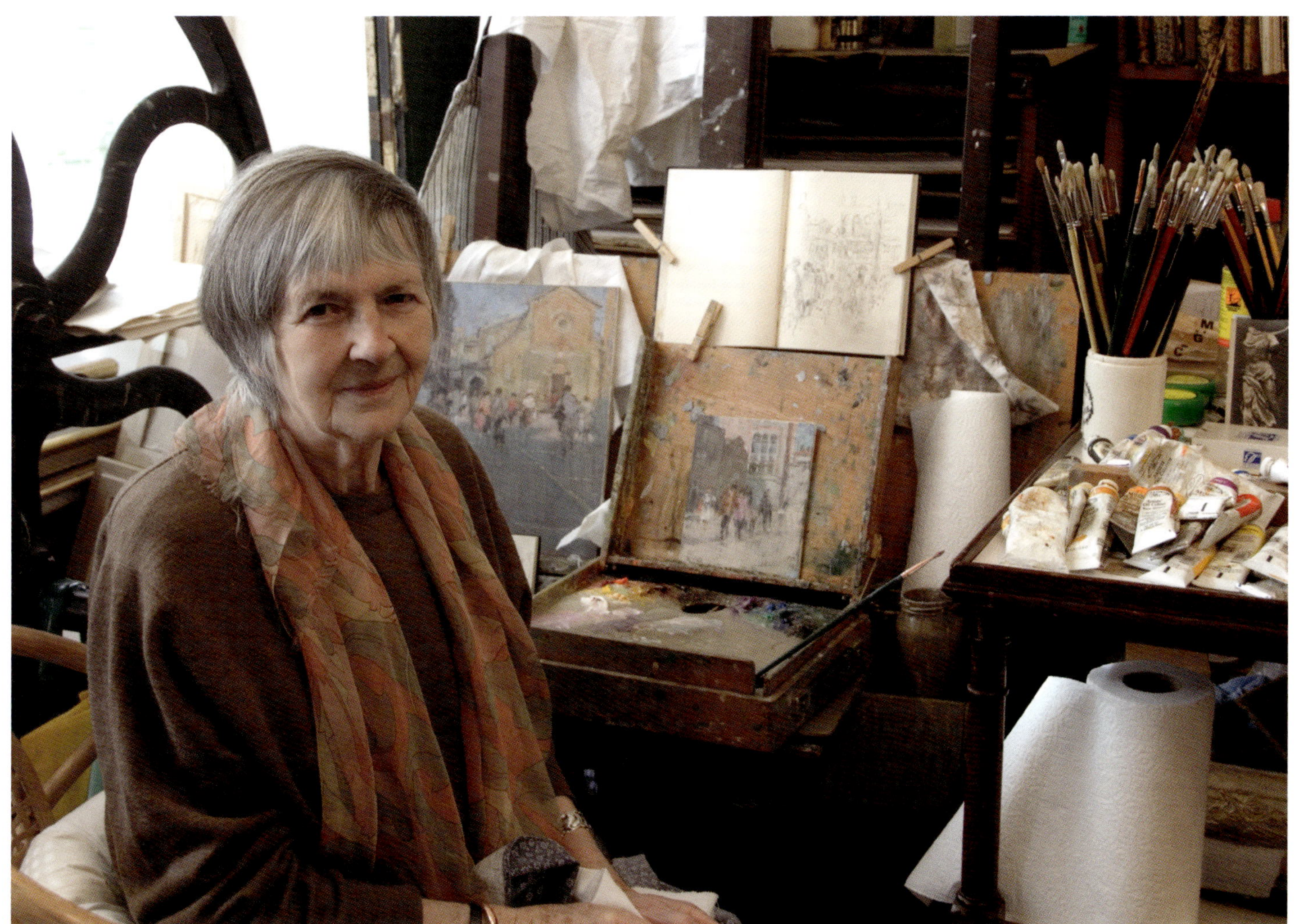

DIANA ARMFIELD RA

GILLIAN AYRES OBE RA

Elected ARA 5th May 1982
Elected RA 29th May 1991

Heliogoland II 2005
Oil on canvas
Courtesy of the artsist
198 x 305 cm

Born 3rd February 1930
London

Gillian Ayres studied at Camberwell School of Art 1946-50 and went on to teach at Bath Academy of Art, Corsham until 1965 after which she taught at St Martin's School of Art 1965-78 before becoming Head of Painting at Winchester School of Art until 1981.

She was awarded an OBE in 1986, made an Honorary Doctor of English Literature by London University in 1994, Senior Fellow of the Royal College of Art 1996, received a Sargent Fellowship from the British School in Rome in 1997 and was made Honorary Fellow by London's University of the Arts in 2005.

Gillian Ayres lives and works in Cornwall.

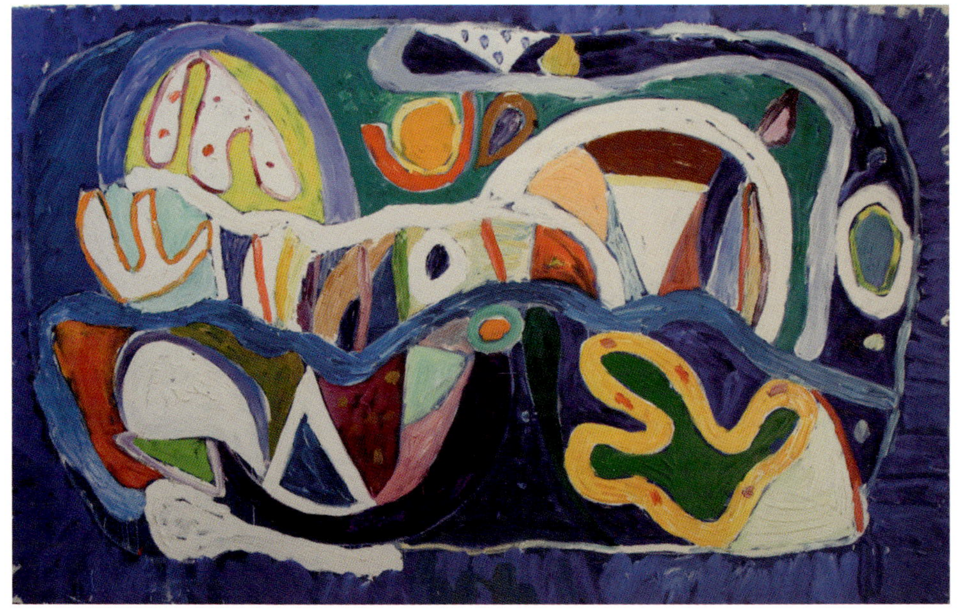

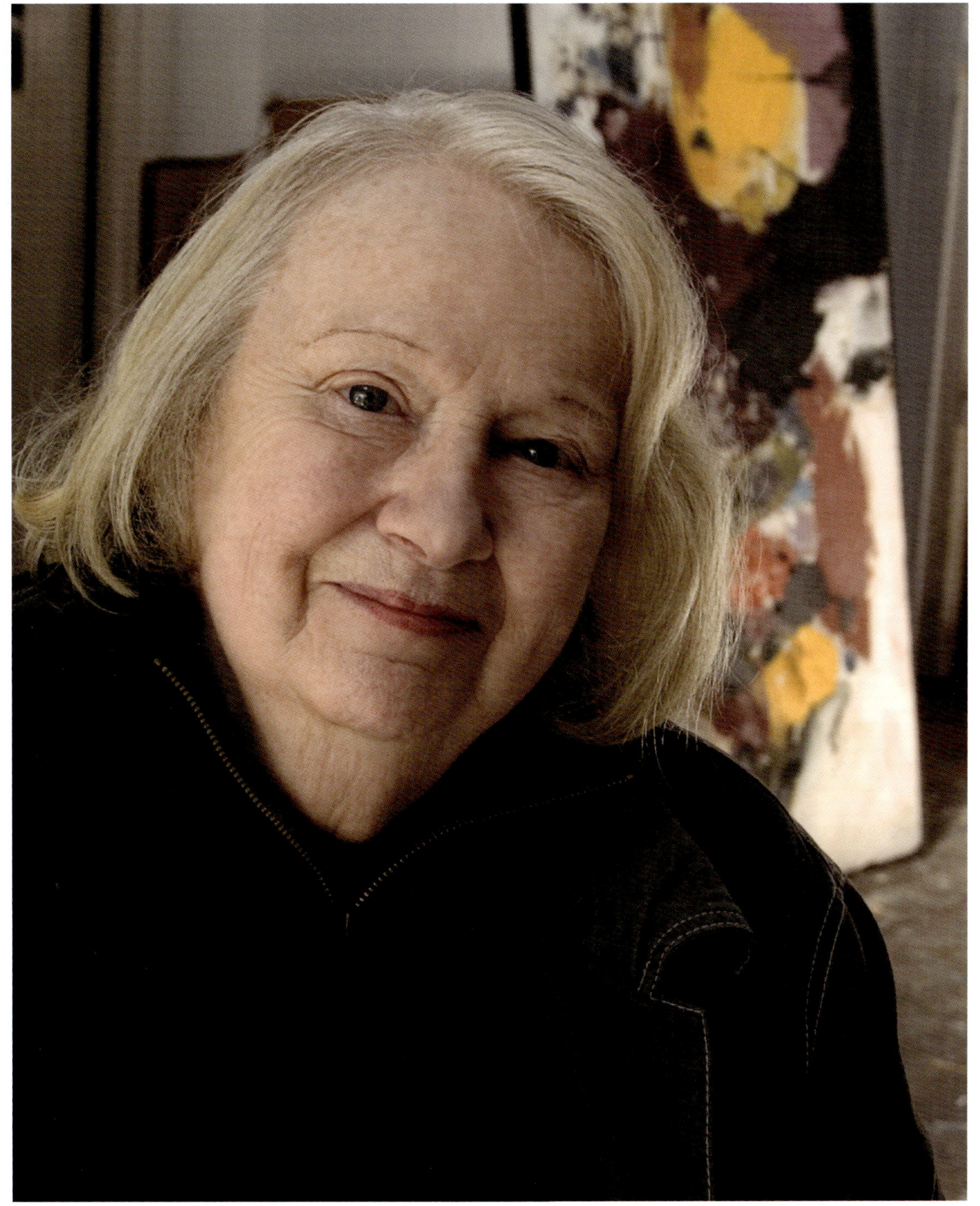

GILLIAN AYRES OBE RA

BASIL BEATTIE RA

Elected RA 7th June 2006

Rendezvous I
Oil on canvas
Courtesy of the artist
51 x 81 cm

Born 9th January 1935
West Hartlepool

Basil Beattie studied at the West Hartlepool College of Art and the Royal Academy Schools. He taught at Goldsmiths College in London until 1998 and is now Emeritus Reader in Painting.

His work has been exhibited widely throughout Britain and abroad and is in many public collections including Tate and the Arts Council.

Basil Beattie lives and works in London

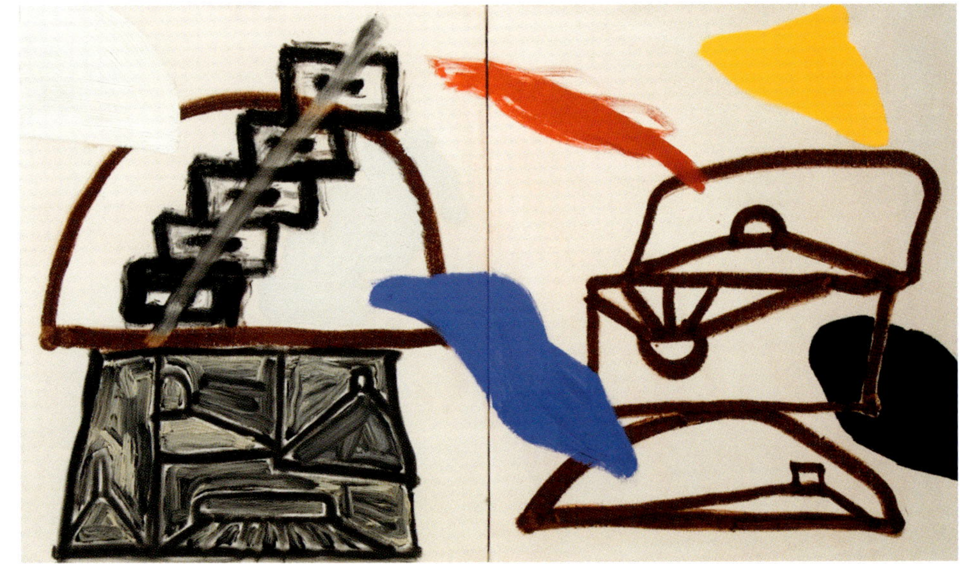

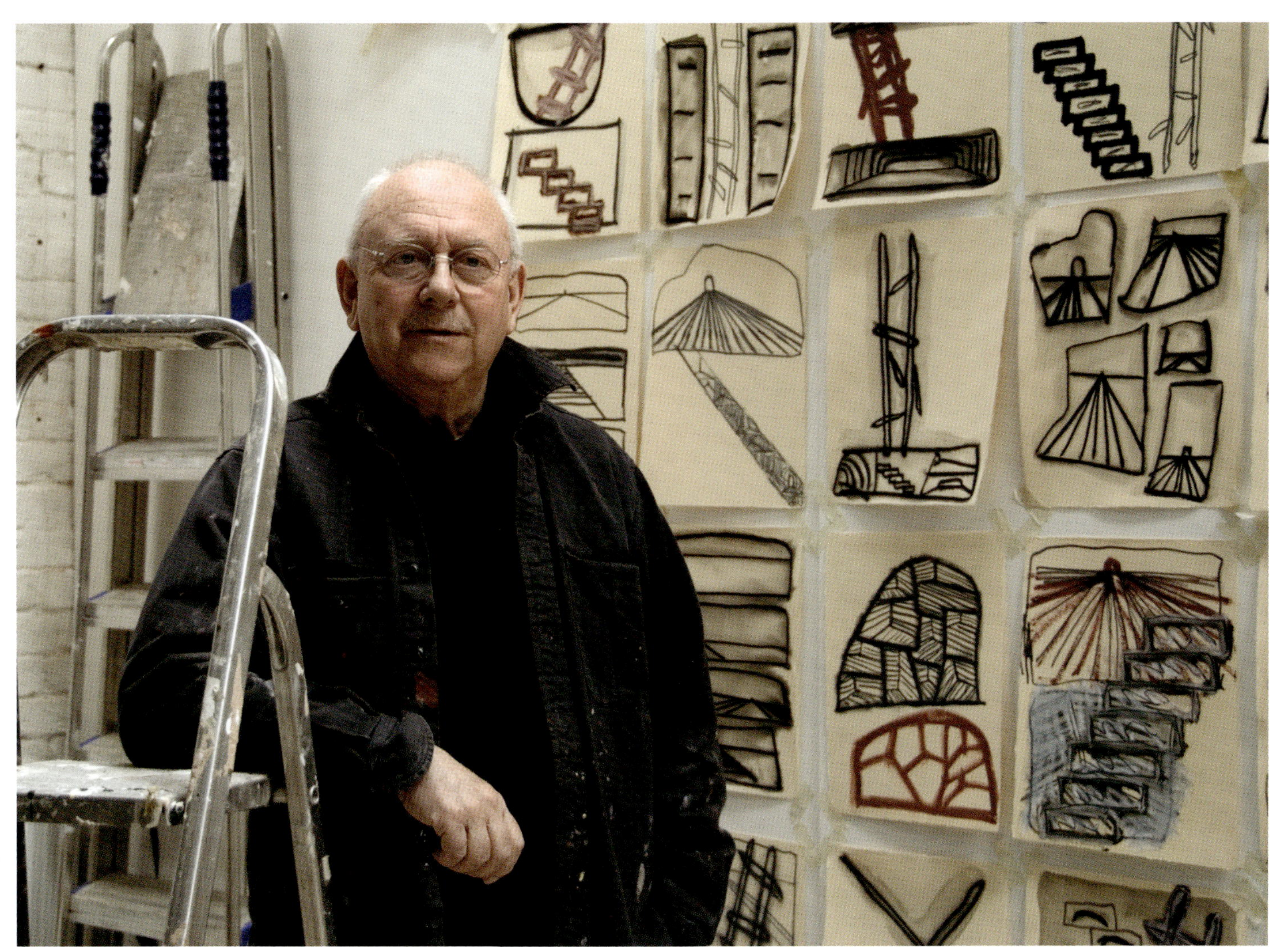

BASIL BEATTIE RA

JOHN BELLANY CBE RA

Elected ARA 20th November 1986
Elected RA 26th June 1991

The Three Sisters
Oil on canvas
Courtesy of the artist
173 x 153 cm

Born 18th June 1942
Port Seton, Scotland

Studied at Edinburgh College of Art from 1960-65 when he won scholarships taking him to Paris, Holland and Belgium. Studied at the Royal College of Art from 1965-68. Lecturer in Painting at Winchester College of Art from 1968-73, he was then lecturer at the Royal College of Art and at Goldsmiths College of Art 1978-84 and Artist in Residence at Victoria College of the Arts in Melbourne 1983. He was elected Fellow of Trinity Hall, Cambridge in 1988 and made CBE in 1994, receiving an Honorary Doctorate from Heriot Watt University in 1998. Made an Honorary Member of the Royal Scottish Academy in 1986 he became a Senior Fellow of the Royal College of Art in 1998 and Fellow of Edinburgh College of Art in 2005.

John Bellany's paintings depict the harsh lives of the Scottish fishing community from which he comes. His work contains allegories and enigmas to do with religious domination, sacred and profane love and hate and the tranquillity and storms of life.
He is represented in the collections of Tate, The Scottish National Galleries, The British Museum, The Metropolitan Museum, New York, National Gallery, Melbourne, Australia and the Fitzwilliam Museum, Cambridge.

John Bellany lives and works in Cambridge, Edinburgh and Barga (Italy).

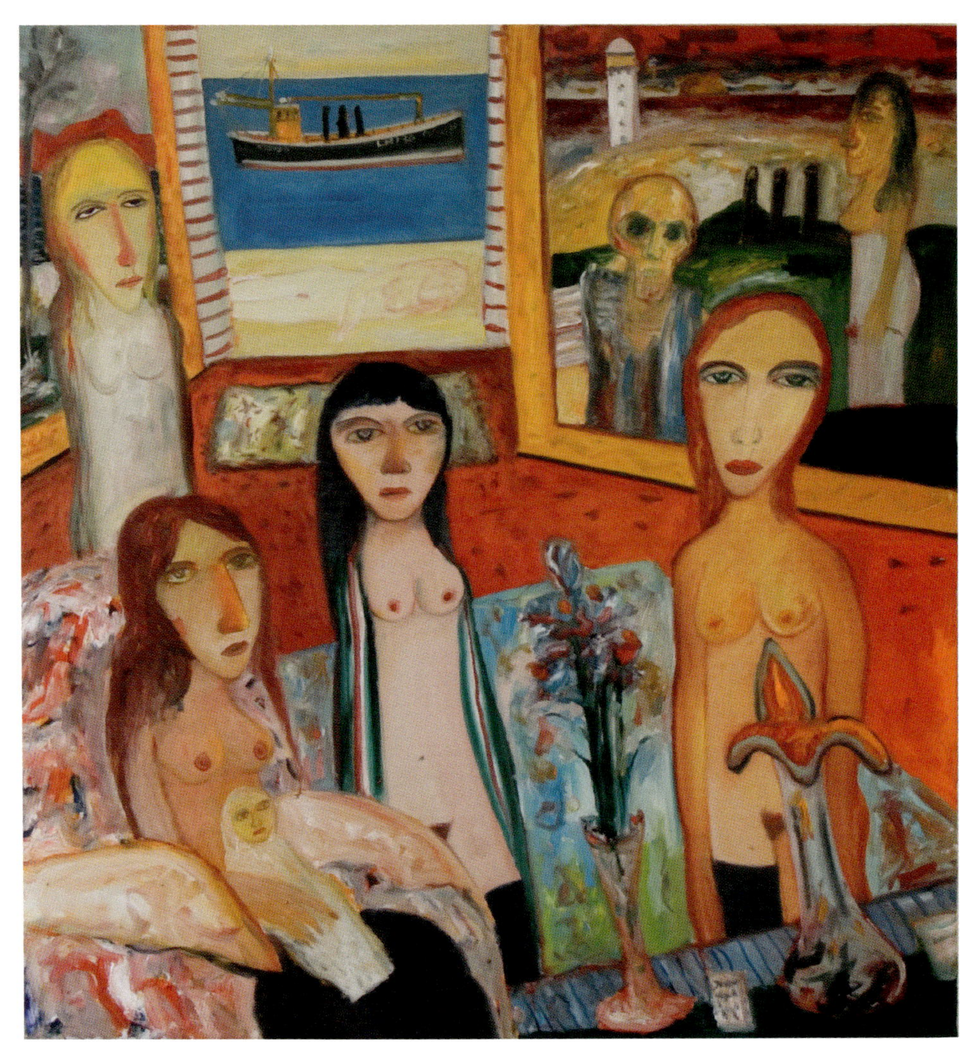

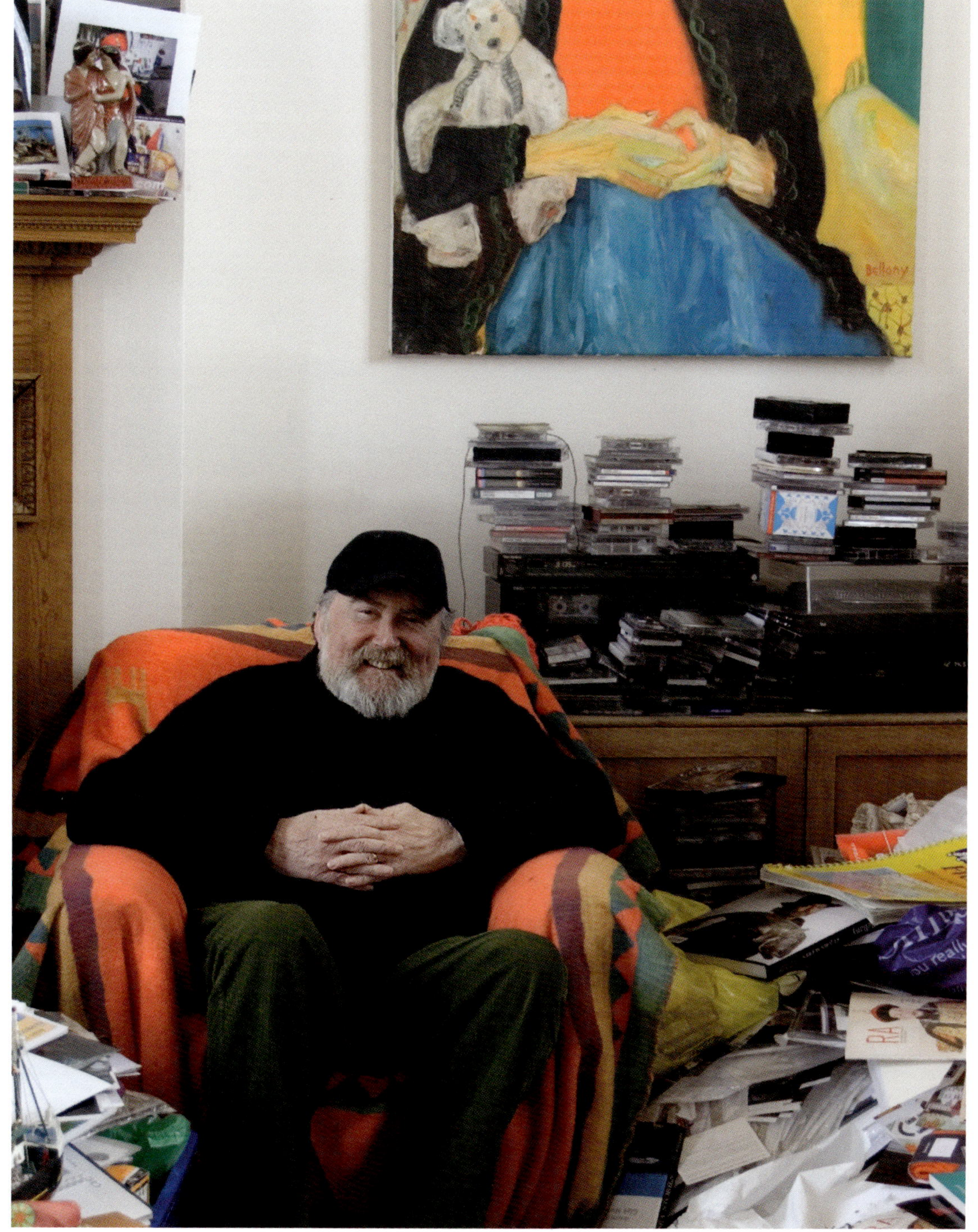

ADRIAN BERG RA

Elected RA 29th June 1992

Stourhead 16th August
Oil on canvas
Courtesy of the artist
102 x 142 cm

Born 12th March 1929
London

Adrian Berg studied Medicine then English at Cambridge University 1949-52 and obtained a Higher Diploma in Education at Trinity College, Dublin before teaching and then studying at St Martin's, Chelsea School of Art and the Royal College of Art from 1955-61. He returned to the Royal College of Art as Senior Tutor from 1987 to 1988.

Adrian Berg is a landscape painter, using a rich palette of colour. He is represented in most major British collections and lives and works in Brighton.

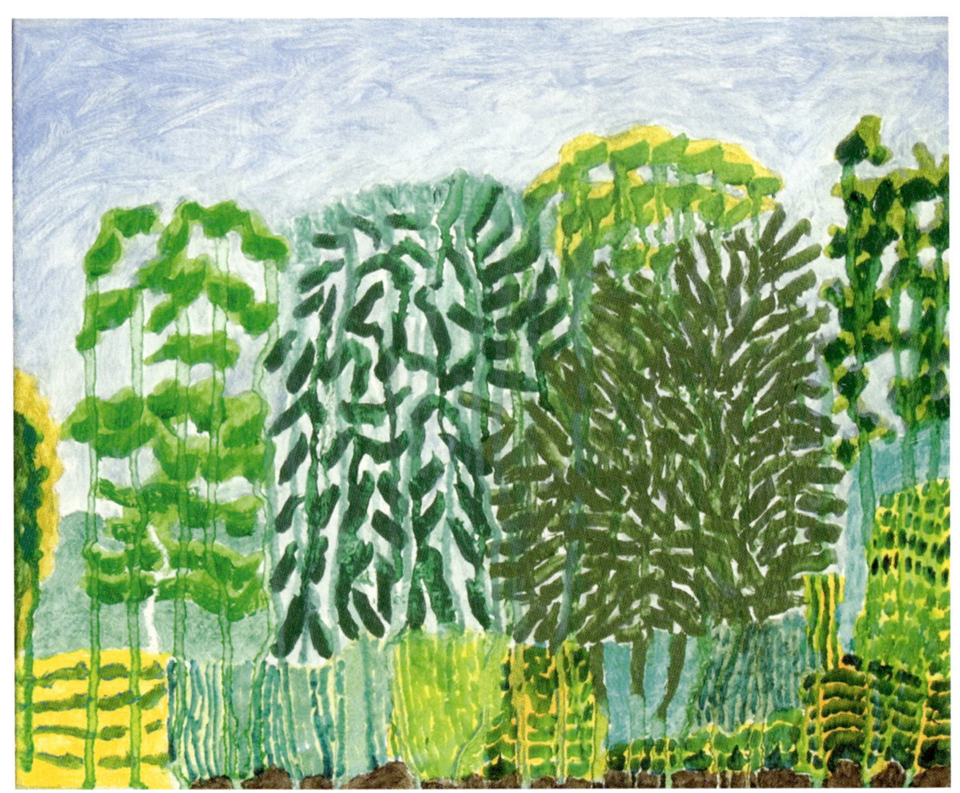

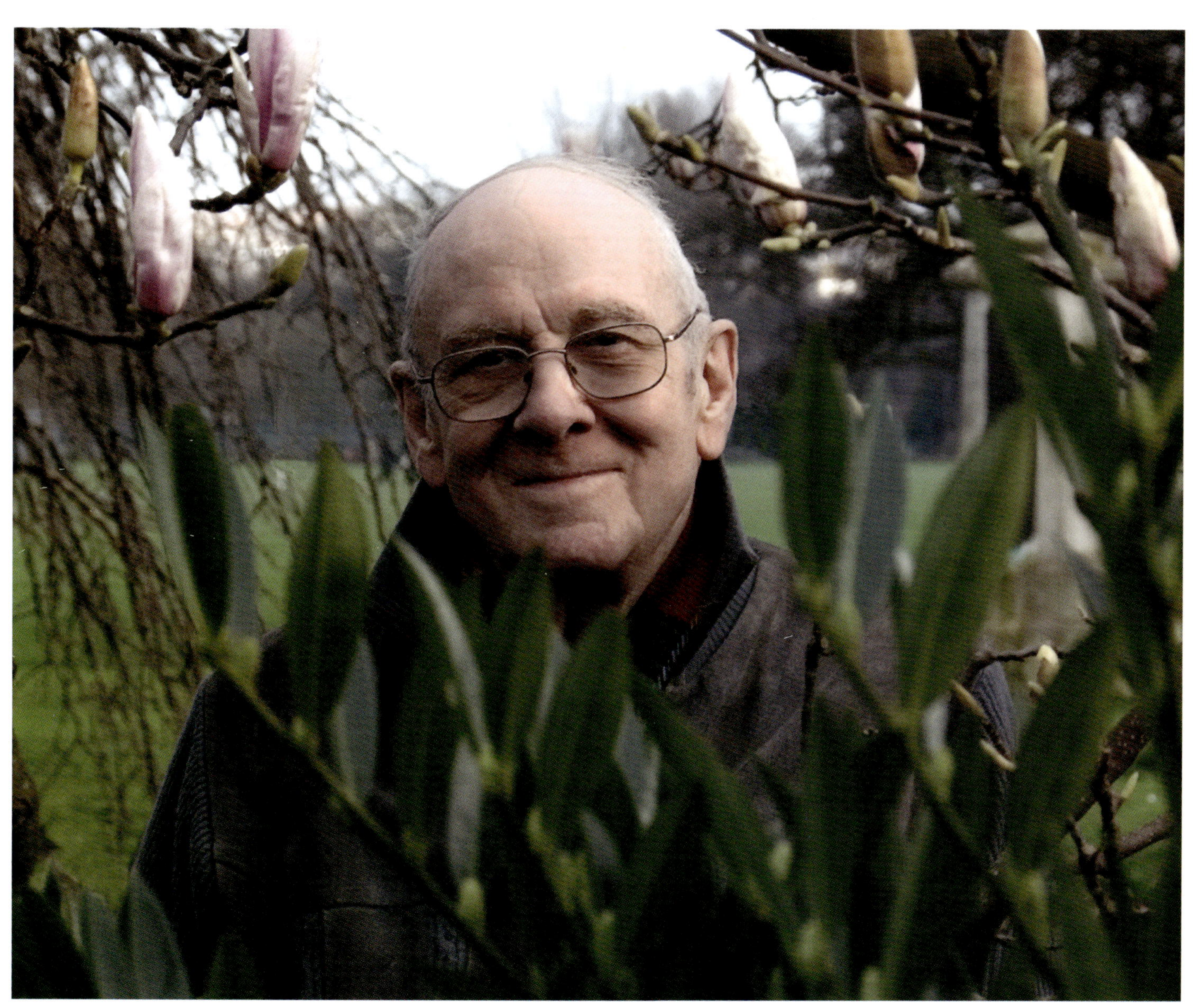

ADRIAN BERG RA

TONY BEVAN RA

Head and Neck 2007
Acrylic on canvas
Courtesy of the artist
90 x 74 cm

Born 22nd July 1951

Tony Bevan studied at Bradford School of Art from 1968-71,then at Goldsmiths College, 1971-74, and the Slade School of Fine Art from 1974-76 since when he has had numerous exhibitions in Europe and the USA. A major retrospective of his paintings was held at IVAM, Valencia, in 2005.

In his well-lit but windowless studio in Deptford he immerses himself in a world of his imagination that is the source of the energy and imagery of his bold representational paintings. Working on the floor on unstretched canvases, he places himself physically inside the spaces mapped out on their surfaces. The raw pigment and charcoal are manipulated by his hand with ferocious attack. Faces and abstracted heads are among the most arresting of his signature motifs. Architectural forms also figure prominently, their plunging perspectives adding to the anxiety that gives the paintings a sometimes frightening power. He uses a palette of black, ultramine blue or blood red and embeds within the surface of the paint the shards of charcoal with which he has drawn out the motifs 'working into an area of the invisible, into this pictorial space that you can only bring about through painting.'

Tony Bevan lives and works in London
www.tonybevan.com

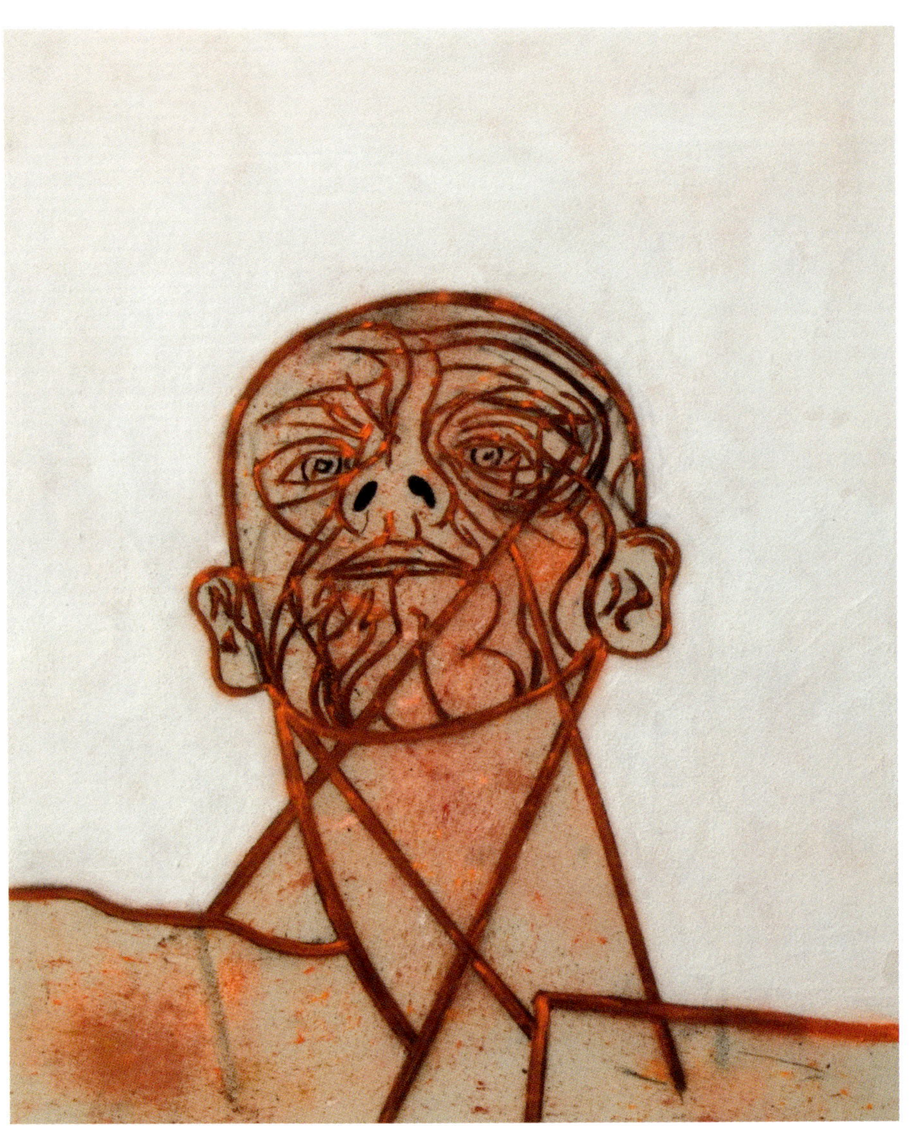

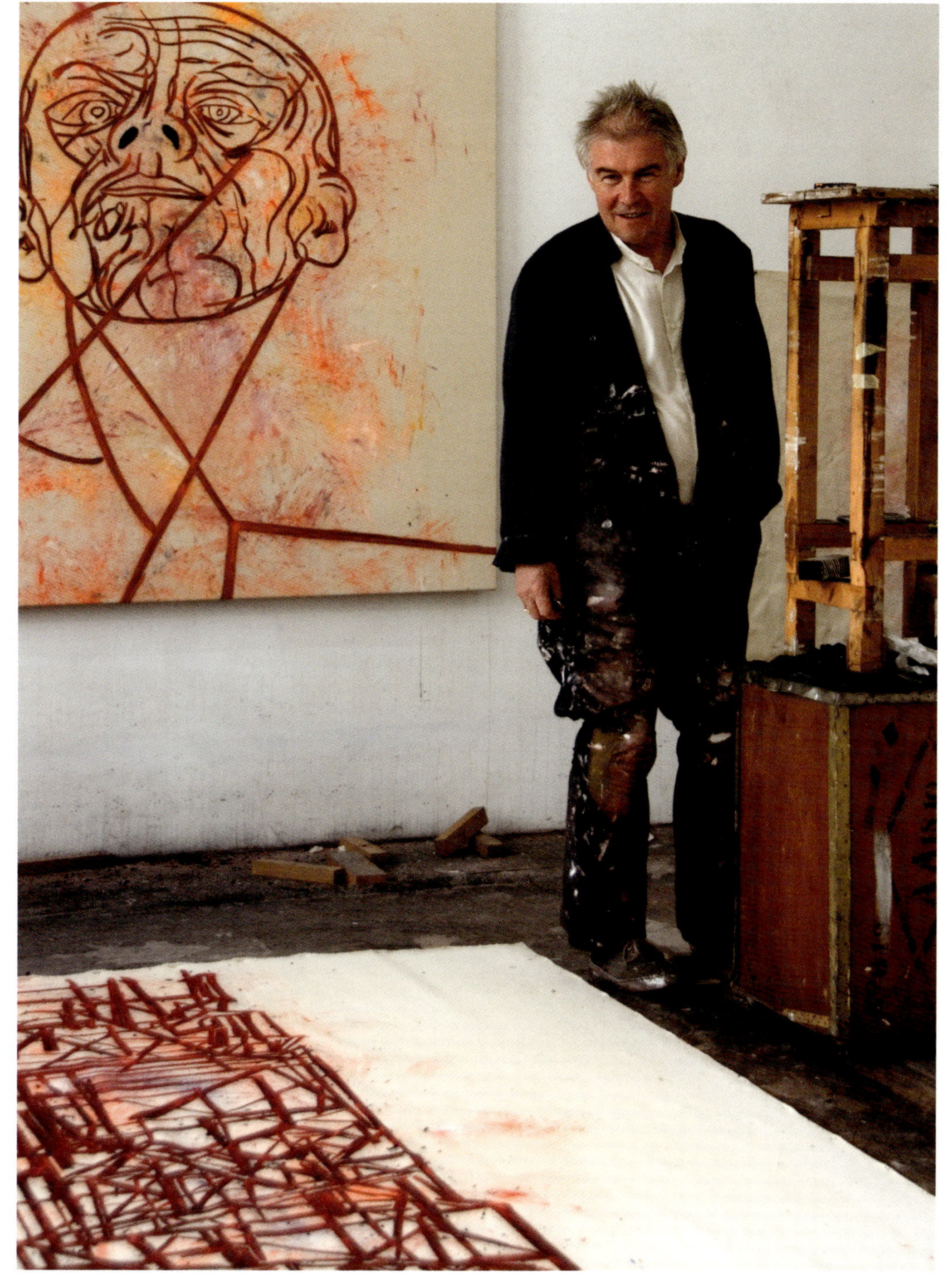

TONY BEVAN RA

ELIZABETH BLACKADDER DBE RA RSA

Elected ARA 22nd April 1971
Elected RA 29th April 1976

Irises
Watercolour on paper
Courtesy of the artist
57 x 79 cm

Born 24th September 1931
Falkirk

Elizabeth Blackadder studied at Edinburgh University and Edinburgh College of Art from 1949-54 when she received her MA Hons Fine Art. In 1954 she was also awarded a Carnegie Travelling Scholarship by the Royal Scottish Academy which took her to Southern Europe. She also received an Andrew Grant Post Graduate Scholarship and then spent 9 months in Italy. She lectured in Drawing and Painting at Edinburgh College of Art from 1962-86 and was awarded OBE in 1982 and made DBE in 2003. Elected Member of the Royal Scottish Academy in 1972, Member of the Royal Glasgow Institute of Fine Art in 1983. She is an Honorary Member of the Royal West of England Academy, the Royal Watercolour Society and the Royal Society of Painter-Printmakers and an Honorary Fellow of the Royal Incorporation of Architects in Scotland and the Royal Society of Edinburgh. She was the first woman to be elected to both the Royal Scottish Academy and the Royal Academy, and in 2001 was appointed Her Majesty's Painter and Limner in Scotland. She has experimented in all types of media through which she depicts landscapes, animals and flowers in her works.

Elizabeth Blackadder lives and works in Edinburgh.

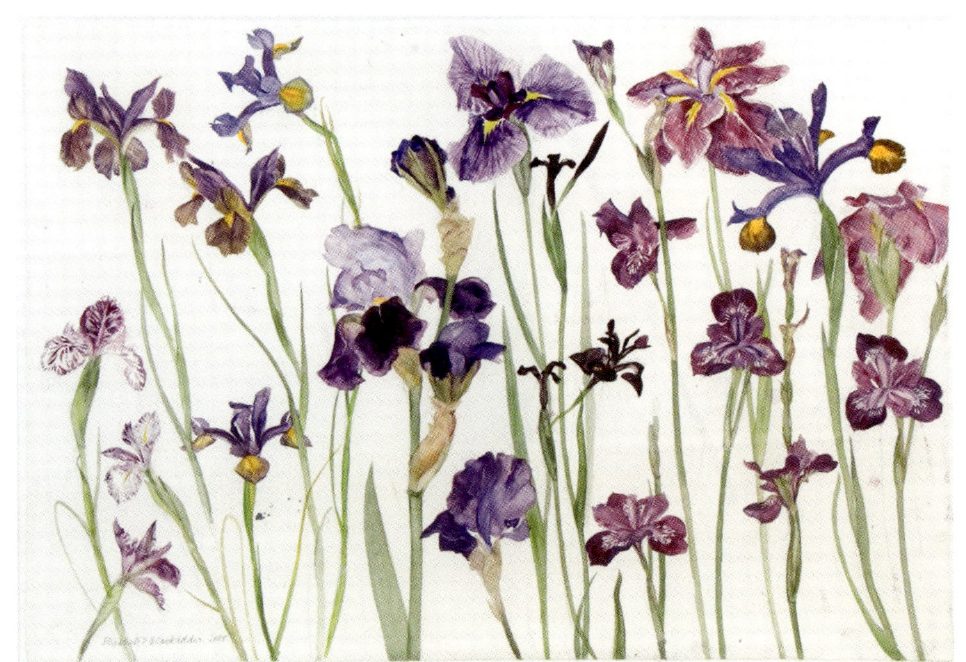

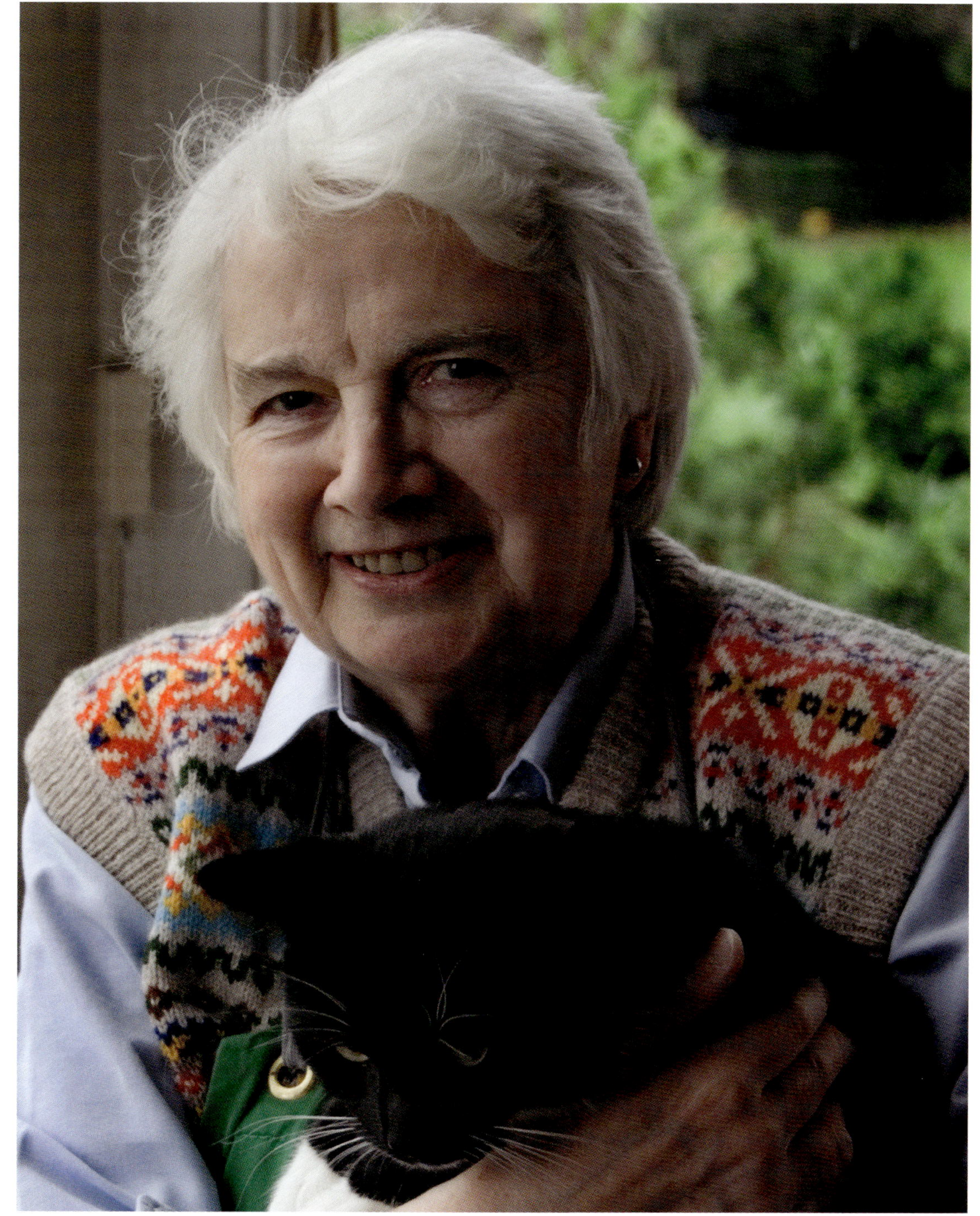

ELIZABETH BLACKADDER DBE RA RSA

OLWYN BOWEY RA

Elected ARA 24th April 1970
Elected RA 24th April 1975

Dried Flowers & Pots
Oil on board
Courtesy of the artist
50 x 50 cm

Born 10th February 1936
Stockton-on-Tees, Durham

Olwyn Bowey studied at the West Hartlepool School of Art and the Royal College of Art under Sir Roger de Grey and Carel Weight where she received a First Class Diploma and a Continuation Scholarship as well as a David Murray Landscape Scholarship.

Olwyn Bowey is an Honorary Member of the Royal West of England Academy and an Associate of the Royal College of Art.

She is particularly interested in the tradition of artist/plantsman and now concentrates on still life which can incorporate landscape, lush foliage and flowers, frequently presented in a greenhouse setting.

Olwyn Bowey lives and works in Sussex.

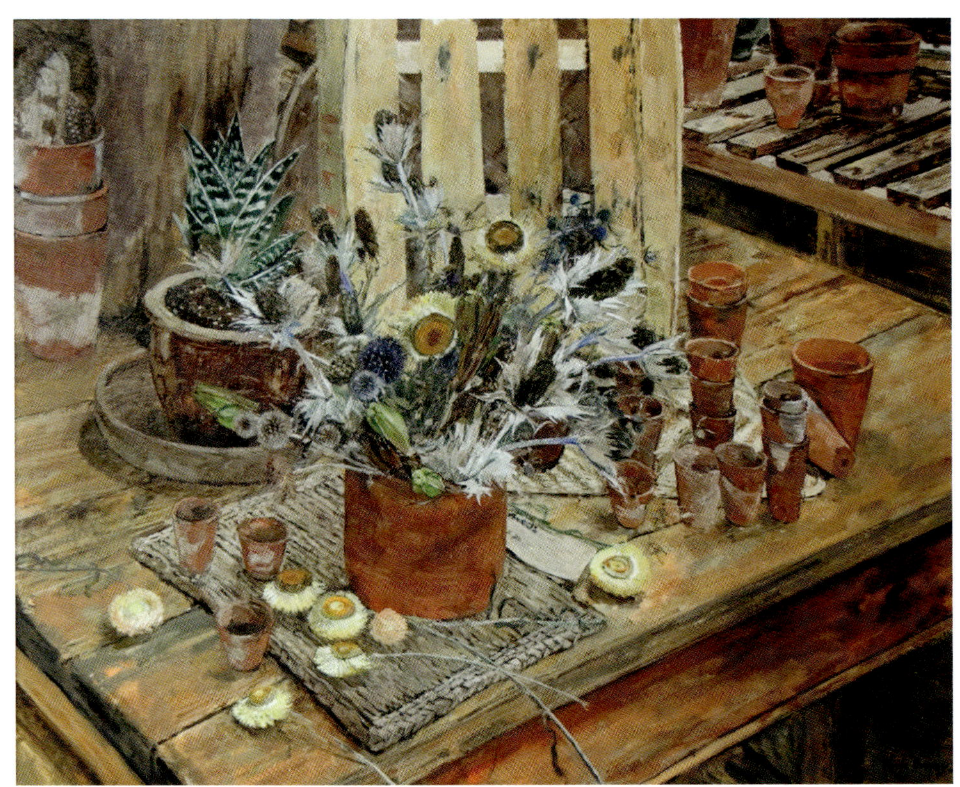

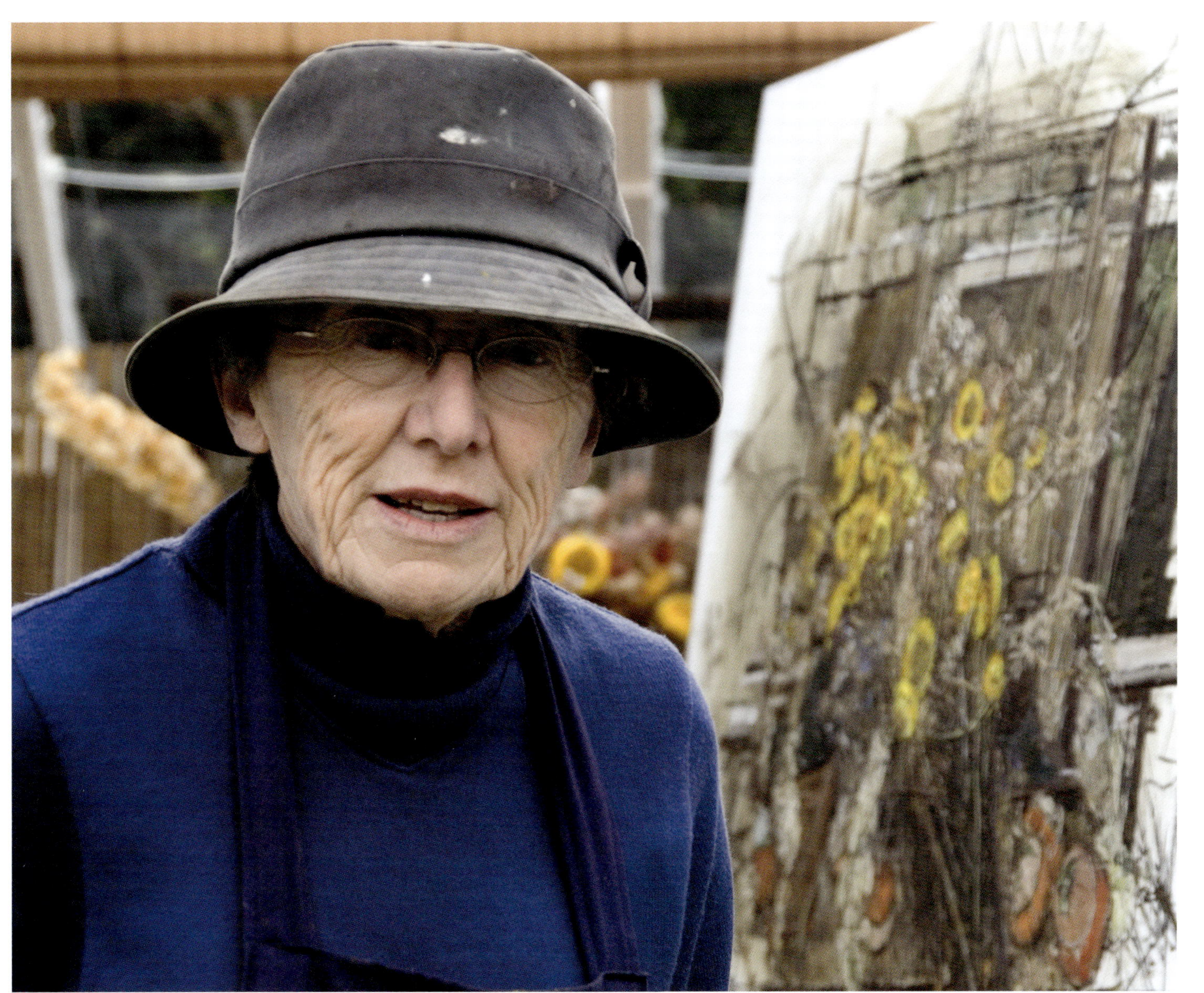

OLWYN BOWEY RA

FRANK BOWLING RA

Thicket
Acrylic on canvas
Courtesy of the artist
130 x 131 cm

Born 29th February 1936
Bartica, British Guiana

Frank Bowling came to England in 1950. He 'discovered' art in 1953 and became 'hooked' when, during his National Service, he and his RAF colleagues waited in the National Gallery for the Naafi club to open across the road near Charing Cross Station. After completing his National Service he won a scholarship to the Royal College of Art in 1959, joining the class which became famous for Pop Art in Britain and included David Hockney, the late Ron Kitaj and Allen Jones. He graduated in 1962 with a Silver Medal, and a travelling scholarship which took him to South America and the Caribbean. Instead of joining his RCA friends in the Pop Art movement, he took a path from Bacon–inspired figurative work to abstract art touched by personal memory and history.

Frank Bowling's early works were figurative but in the mid 1960s they became more geometric and overtly abstract. At the same time he started to use new working methods on larger canvases. He has taught widely and lectured at the University of Reading and Columbia University in New York. He has won many awards and mantains studios in London and Brooklyn.

www.frankbowling.com

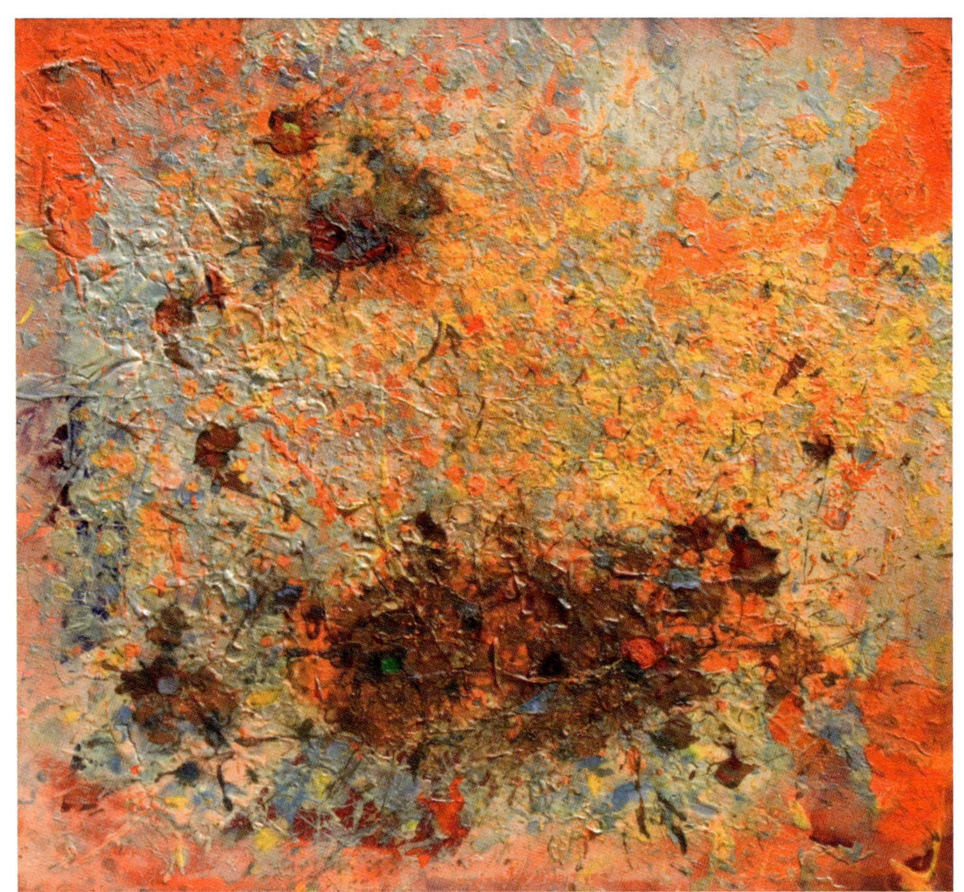

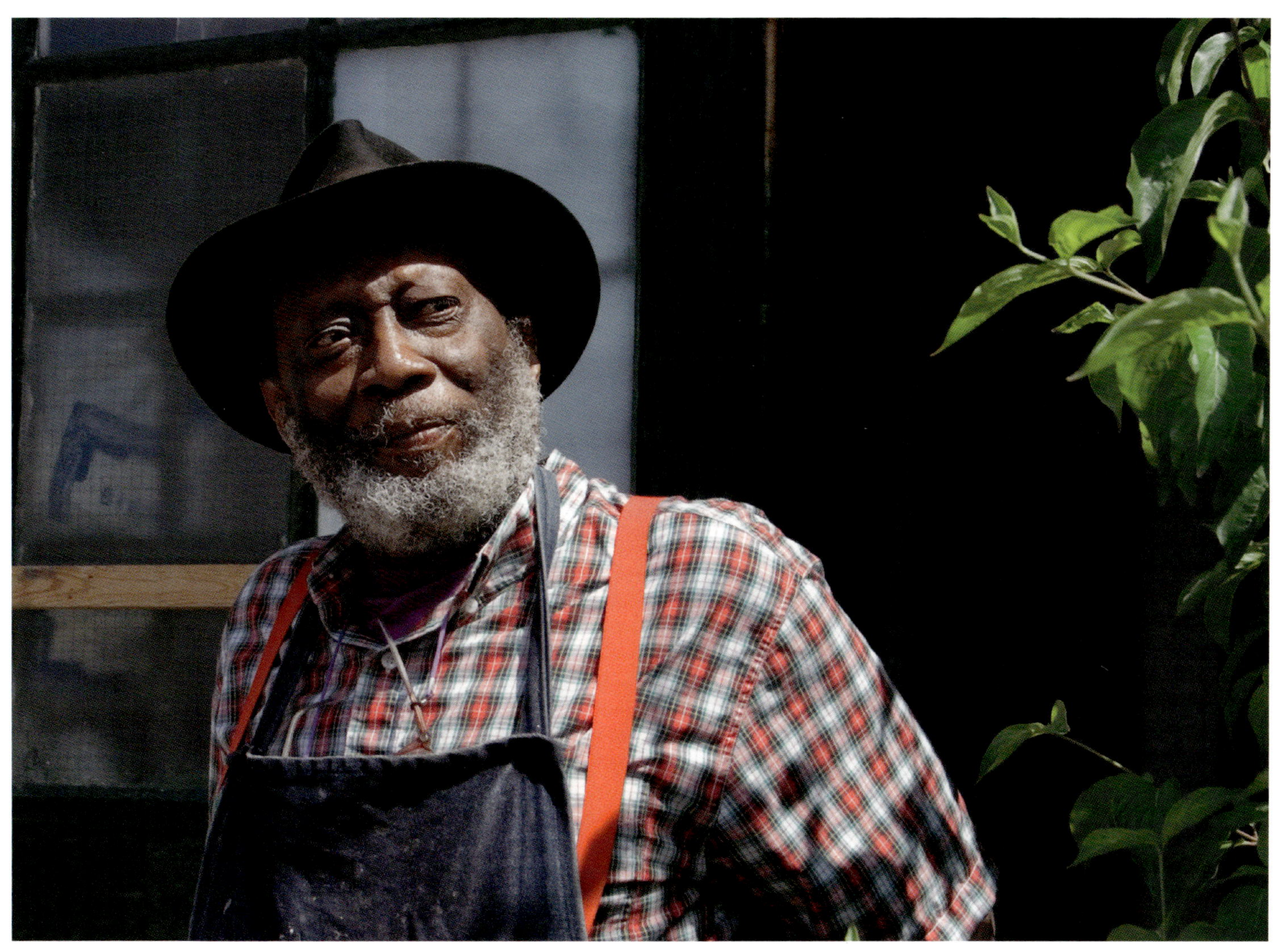

FRANK BOWLING RA

WILLIAM BOWYER RA

Fetters Lane
Oil on canvas
Courtesy of the artist
102 x 127 cm

Born 25th May 1926
Leek, Staffordshire

William Bowyer studied at Burslem School of Art and the Royal College of Art where he was taught by Carel Weight and Ruskin Spear. He works in the tradition of English figurative painting and English landscape painters, particularly Constable and Turner, have strongly inspired his work. He is also a member of the Royal Institute of Painting in Watercolours, the Royal Society of Portrait Painters and, for 30 years, was a leading figure in the New English Art Club.

Ken Howard says of William Bowyer's work that 'it communicates with us directly. It gives us a way of seeing the World and above all it is life enhancing'.

William Bowyer works in London and Suffolk.

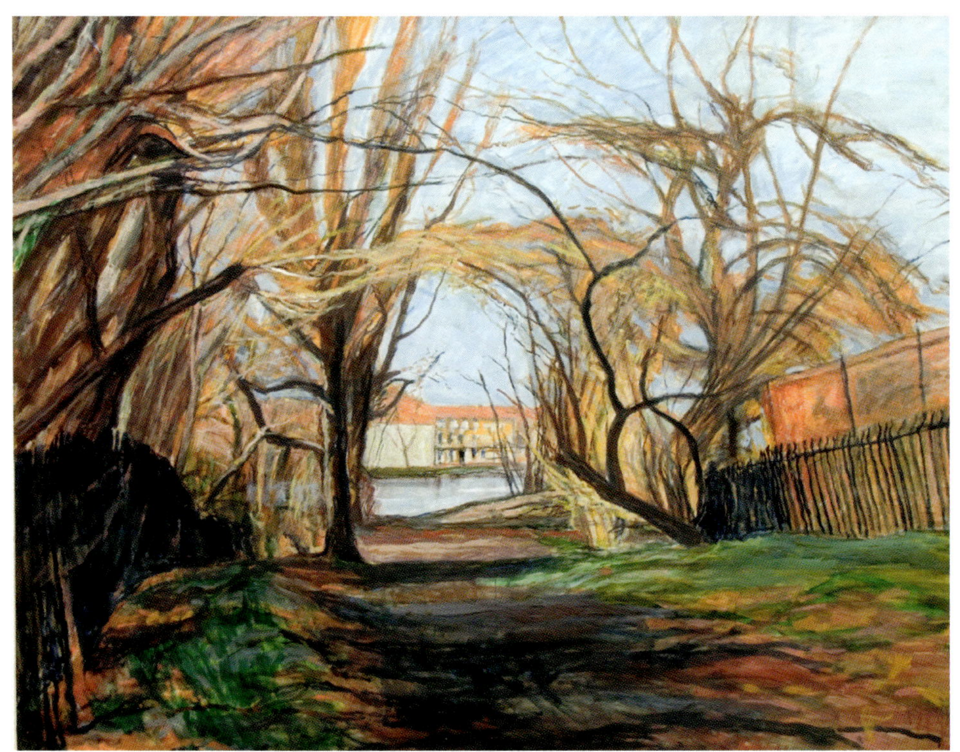

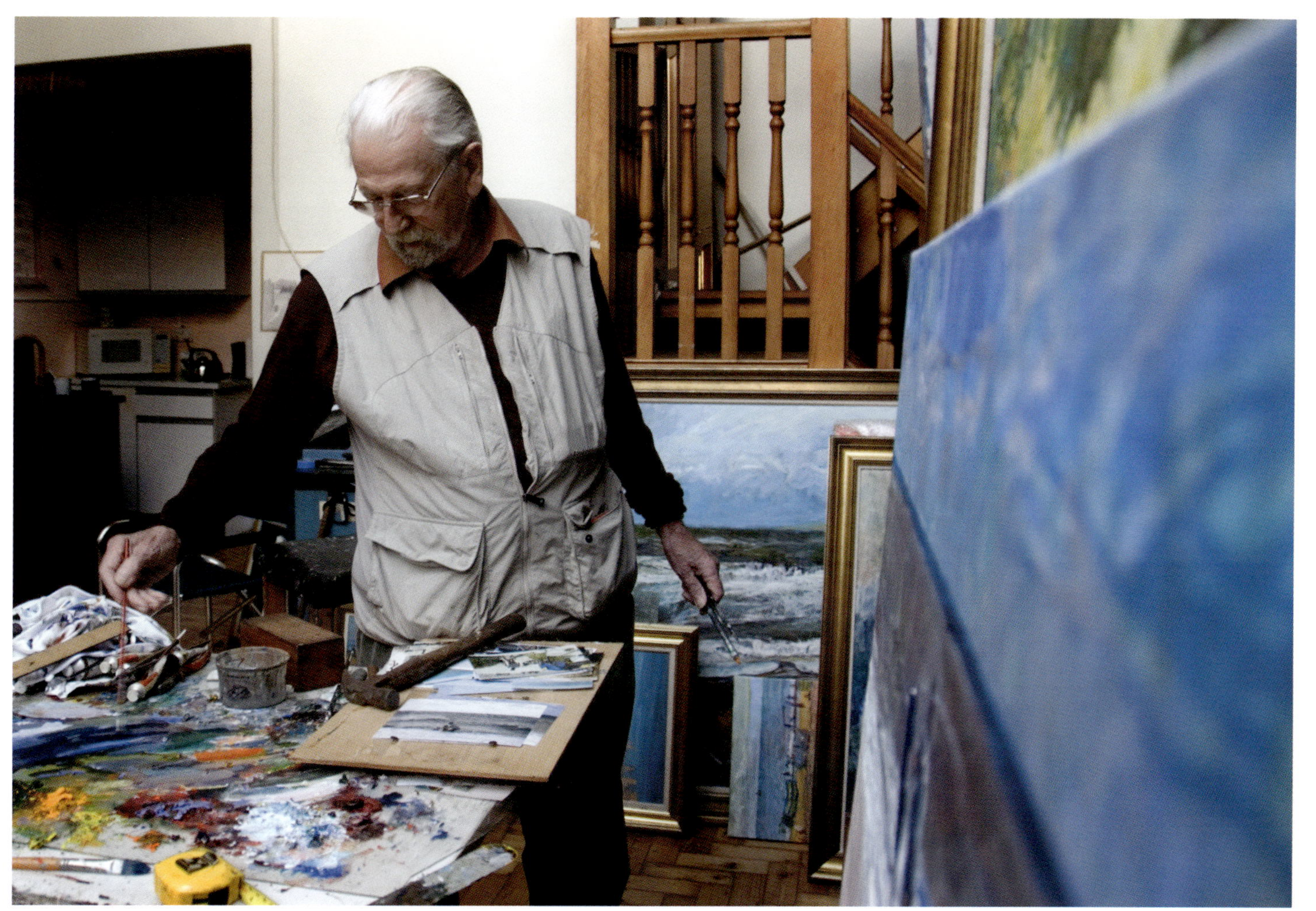

WILLIAM BOWYER RA

JEFFERY CAMP RA

Elected ARA 26th April 1974
Elected RA 9th May 1984

Cuckmere
Oil on canvas
Courtesy of the artist

Born 17th April 1923
Broad, Suffolk

Jeffery Camp studied at Lowestoft and Ipswich Schools of Art from 1939-40 and subsequently at Edinburgh College of Art from 1941-44. He was awarded Travelling Scholarships in 1944 and 1945 and went on to teach at Chelsea School of Art from 1960-81 and at the Slade School of Art from 1963-88.

In latter years a warm dreamlike note has spread through Jeffery's lyrical reaction to the world with entwined couples in rainbow colours contrasting with his landscapes of Beachy Head, Birling Gap or the Seven Sisters. After presenting works on small irregular shaped canvases he has recently returned to large-scale coastal paintings.

Jeffery Camp lives and works in London.

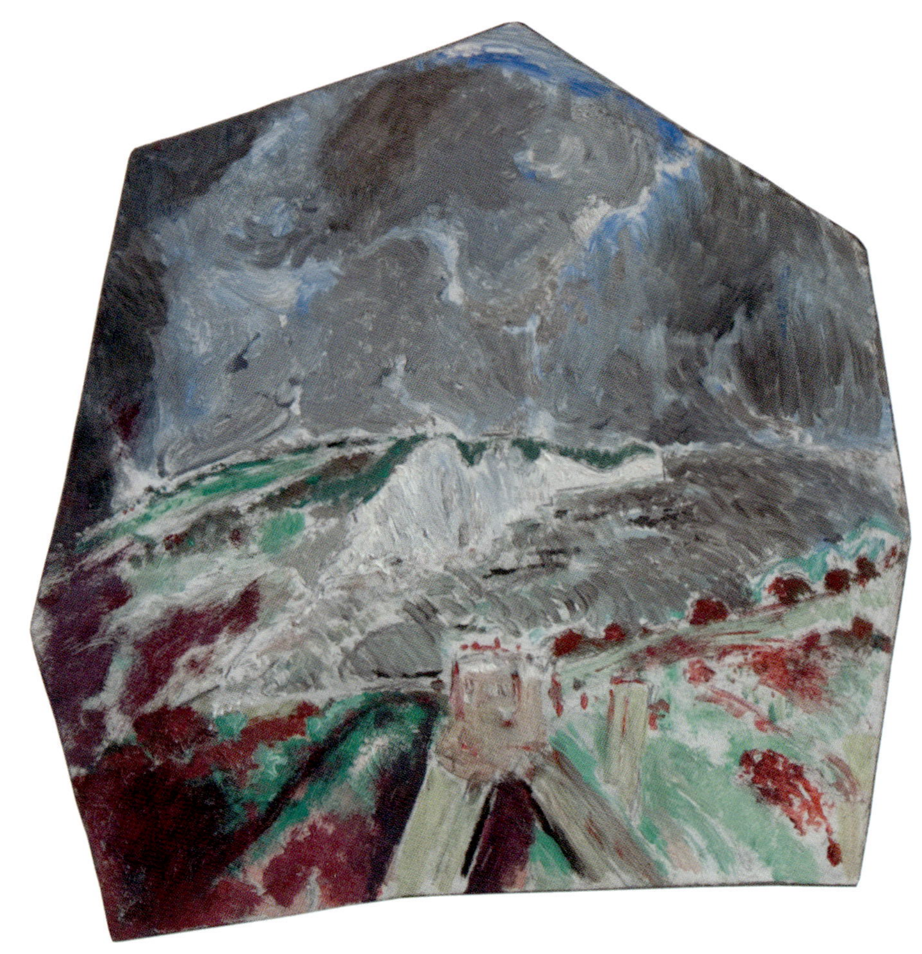

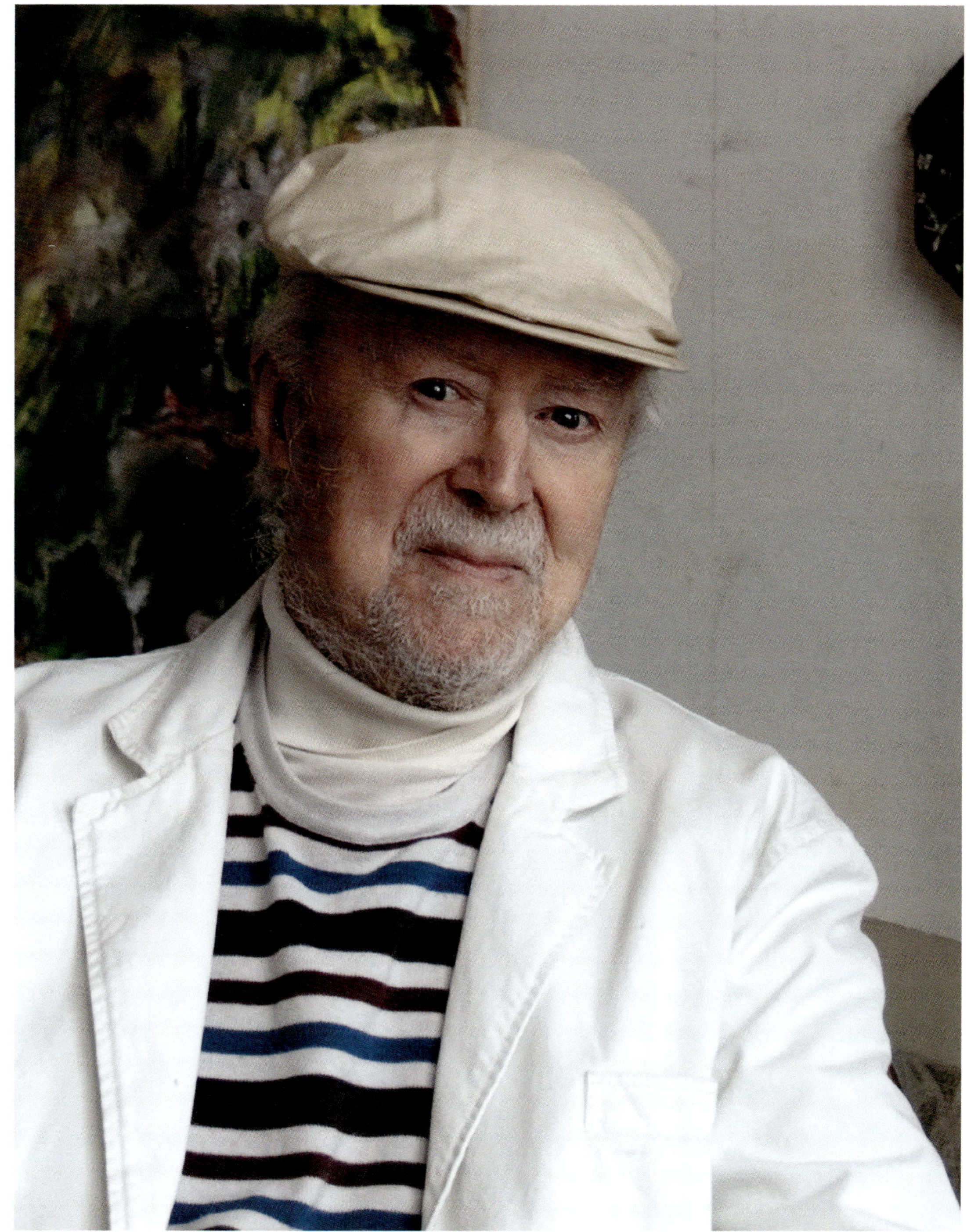

JEFFERY CAMP RA

STEPHEN CHAMBERS RA

Elected RA 13th December 2005

Shack Life
Etching on Chile-Collé
Courtesy of the artist
50 x 53 cm

Born 20th July 1960
London

Stephen Chambers studied at Winchester School of Art from 1978-79 and St Martin's School of Art from 1979-82. He graduated from Chelsea School of Art with a Masters Degree in 1983, won a Rome Scholarship, a Fellowship of Winchester School of Art and a Mark Rothko Memorial Trust Travelling Award.

Stephen says that his works 'speak of states of mind, behaviours and sensibilities.' They are about people even though they do not always appear. When viewing his paintings he wants us to develop a curiosity, experience his feelings and experiences in a silent conversation with him.

Stephen Chambers lives and works in London.

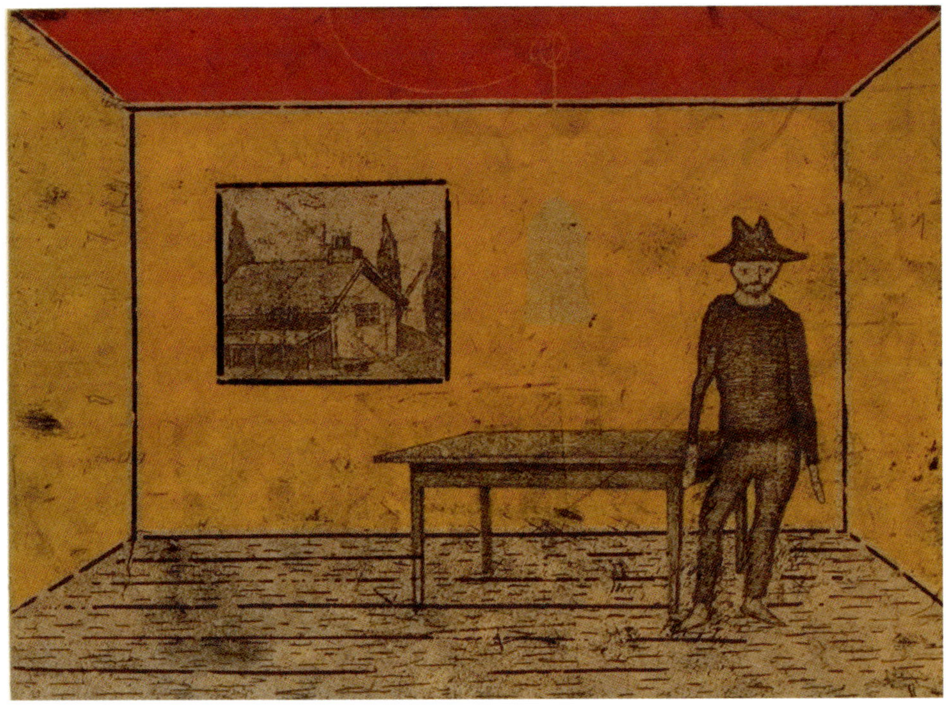

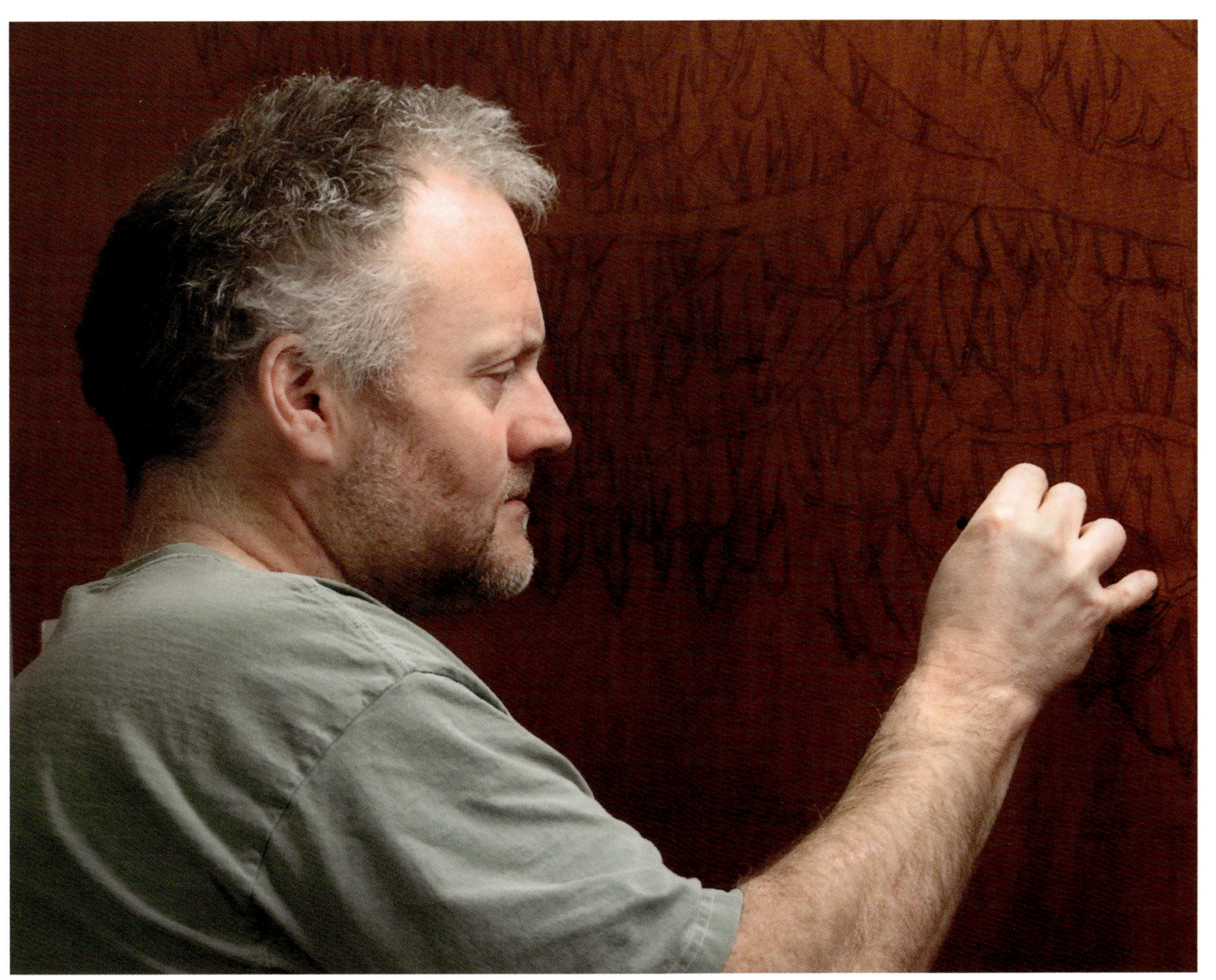
STEPHEN CHAMBERS RA

MAURICE COCKRILL RA

Elected RA 8th October 1999

Güten Tag
Oil & acrylic on canvas 1995
Courtesy of the artist
214 x 184 cm

Born 8th October 1936
Hartlepool, County Durham

Maurice Cockrill studied at Wrexham School of Art, then Denbigh Technical College and the University of Reading from 1960-64. His teaching career commenced at Liverpool College of Art from 1967-80 and Liverpool Polytechnic. From 1982 and 1985 he was visiting Tutor at Schools of Art in Manchester, Portsmouth, Farnham, Winchester and Nottingham going on to become Visiting Tutor at the Royal College of Art and St Martin's School of Art from 1984-94.

He was Artist in Residence at GOFA University of NSW Australia and visiting Tutor at the Royal Acadeny Schools from 1994-98 becoming Keeper of the Schools in 2004.

Maurice Cockrill's extensive list of past exhibitions and awards runs into many pages despite his having destroyed all his work in 1968. The consistency of themes, motifs and visions underlying his recent work and its depth of meaning reinforce his position as a 'Painter's Painter'.

Maurice Cockrill lives and works in London.
www.cockrill.co.uk

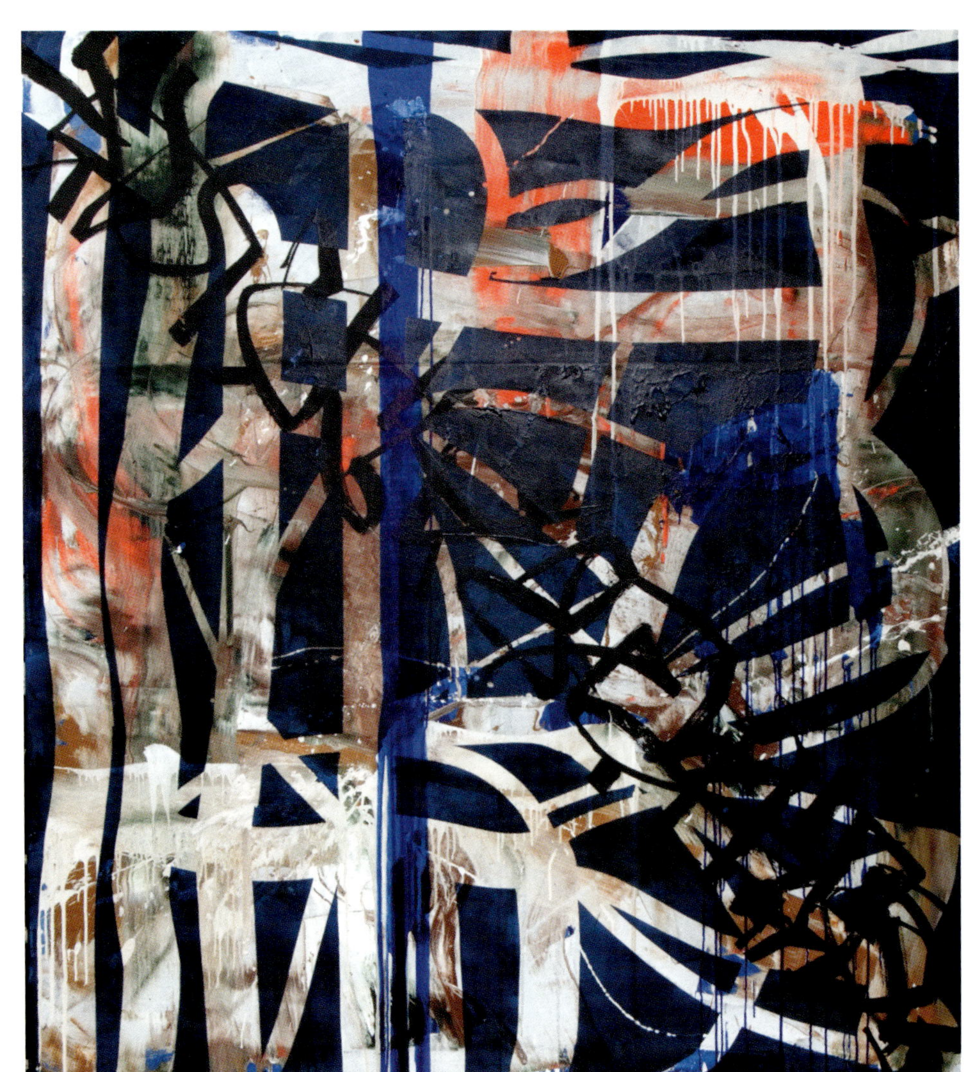

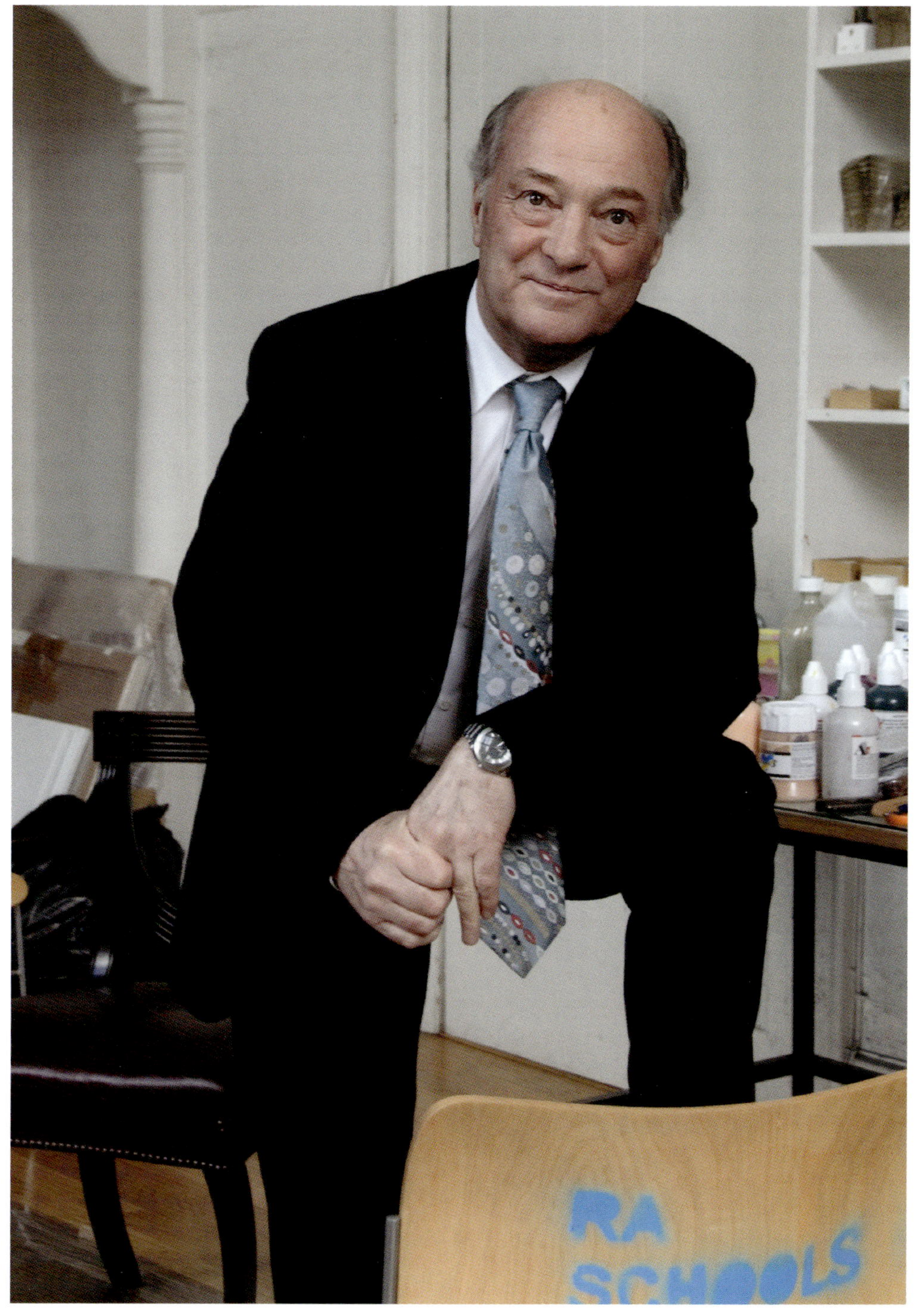

RA
SCHOOLS

JEAN COOKE RA

Elected ARA 23rd April 1965
Elected RA 15th June 1972

*Burned my Broomstick, slashed my Golden
Gown, c'mon Darling fly me down-town*
Oil on canvas
Self portrait, courtesy of the artist

Born 18th February 1927
London

Jean Cooke studied at the Central School of Arts and Crafts in Camberwell from 1943-45, Goldsmiths College School of Art from 1945-49 and at the Royal College of Art from 1949 returning as Lecturer 1964-74. She was a member of the Academic Board of Blackheath School of Art from 1986-88 and a Governor of the Central School of Art and Design from 1984-86.

Whilst painting a wide variety of subjects, Jean Cooke has returned time and time again to self-portraiture of which she has written: *'Sometimes I paint to show off, sometimes to hide away in solitude; sometimes to say 'Here I am', sometimes to say 'I want to be alone'. But always there is a searching for the unknown, the previouly unperceived.'*

Jean Cooke was married to John Bratby from 1953-73 and appeared in many of his works.

Jean Cooke lives and works in London and Sussex.

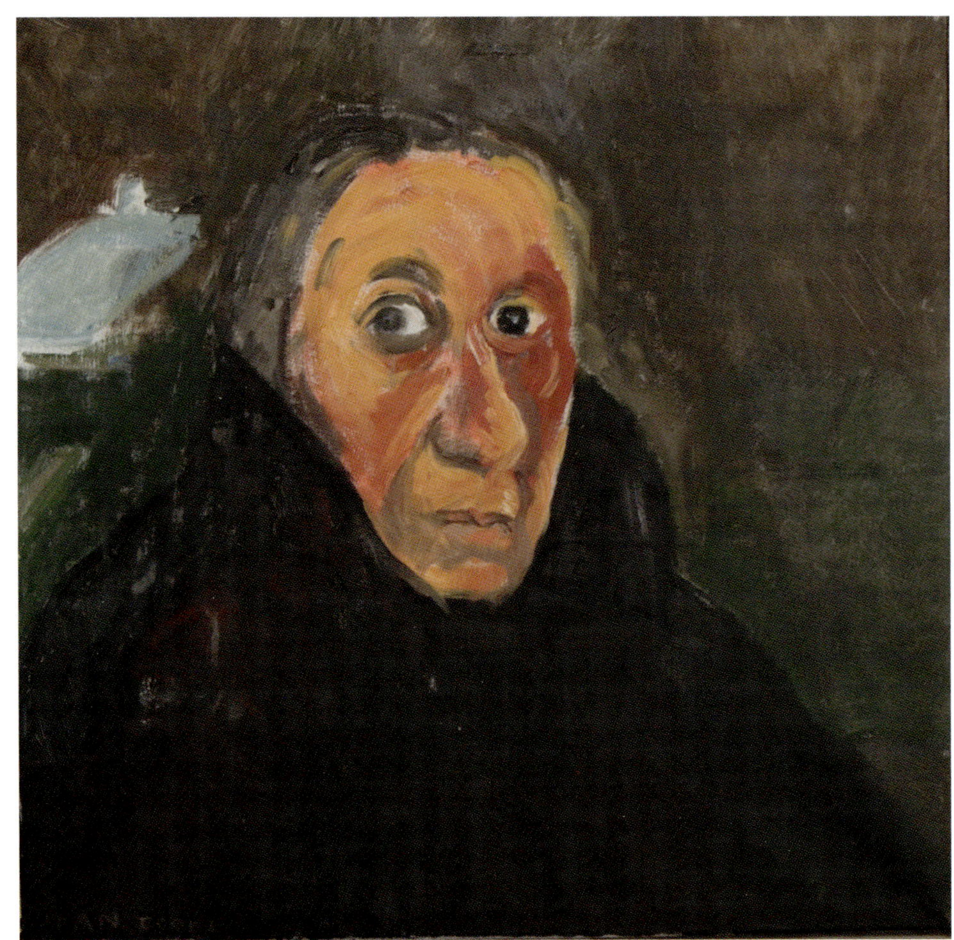

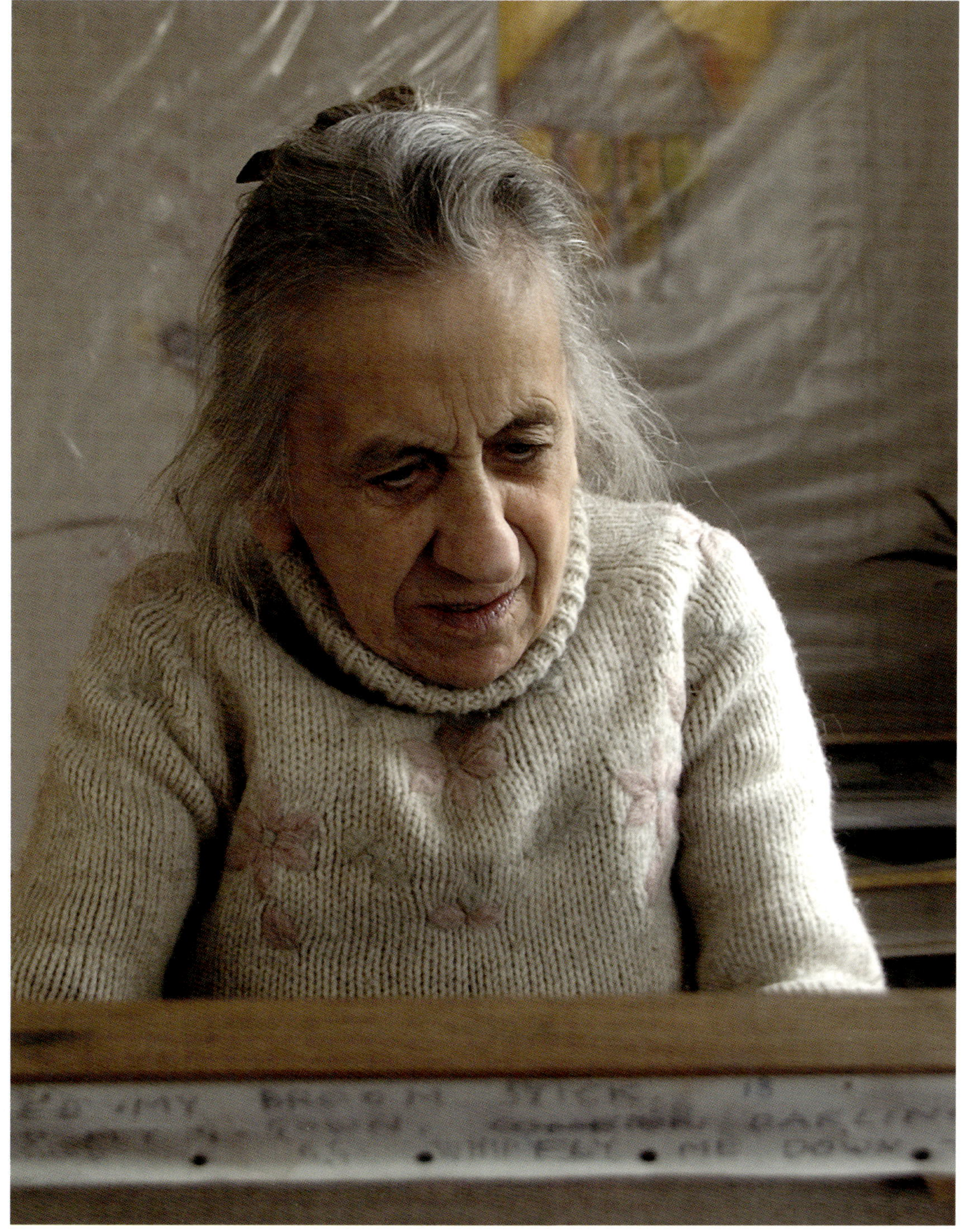

JEAN COOKE RA

EILEEN COOPER RA

Deeper Water 2007
Oil on canvas
Courtesy of the artist
122 x 153 cm
Computer-aided programme

Born 10th June 1953
Glossop, Derbyshire

Eileen Cooper studied at Goldsmiths College from 1971-74 and the Royal College of Art from 1974-77. She has been Visiting Lecturer at the Royal College of Art since 1998. and is also currently teaching at the Royal Academy Schools.

Eileen Cooper has had numerous solo exhibitions since her first in 1979 at the Air Gallery in London, and has also participated in many group exhibitions. She has work in many public and private collections in the UK and USA.

She writes, *'Lots of people are thrown together in my pictures, but there is also a strong sense of separateness. I find it fascinating that, in the busy lives that everyone leads, people have a sense of their own time, their own moments of reverie.'*

Embracing change and innovation, her style is a very personal one reflecting stages in her own life which evolve into imaginative narratives executed in a playful spirit with tenderness and passion.

Eileen Cooper lives and works in London
www.eileencooper.co.uk

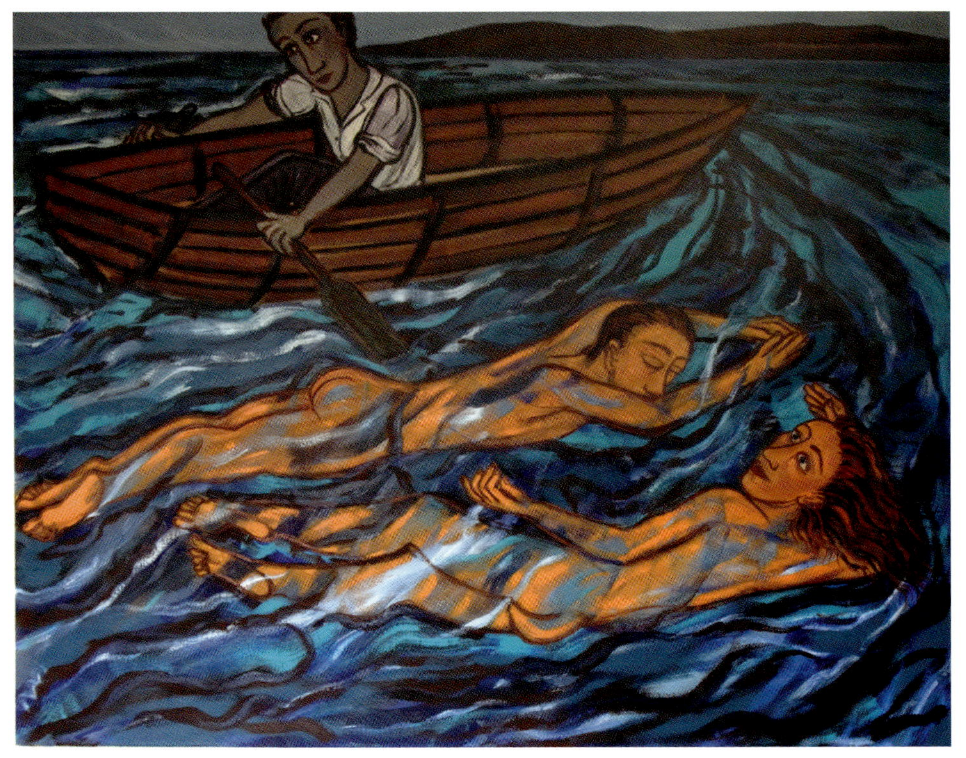

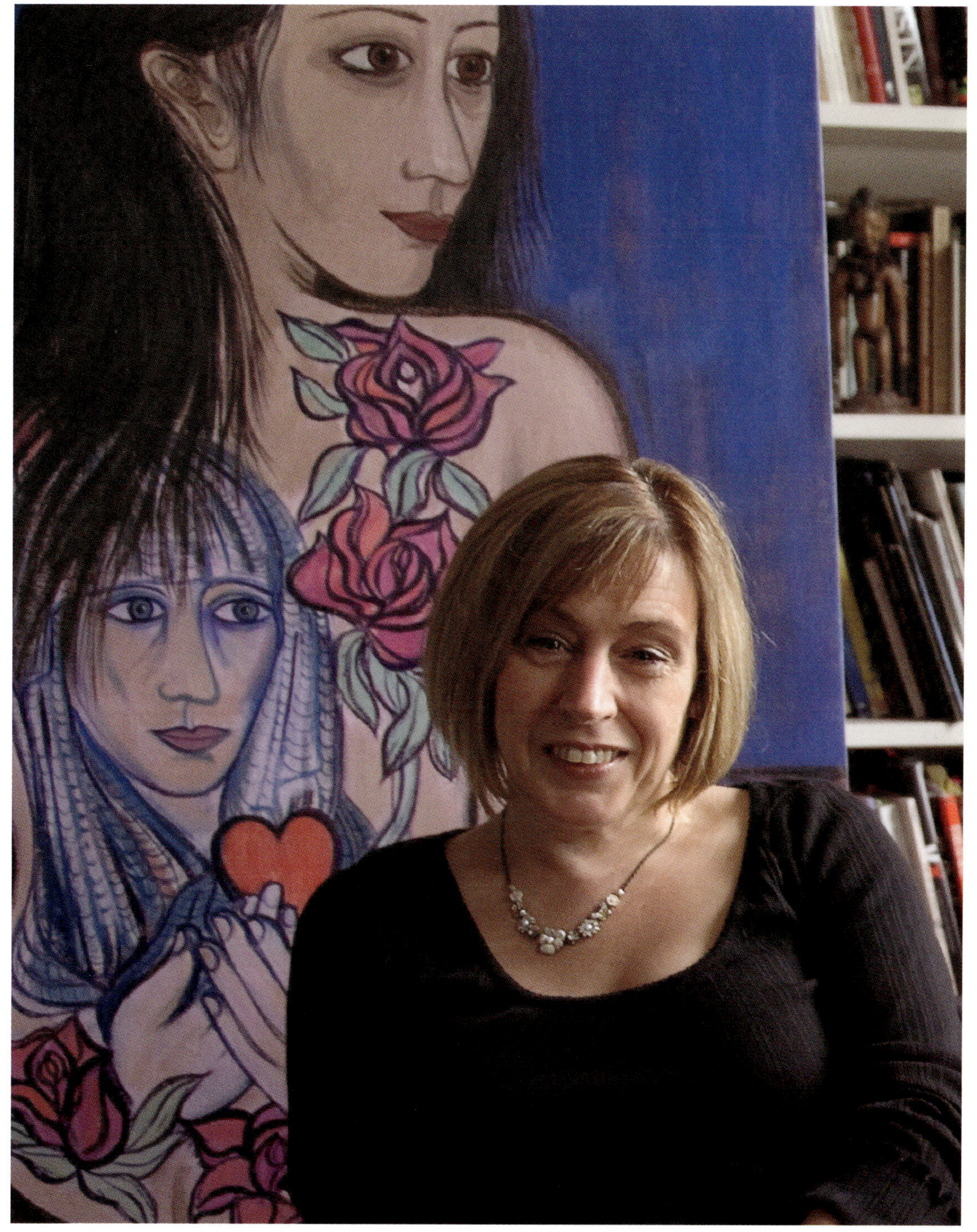

MICHAEL CRAIG-MARTIN CBE RA

Elected RA 12th December 2006

Inhale/Exhale, 2002
Acrylic on canvas
Courtesy of Gagosian Gallery
307 x 371 cm
© Michael Craig-Martin

Born 28th August 1941
Dublin

Michael Craig Martin grew up in the USA where he obtained his MFA from Yale in 1996. Returning to Europe in the mid 1960s he was a key figure in the first generation of British conceptual artists. He taught at Bath Academy of Art from 1966-69, Canterbury College of Art from 1969-70 and again from 1972-73. He taught at Goldsmiths College of Art from 1974-88 and again from 1994 to 2000 becoming Professor in 1995.

At Goldsmiths he taught, among others, Gary Hume, Fiona Rae and Damien Hirst who were among those artists who became known as the YBAs (Young British Artists). He was appointed Trustee of the Tate Gallery from 1989-99, Honorary Fellow and Professor Emeritus of Fine Art at Goldsmiths College in 2000 and was made CBE in 2001. Michael has had more than 60 solo exhibitions and participated in more than 80 group exhibitions worldwide, written many articles and essays and undertaken numerous commissions in Europe, Japan, Australia and the USA. His work formed the theme for the Royal Academy's Summer Exhibition 2007. He is fascinated with the dialogue between representation and reality within art.

Michael Craig Martin lives and works in London.
www.michaelcraig-martin.com

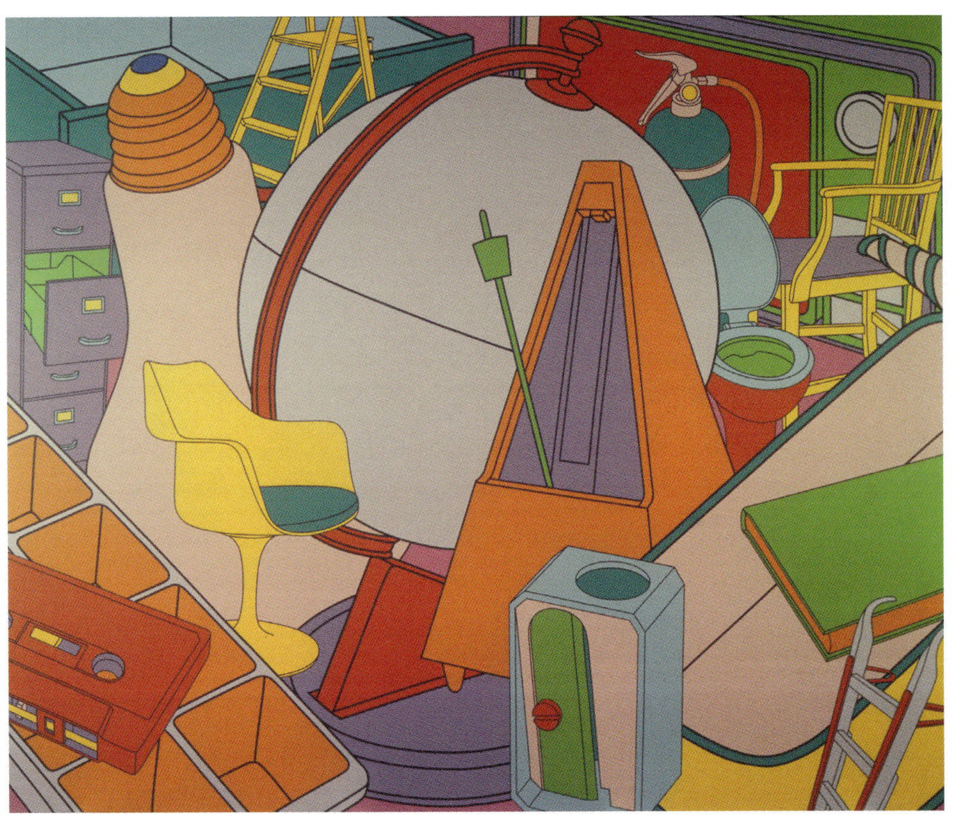

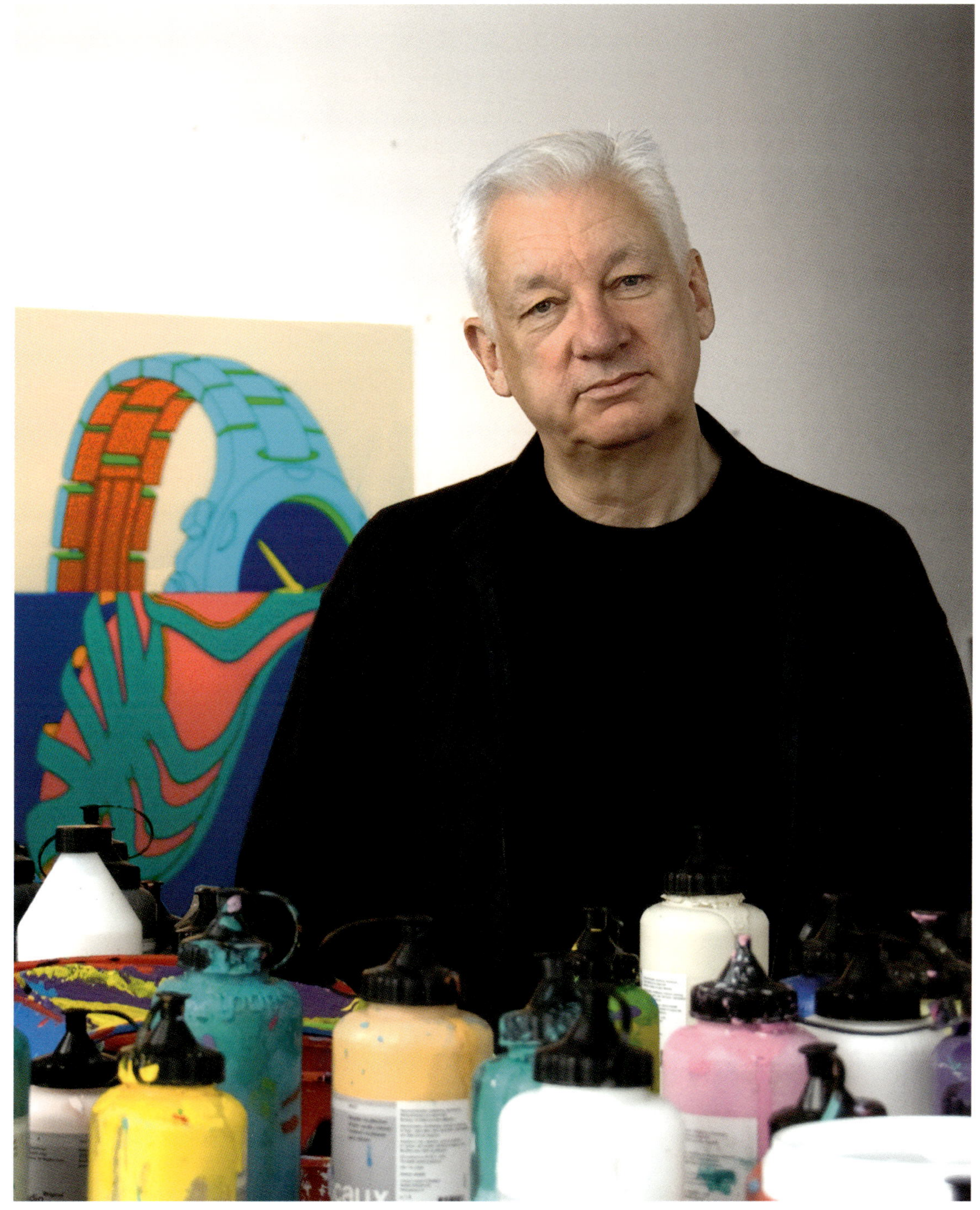
MICHAEL CRAIG-MARTIN CBE RA

JOHN CRAXTON RA

Cat and Mouse
Acrylic tempera on canvas
Courtesy of the artist
30 x 56 cm

Born 3rd October 1922
London

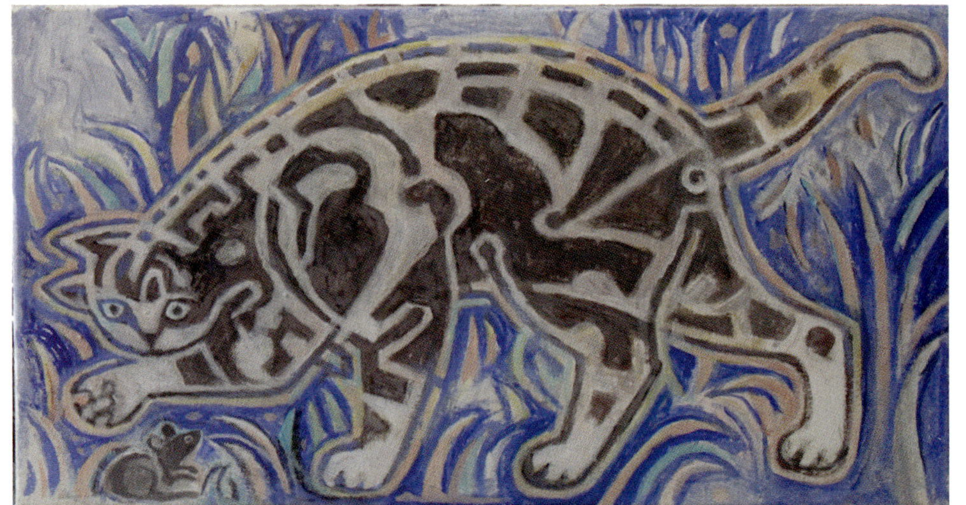

John Craxton knew he wanted to be a painter when he was 7 years old. At Betteshanger School he was taught by Elsie Barling, inspired art teacher and close friend of Frances Hodgkins. He was just 10 when in 1932 the school exhibited their work at the Bloomsbury Gallery. At 17 he applied for a place at Chelsea School of Art but was considered too young to attend life classes. He left for Paris and enrolled at the Academie de la Grande Chaumière. Forced by the onset of war to leave Paris in 1939, he joined the Central School of Art under Roberts, Meninsky, Schilsky, and P F Millard. Rejected for military service he studied with his friend Lucian Freud at Goldsmiths College from 1942-44 after advice and help from Graham Sutherland.

John Craxton regards himself as English by birth but European by choice. His paintings combine a love of line with an almost spiritual use of colour and light which mixes new ideas with tradition. He designed sets and costumes for the Royal Ballet's performance of Daphnis and Chloë in 1951. He worked on a condensed version for the Birmingham Royal Ballet which toured the UK in 2007.

After first visiting Greece in 1946, he has lived in Crete since 1965 while maintaining a studio in London.

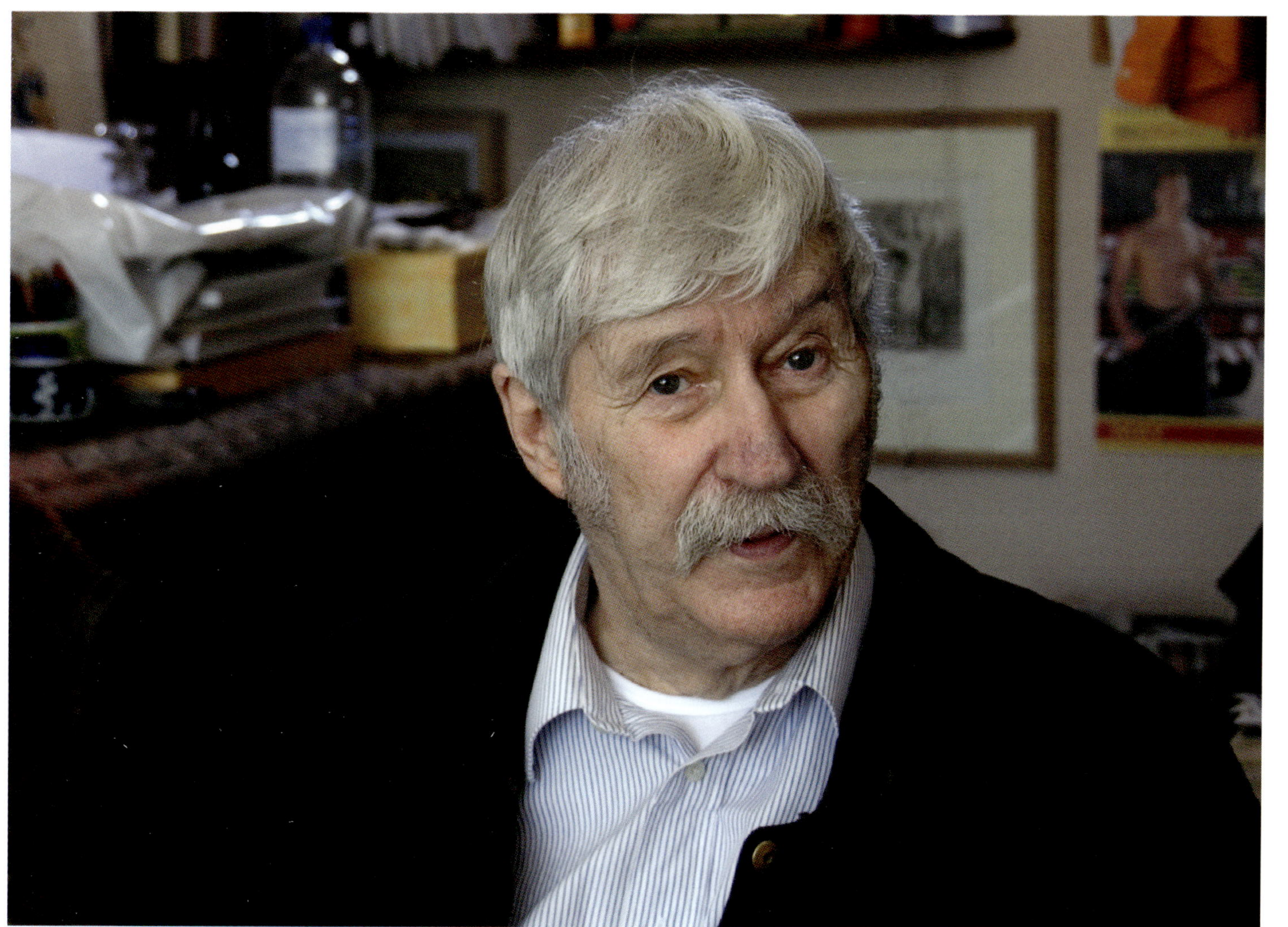

JOHN CRAXTON RA

FREDERICK CUMING RA

Elected ARA 25th April 1969
Elected RA 12th February 1974

Fowey, Cornwall
Oil on canvas on board
Courtesy of the artist
76 x 76 cm

Born 16th February 1930
London

Frederick Cuming studied at Sidcup School of Art from 1945-49 before doing his National Service from 1949-51, returning to study at the Royal College of Art from 1951-55. He gained a Rome Scholarship and an Abbey Minor Scholarship. He was awarded an Honorary Doctorate of Letters by the University of Kent in July 2004

'My work is about responses to the moods and atmosphere generated by landscape, still life or interiors. I am interested in the developments of 20th Century painting in abstraction and in the new ideas and art forms the more I work the more I discover'.

Fred Cuming lives and works in East Sussex.

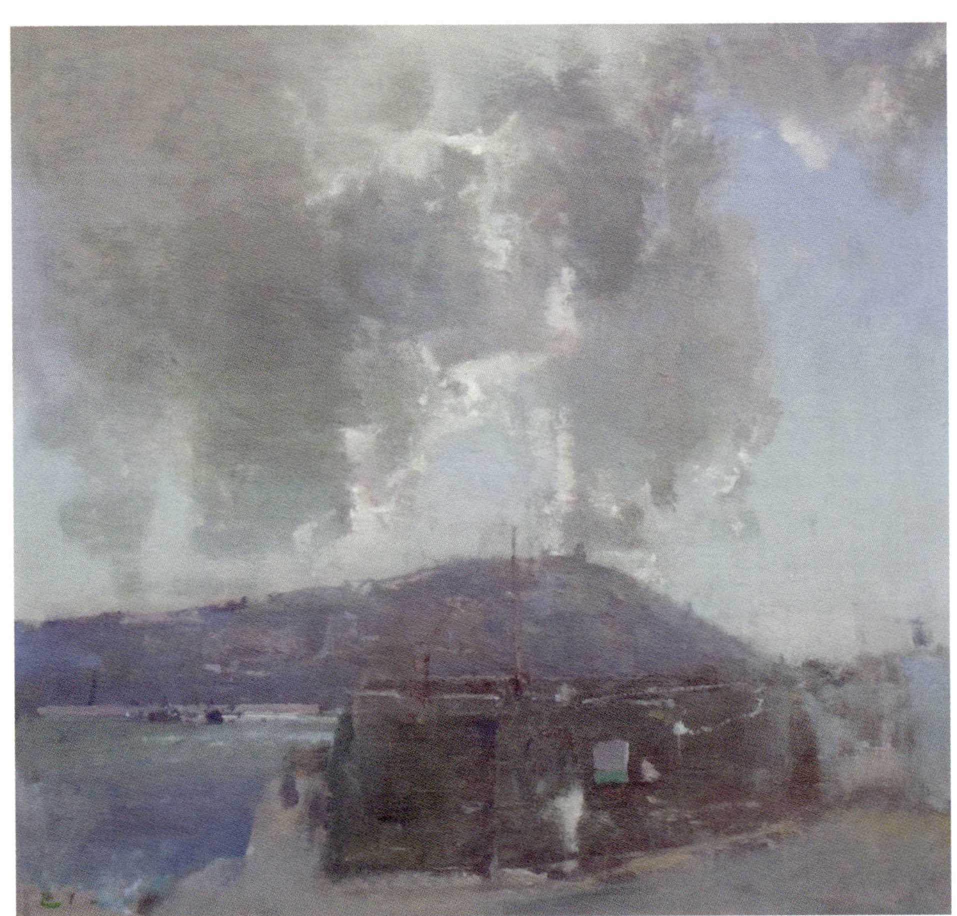

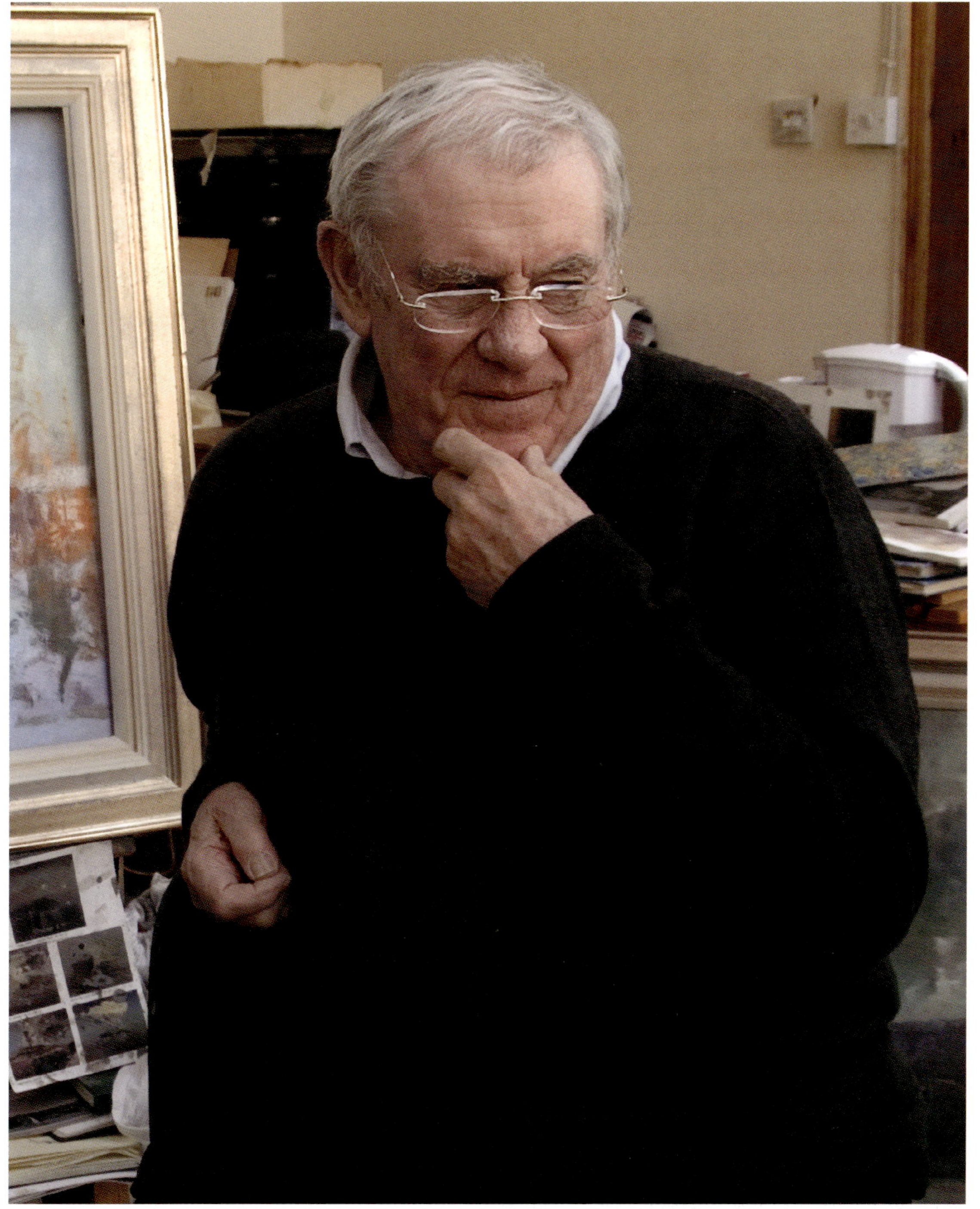

FREDERICK CUMING RA

GUS CUMMINS RA

Preliminary model of 'OFF THE WALL'
for installation
Courtesy of the artist
model 30 x 36 x 8 cm
full installation 256 x 270 x 65 cm

Born 28th January 1943
London

Gus Cummins studied at Sutton School of Art from 1958-61, Wimbledon School of Art from 1961-64 where he received a Senior Drawing Prize, and subsequently at the Royal College of Art from 1964-67.

He went on to teach at Hammersmith College of Art and Building, Sutton College of Liberal Arts and Technology, Wimbledon School of Art and Ravensbourne College of Art and Communications in the 1980s.

Throughout the 1980s and 1990s he taught at Chelsea School of Art and at City & Guilds of London Art School and during 2000 at the Prince's Foundation.
He has also been a tutor at the Royal Academy Schools since the early 1980s.
Gus says *'I try to create a 'parallel' reality: to find an 'overview' by standing slightly to one side and inviting the viewer to engage and speculate. I often feel unsure about what I am working towards. I sense it is an act of faith with anxiousness often in the background. But now and then, an extraordinary exhilaration creeps up which like poetry seeks to reinvent both an individual and universal language'.*

Gus Cummins lives and works in East Sussex.

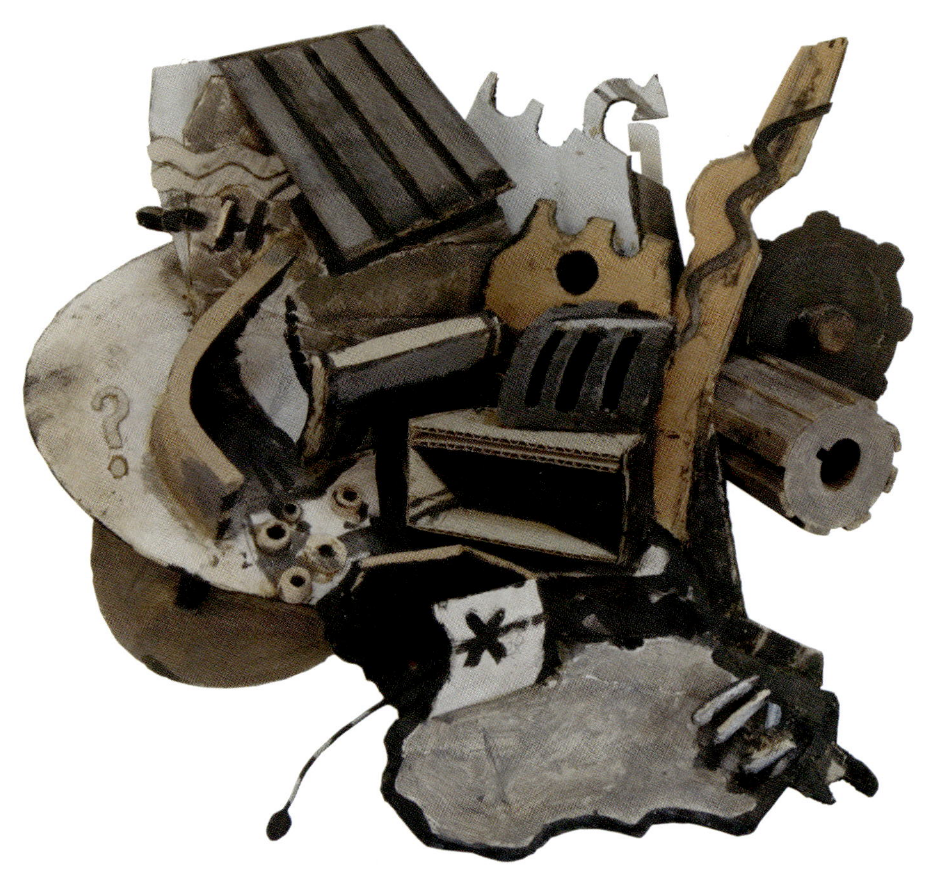

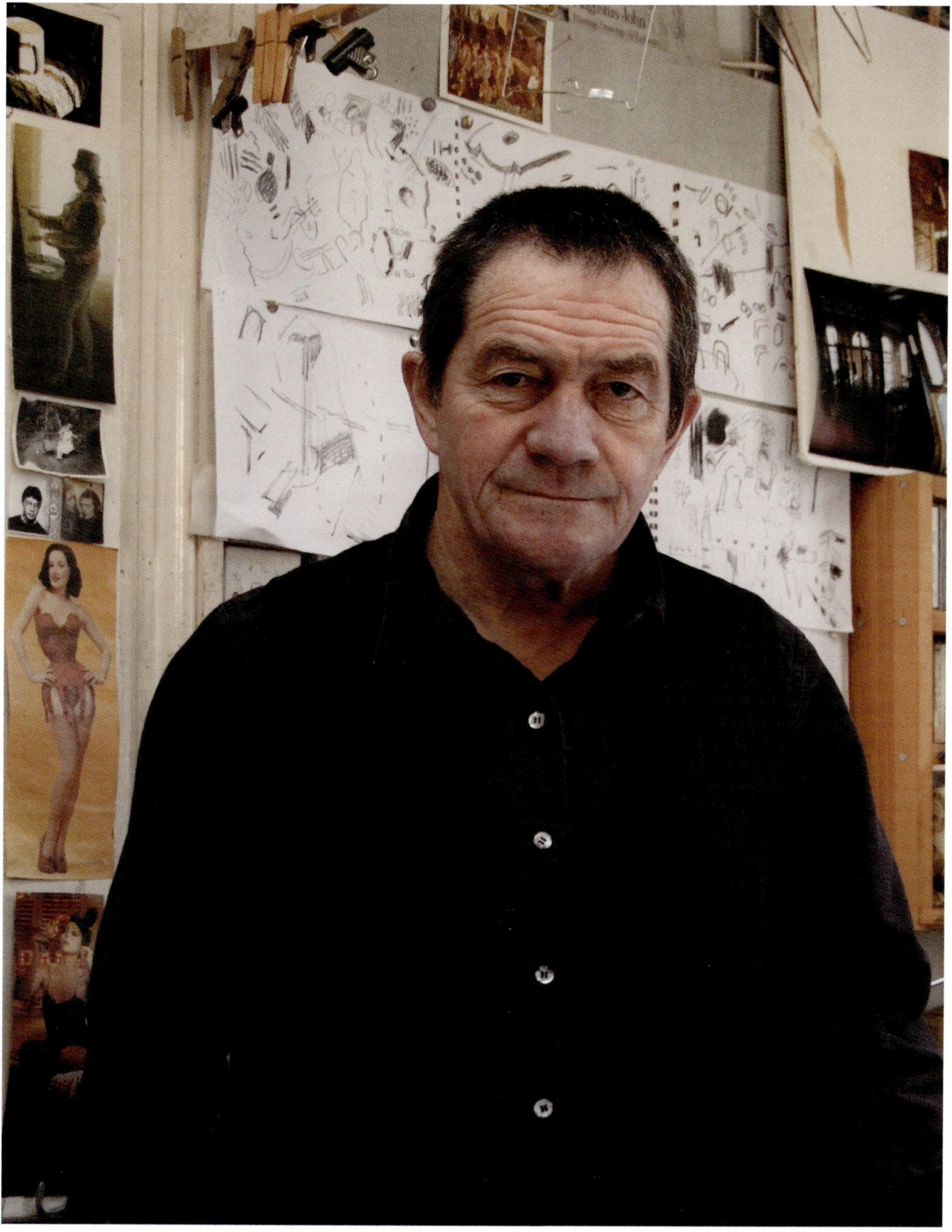

JENNIFER DICKSON RA

Elected ARA 24th April 1970
Elected RA 29th April 1976

Time is the Thief of Time
(Valsanzibio, Veneto) 2005
Giclée & watercolour on paper
Courtesy of the artist
57 x 77 cm

Born 17th September 1936
Piet Retief, South Africa

Jennifer Dickson trained as a painter and printmaker at Goldsmiths College School of Art from 1954-59 and her graduate studies in etching were under Stanley William Hayter at Atelier 17, Paris from 1960-65.

Jennifer Dickson went on to found and direct the Graduate Printmaking programme at Brighton College of Art (now Brighton University) integrating photography into the programme in the early 1960s. She moved to Canada in 1969 where she taught at the Saidye Bronfman Centre in Montreal. Her first exhibition in London in 1962 was followed by annual solo exhibitions in the UK, Belgium, South Africa, Jamaica, the USA and Canada and many international group exhibitions. Jennifer Dickson received an Honorary Doctorate of Law from the University of Alberta and was appointed a Member of the Order of Canada in 1995. She has won numerous awards and her work is in the collections of more than 40 Museums and Public Galleries. Since 1970 she has experimented with many modes of the application of photography to printmaking, combining her love of watercolour with etching and most recently, the giclée process.

Jennifer Dickson lives and works in Ottawa, Canada.

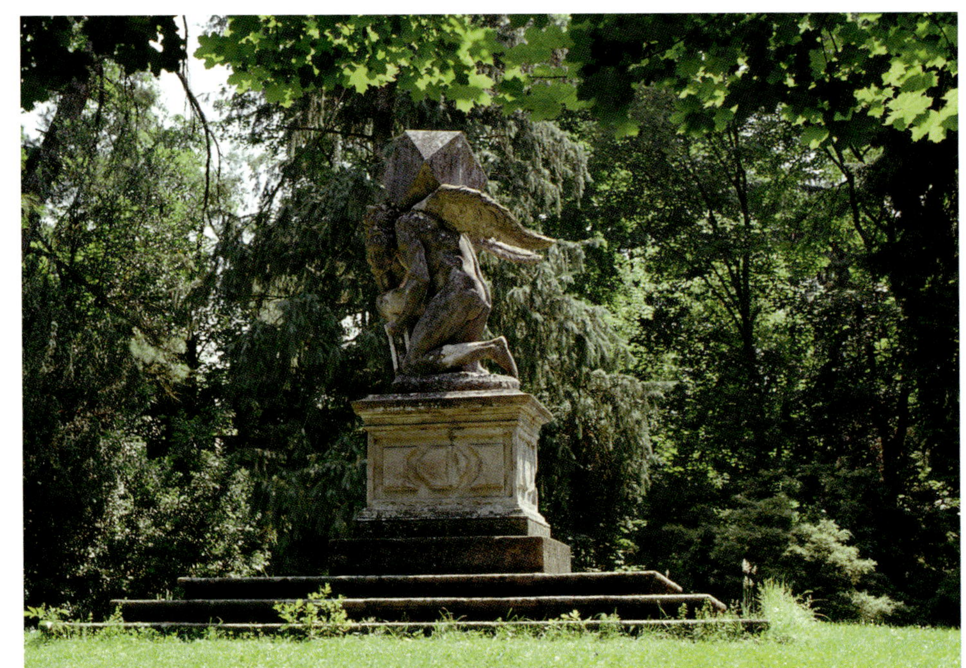

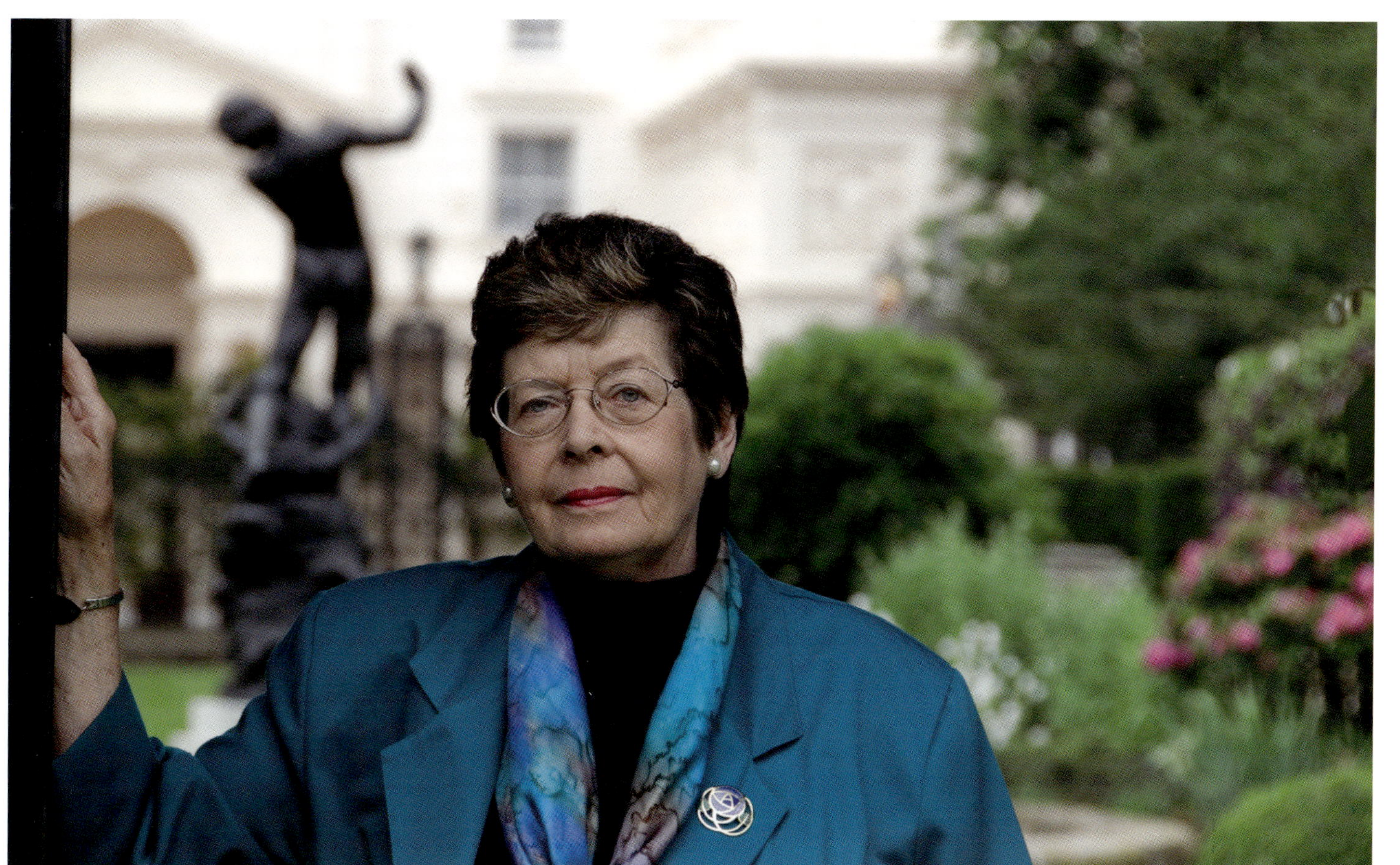

BERNARD DUNSTAN RA

Elected ARA 24th April 1959
Elected RA 9th July 1968

The Sargent Portrait
Oil on panel
Courtesy of the artist
36 x 33 cm

Born 19th January 1920
Teddington, Middlesex

Bernard Dunstan studied at the Byam Shaw School of Art in 1939 and the Slade School of Art from 1939 to 1941. He taught at the West of England School of Art in Bristol from 1946-49, the Camberwell School of Art from 1950-64, Byam Shaw School of Art from 1953-74, Ravensbourne Art College from 1959-64 and the City & Guilds of London Art School from 1964-69.
He was President of the Royal West of England Academy from 1979-84.

One of the last of the followers of Sickert and Vuillard, Bernard Dunstan's work has a timeless quality. He says that his motto is Ruskin's *'Paint what you love and love what you paint'*. He is married to Diana Armfield RA, they are the only married couple in the current RA membership and have been described as 'quintessentially English artists'. They have been creatively and romantically connected since 1947, sharing a relationship which radiates warmth and affection.

Bernard Dunstan and Diana Armfield live and work in London and Wales.

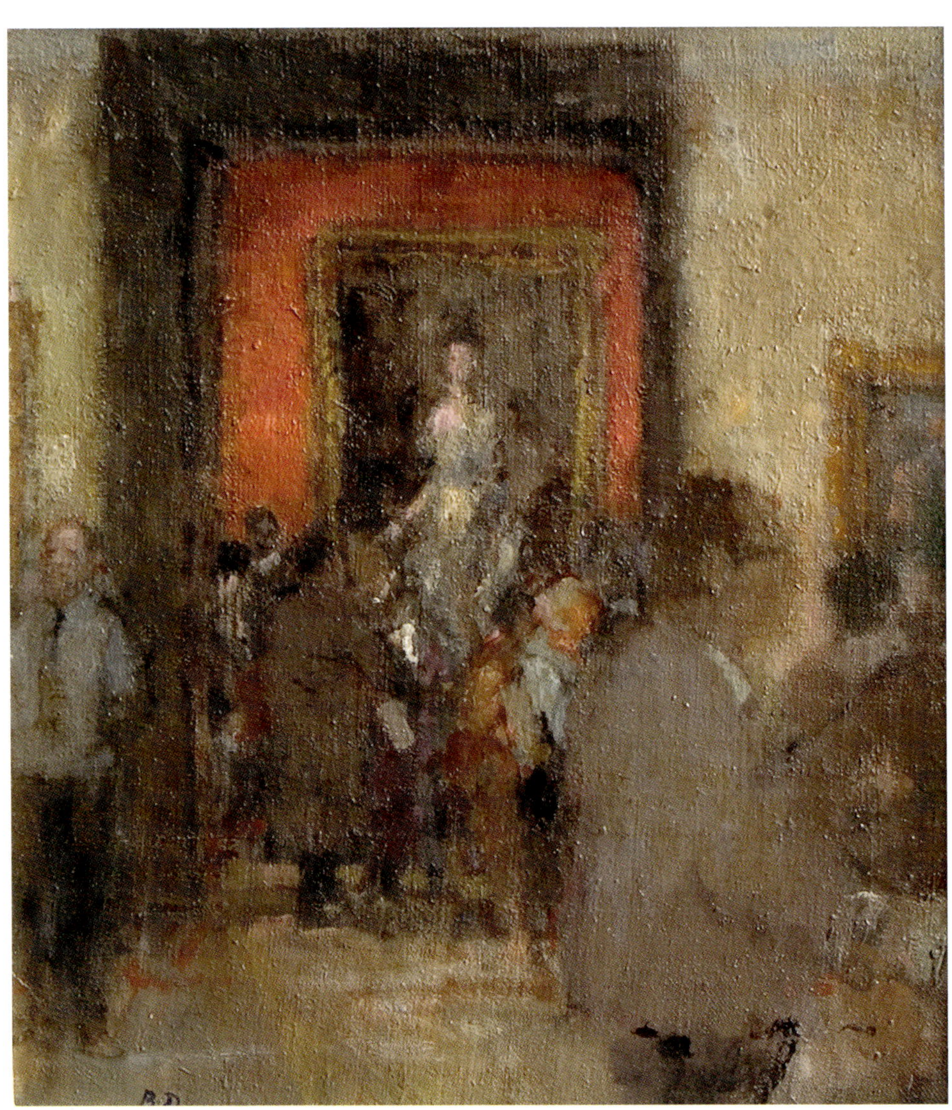

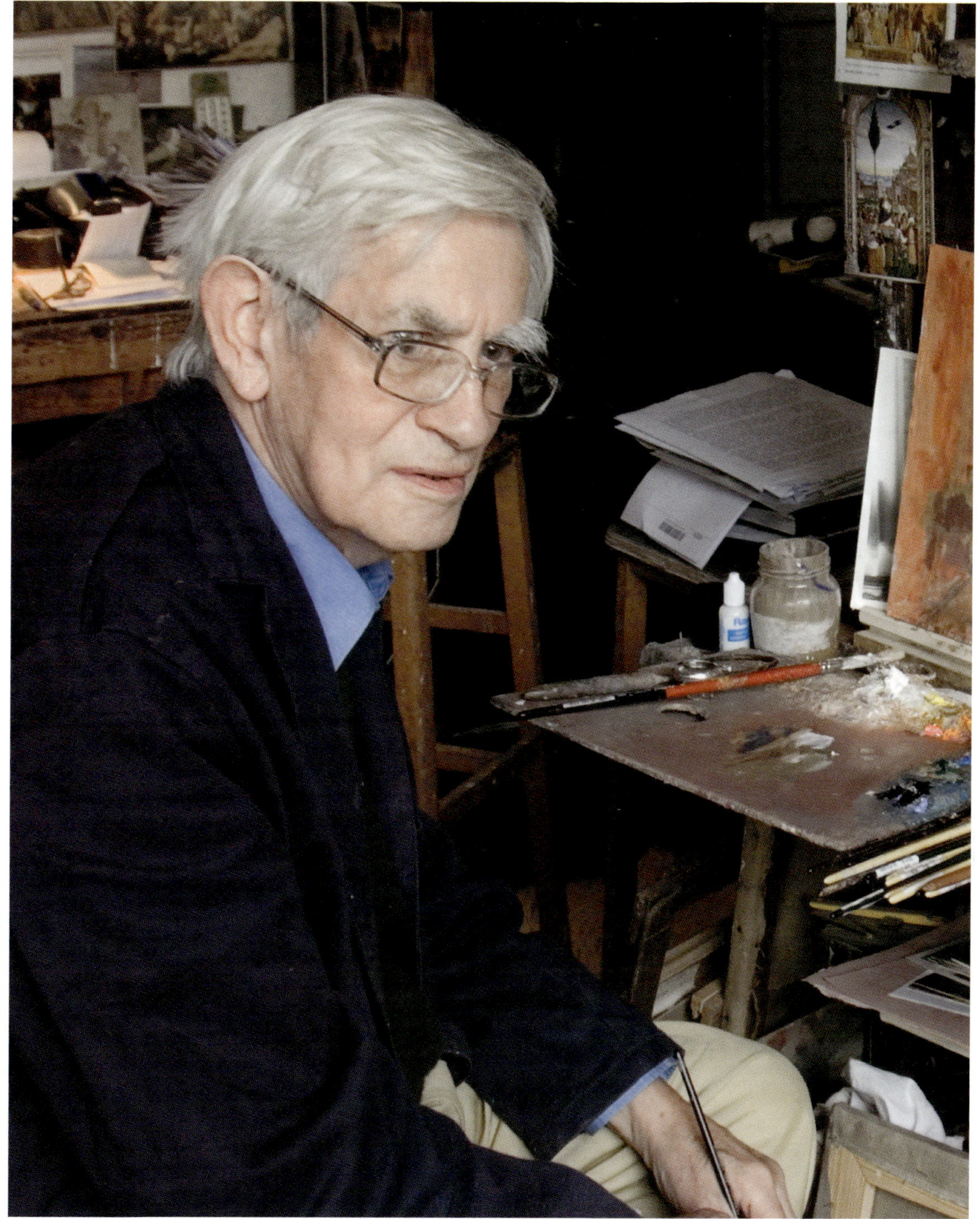

BERNARD DUNSTAN RA

JENNIFER DURRANT RA

From a series 'Last Conversations'
(Venti Furiosi), 2006
Acrylic and gouache on paper on card
38 x 18 cm

Born 17th June 1942

Jennifer Durrant studied at Brighton College of Art from 1959-63 and at the Slade School of Art from 1963-66. In 1972 she visited the United States where she experienced for the first time (and identified with) the large-scale works of Pollock, Gorky, Newman, Rothko and Morris Louis. She 'discovered' the works and ideas of Arthur Dove, Kandinsky and other great moderns and was introduced to the art critic Clement Greenberg.

Since appearing as a prizewinner in the Young Contemporaries in 1966, Jennifer Durrant has won a number of important art prizes and awards and has exhibited her large-scale canvases widely in major group exhibitions and solo shows in the UK and abroad including Europe, Canada and the USA. Since the 1970s She has produced a significant body of non-figurative lyrical acrylic/canvas works responding to her experiences of the natural world, cycles of change and her interest in music and eastern philosophy.

Jennifer Durrant lives and works in Umbria, Italy.

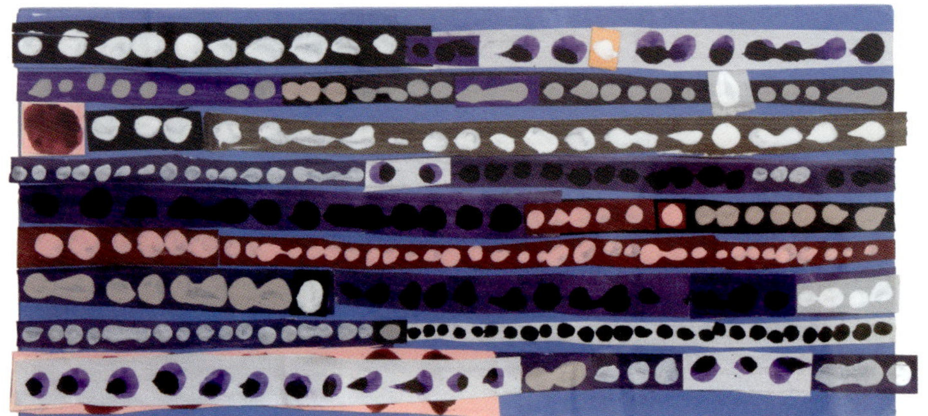

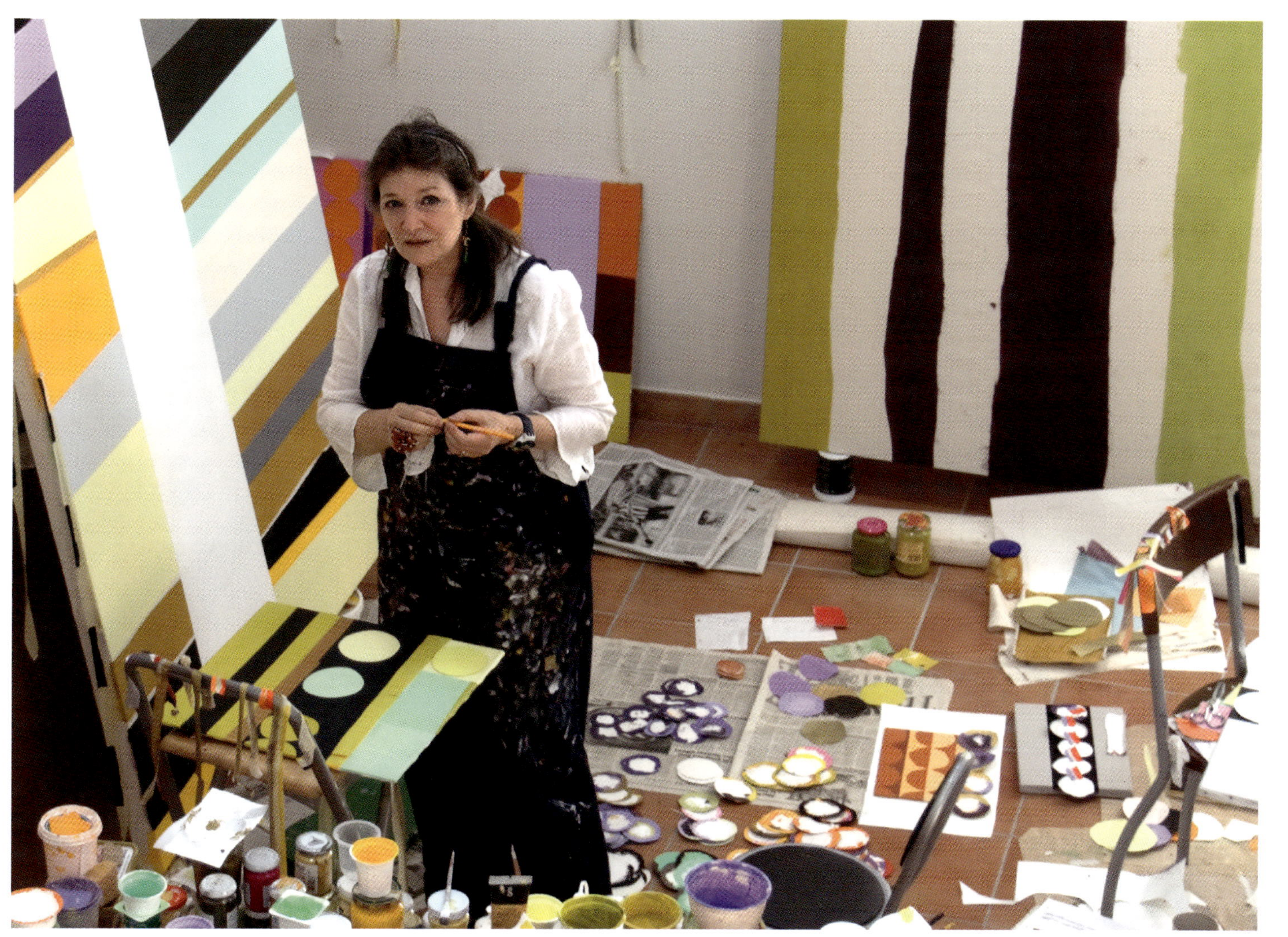

JENNIFER DURRANT RA

TRACEY EMIN RA

Elected RA 27th March 2007

More Fun
Pencil on paper
Courtesy of the artist
21 x 30 cm

Born 3rd July 1963

Tracey Emin studied at Maidstone College of Art (BFA),1986, and then at the Royal College of Art (MA),1989. She has exhibited internationally including solo and group exhibitions in Holland, Germany, Japan, Australia and America. In 1999 she was short-listed for the Turner Prize at Tate, London. She has had solo shows at the Stedelijk Museum (Amsterdam), Haus der Kunst (Munich) and Museum of Modern Art Oxford in 2002; Art Gallery of New South Wales (Australia) 2003 and Platform Garanti Contemporary Art Center, Istanbul in 2004. In June 2007 Tracey Emin represented Britain at the 52nd Venice Biennale, becoming only the second female artist to do so. Emin's art is one of disclosure using her life events as inspiration for works ranging from painting, drawing, video and installation, to photography, needlework and sculpture. Emin reveals her hopes, humiliations, failures and successes in candid and, at times, excoriating work that is frequently both tragic and humorous. Her interest in the work of Edvard Munch and Egon Schiele particularly informs her paintings, monoprints and drawings, which explore complex personal states and ideas of selfrepresentation through manifestly expressionist styles and themes.

Tracey Emin lives and works in London.
www.tracey-emin.co.uk

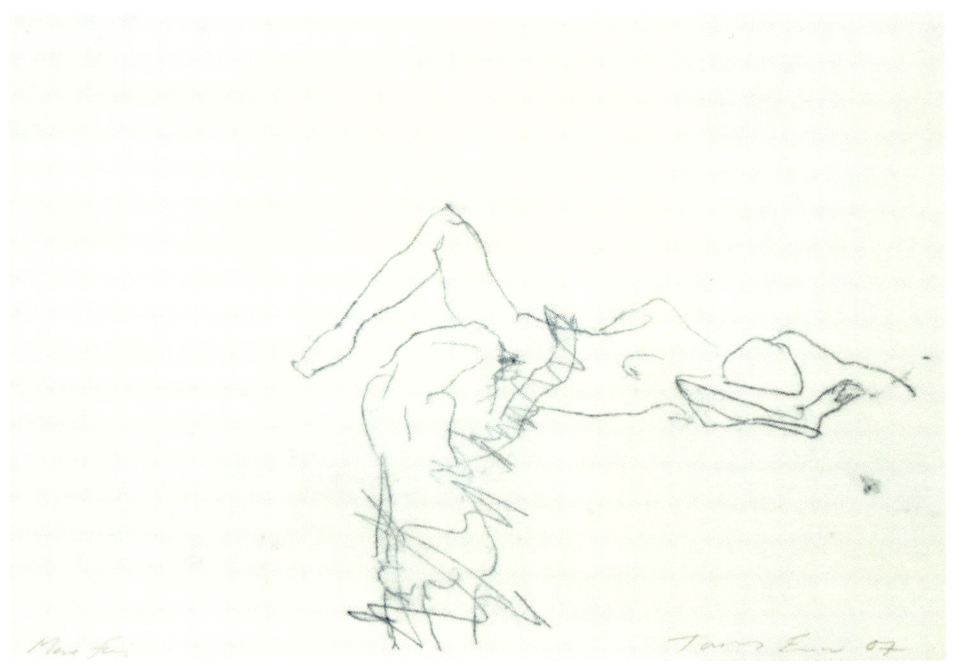

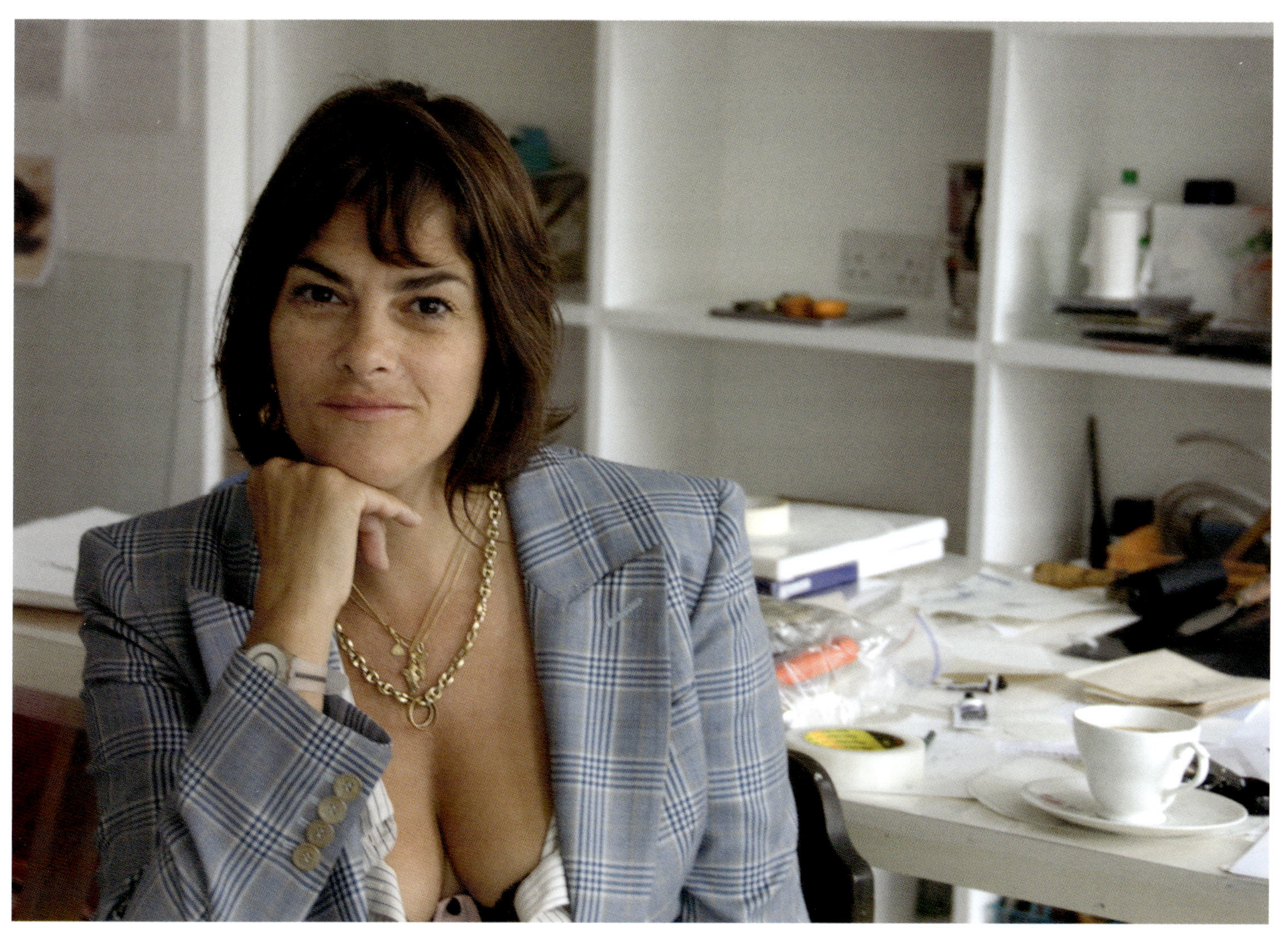

TRACEY EMIN RA

ANTHONY EYTON RA

Elected ARA 30th April 1976
Elected RA 20th November 1986

Morning Light Varinasi (Death and Life)
Oil on canvas
Courtesy of the artist
102 x 154 cm

Born 17th May 1923
Teddington, Middlesex

Anthony Eyton studied Fine Art at Reading University in 1941 before serving in the Army from 1942-47. He studied at Camberwell School of Art from 1947-50 and received an Abbey Major Scholarship in 1951-52 taking him to work in Italy. He was Head of Painting at St Lawrence College, Kingston, Ontario in 1960 and taught at the Royal Academy Schools from 1964-69.

Anthony Eyton has travelled extensively particularly in India, Israel and Sudan and was commissioned by the Artistic Records Committee to observe and paint the Gurkha Regiment in Hong Kong and the New Territories. He was asked to record the building of the Eden Project and the conversion of Bankside Power Station into Tate Modern. He was also commissioned by the Government Art Collection to record the Centenary of the British Embassy in Addis Ababa, Ethiopia. Anthony Eyton says *'I want to reproduce the look of nature as spontaneously and accurately as possible, which entails much redrawing and composing in order to gain the light and structure, together with the continual excitement of observing'*.

Anthony Eyton lives and works in London.

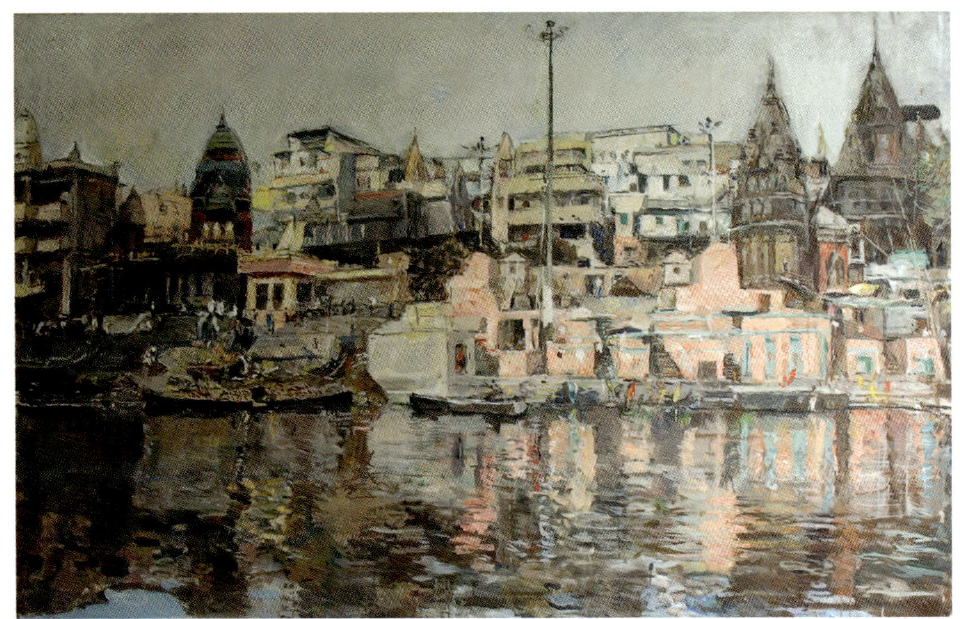

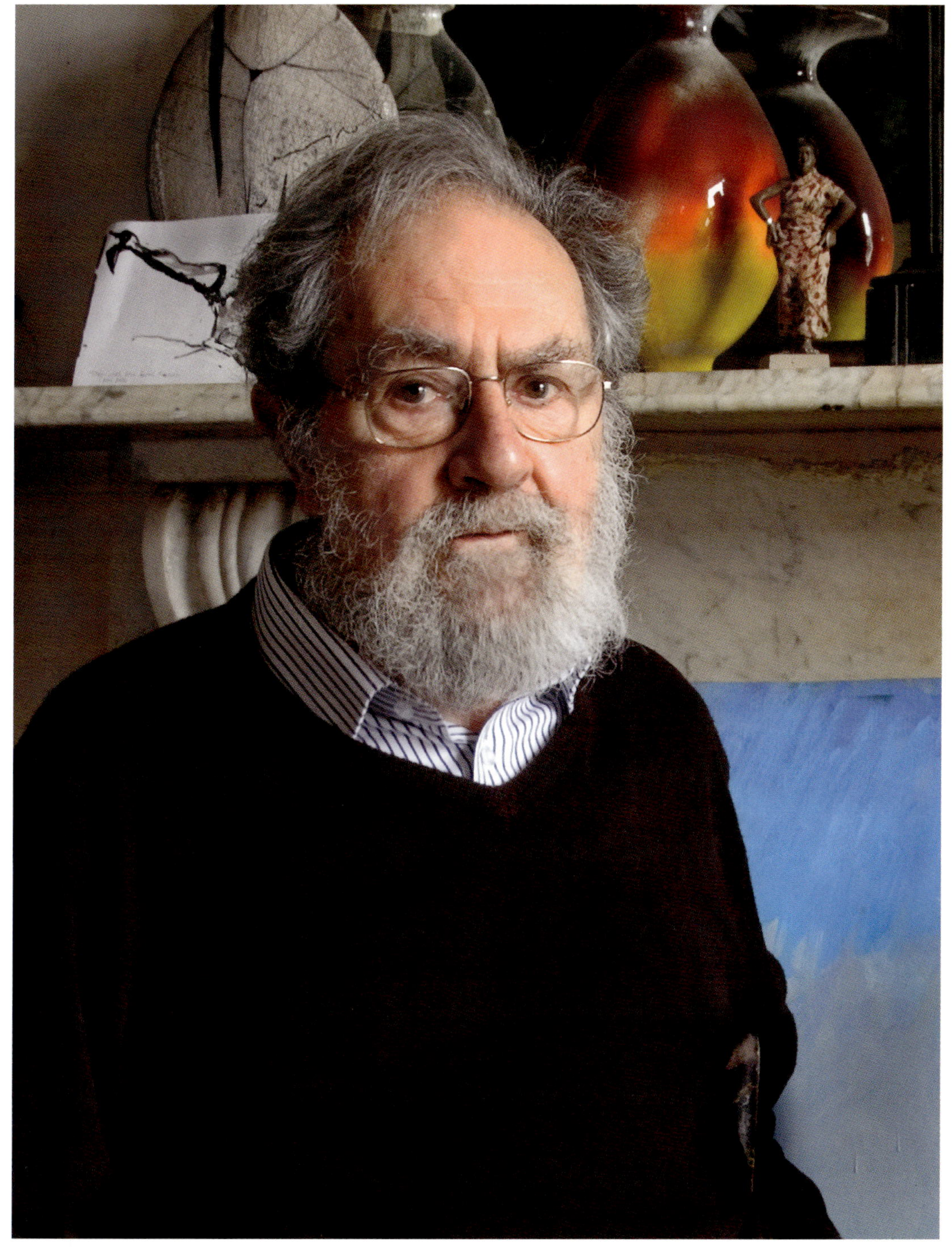

ANTHONY EYTON RA

STEPHEN FARTHING RA

Elected RA 21st May 1998

Painted Duck no 3 2007
Gesso on canvas
Courtesy of the artist
210 x 173 cm

Born 16th September 1950
London

Stephen Farthing studied at St Martin's School of Art from 1969 to 1973 before taking his Masters Degree in Painting at the Royal College of Art from 1973-76. There he received an Abbey Major Scholarship in 1976 taking him to the British School at Rome for a year. He began teaching as a Lecturer in Painting at Canterbury College of Art from 1977-79 after which he was a Tutor in Painting at the Royal College of Art from 1980 to 1985. He became Head of Painting 1985 to 1987 and Head of the Department of Fine Art at West Surrey College of Art and Design. From 1990 he was Ruskin Master at Ruskin College of Fine Art and Professorial Fellow of St Edmund Hall, Oxford. He became Emeritus Fellow in 2000 on becoming Executive Director of the New York Academy of Art. In 2004 he was appointed Rootstein Hopkins Research Professor of Drawing at the University of the Arts in London. Stephen Farthing has been described as an erudite painter with several enthusiams evident in his career. His work is economical using the briefest means to express his view. A critic once said of Stephen Farthing that *'he enjoys a dry, pointed humour enjoying comparison of a painter's trompe l'oeil with a game bird's art of camouflage'.*

Stephen Farthing lives and works in London and New York.

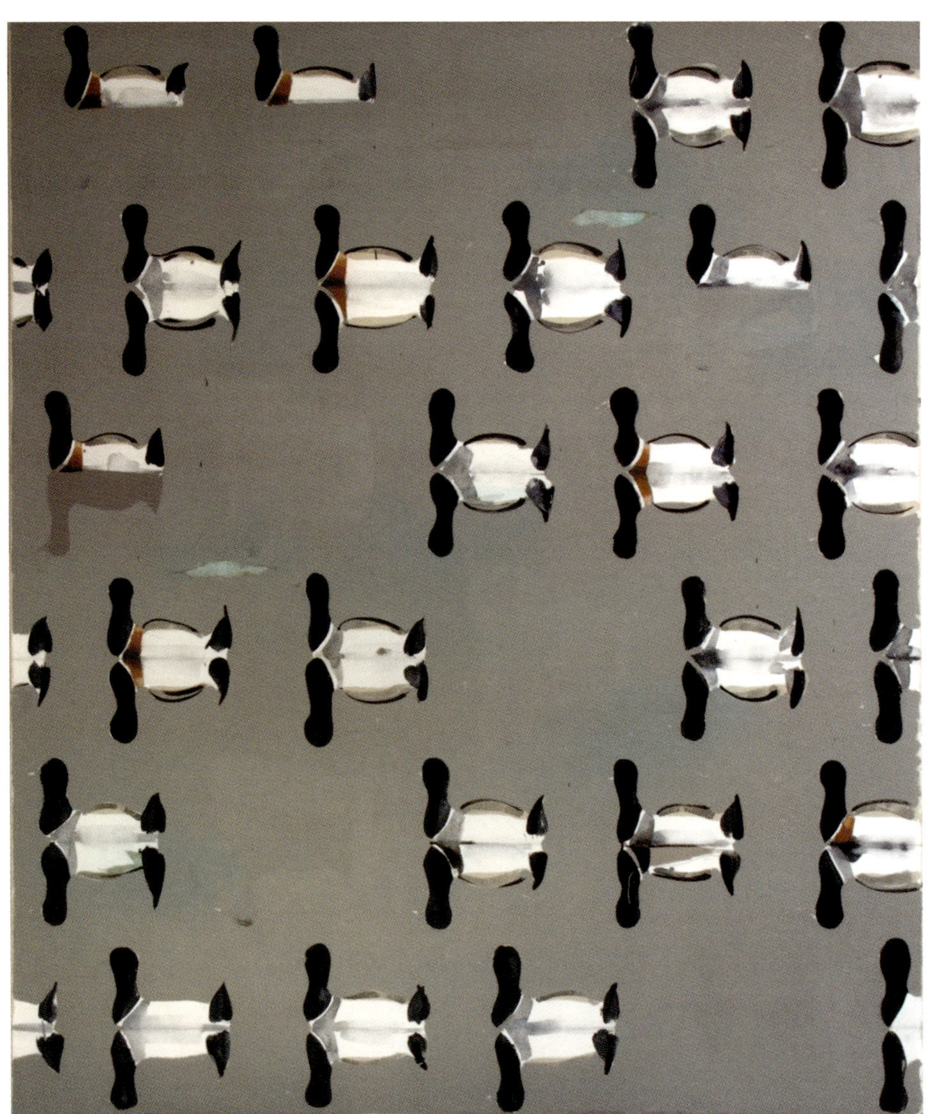

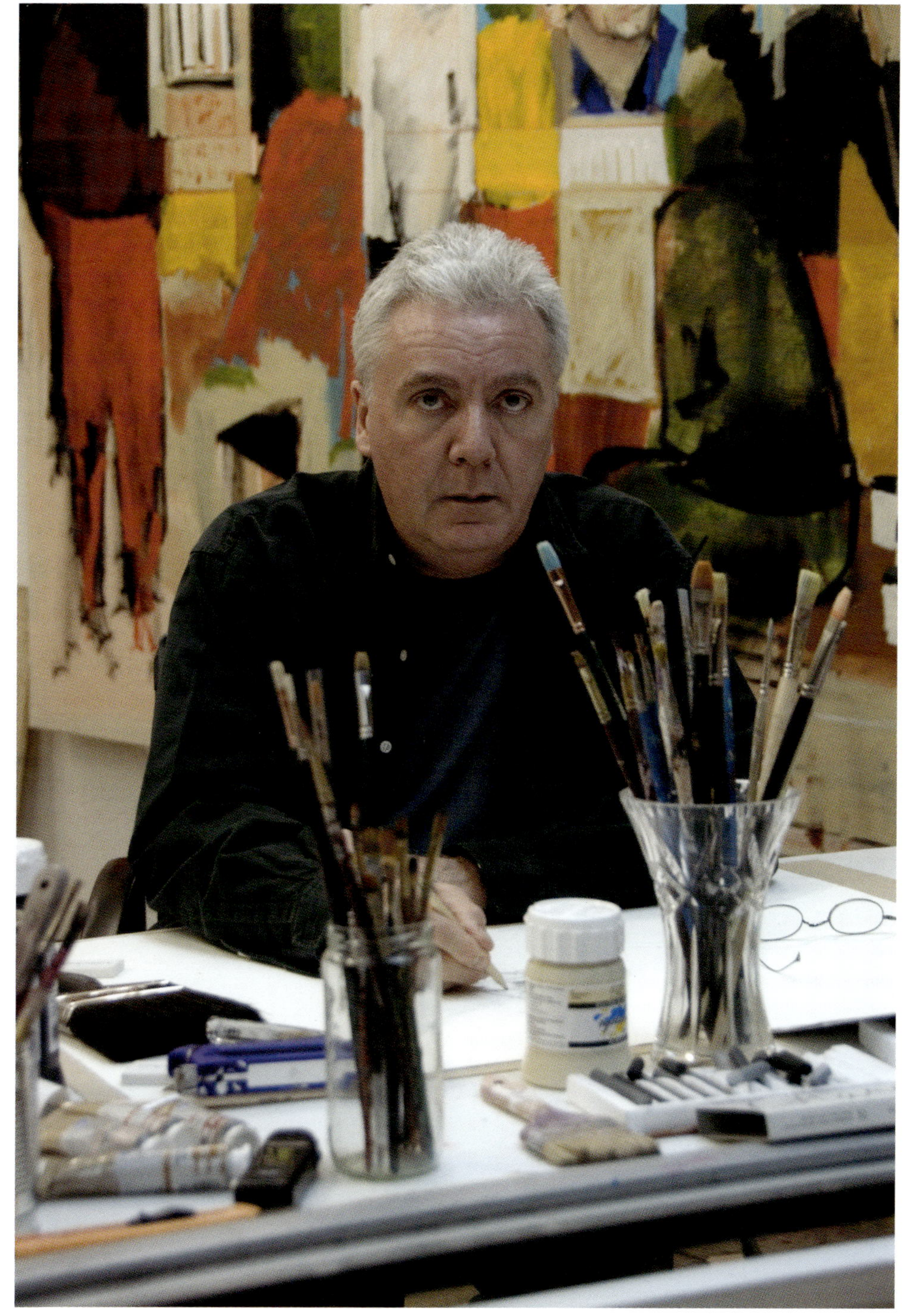

STEPHEN FARTHING RA

MARY FEDDEN OBE RA

Black and White Ball
Oil on canvas
Courtesy of the artist

Born 14th August 1915
Bristol

Mary Fedden studied at the Slade School of Fine Art from 1932-36. She went on to teach Painting at the Royal College of Art from 1958-64 where she was the first woman tutor to teach in the Painting School. She then taught at the Yehudi Menuhin School from 1965-70. Mary Fedden was made a Doctor of Literature by Bath University in 1992. She paints still-lifes, which are often placed in front of a landscape, flowers and animals in a variety of media and enjoys contrasting disparate and even quirky elements. She was married to the late British artist Julian Trevelyan whom she described as *'really changing the direction of my painting'*. She has received many mural commissions, notably the Festival of Britain in 1951, the P & O Liner Canberra in 1961, Charing Cross Hospital in 1980 (along with Julian Trevelyan), and Colindale Hospital in 1985.

Mary Fedden lives and works beside the River Thames in London.

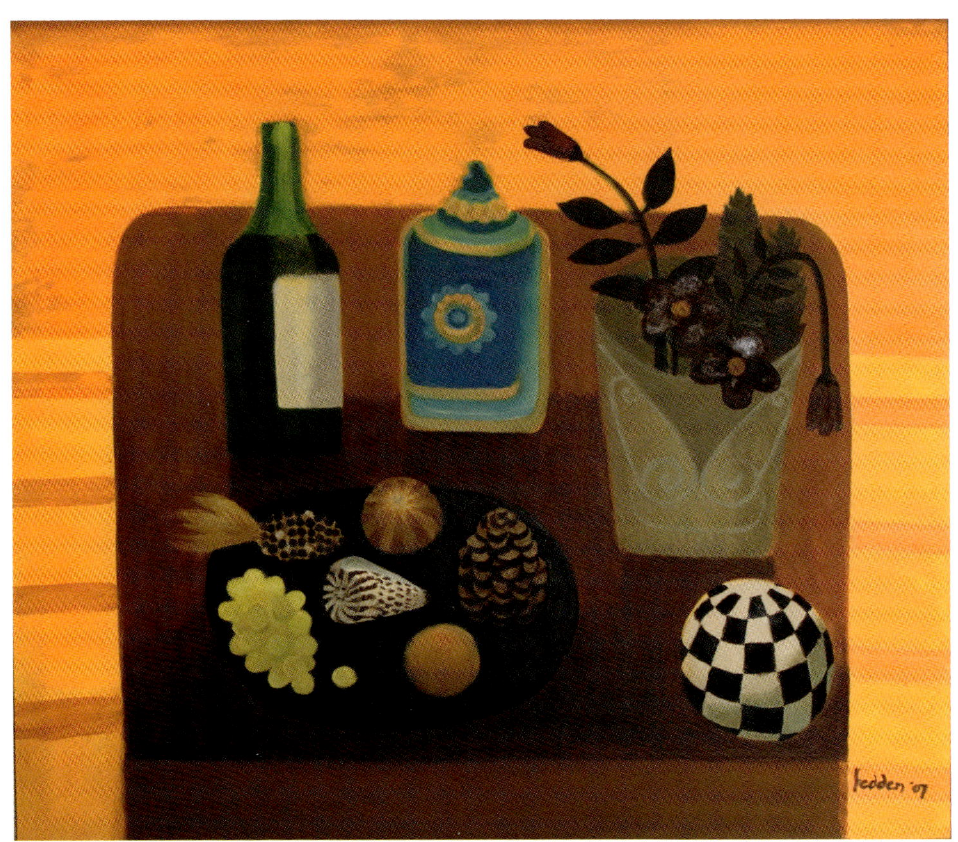

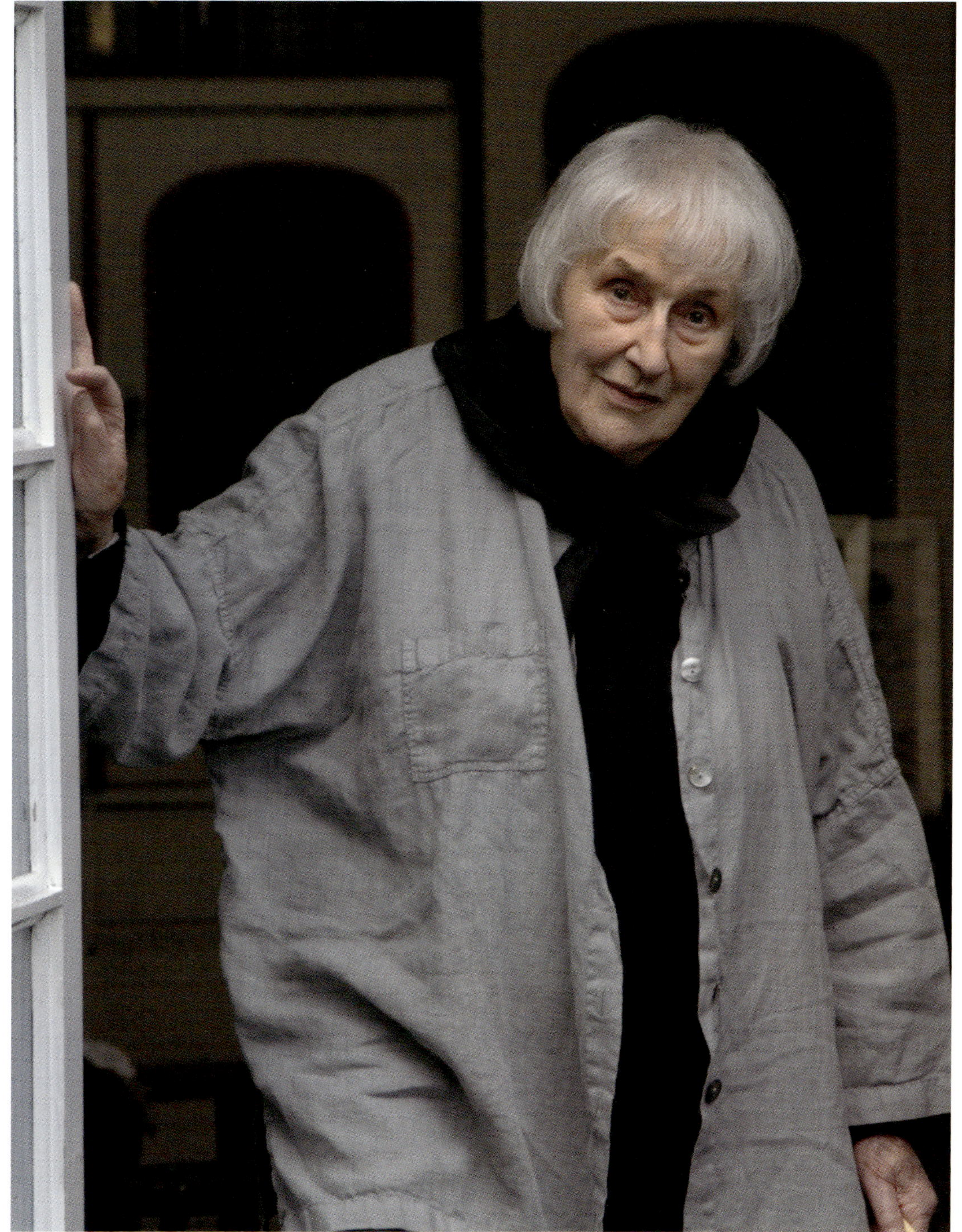

MARY FEDDON OBE RA

PETER FREETH RA

Elected ARA 30th May 1990
Elected RA 26th June 1991

Equus 3
Aquatint
Courtesy of the artist
48 x 60 cm

Born 15th April 1938
Birmingham

Peter Freeth studied at the Slade School of Fine Art from 1956-60 when he won the Prix de Rome in Engraving which took him to Rome for 3 years and enabled him to travel extensively throughout Italy.

Peter Freeth has been Tutor in Engraving at the Royal Academy Schools since 1966 and in 1991 was made a Fellow of the Royal Society of Painter Printmakers. He has exhibited widely in the UK, USA, Europe, India and Asia and his work is held in public collections in both the UK and USA. He works exclusively in black and white on a wide variety of themes drawn from memory, literature, still life and the daily experience of the city dweller. Freeth says *'Sometimes I start work with a precise image in mind, sometimes with a vague general direction, sometimes the title comes before the image. Often I discover that the elusive image I have struggled so hard to define is a distant recollection of something I have seen ten years before..'*

Peter Freeth lives and works in London.

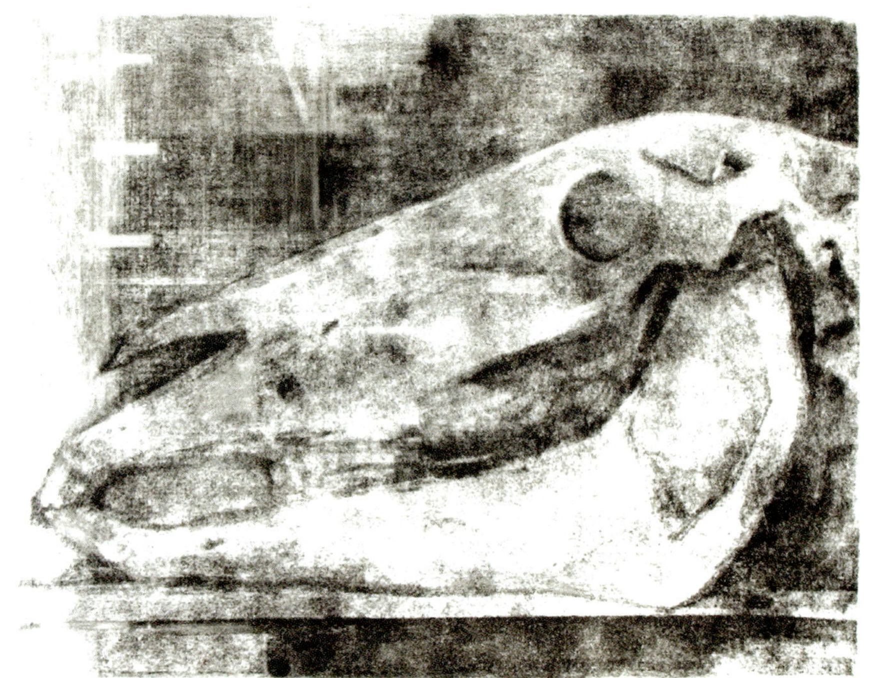

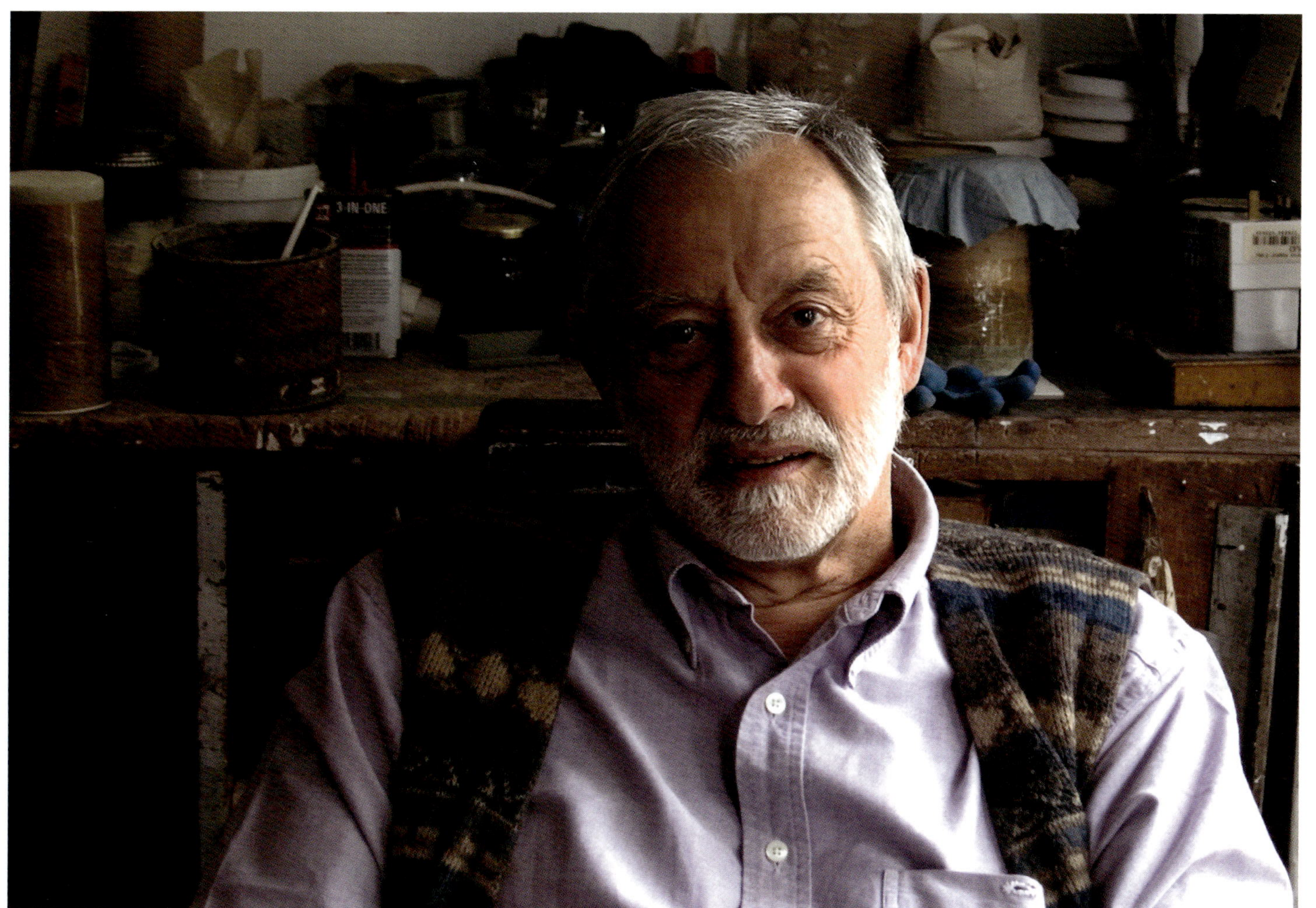

PETER FREETH RA

FREDERICK GORE CBE RA

Elected ARA 23rd April 1963
Elected RA 15th June 1972

Indian Sculpture and the Gauguin Catalogue
Oil on canvas
Courtesy of the artist
61 x 51 cm

Born 8th November 1913
Richmond, Surrey

Frederick Gore studied at the Ruskin School of Drawing, Oxford from 1932-34 and the Westminster School of Art and the Slade School of Fine Art from 1934-37. In World War II he served as a Major in the Royal Artillery and then as camouflage officer before D Day.

In 1946 he taught at St Martin's School of Art, was Head of Painting there from 1951-79 and Vice-Principal from 1961. He was appointed Chairman of the Exhibitions Committee of the RA from 1976-87 and still serves on this Committee. He was a Trustee of the Imperial War Museum from 1967-84 and Chairman of its Artistic Records Committee: one of its longest serving members. He was made CBE in 1987.

Gore has had exhibitions in London, Paris (where he was dubbed 'Fauve' by the art critic Louis Vauxcelles) and New York, he has written on abstract art, principles of painting and on Piero della Franscesca. As Chairman of the Exhibitions Committee his innovative ideas helped rejuvenate the image of the Royal Academy. Always athletic, he was for more than thirty years an active member of the Balalaika (Russian Folk) Dance Group.

Frederick Gore lives and works in London and Provence.

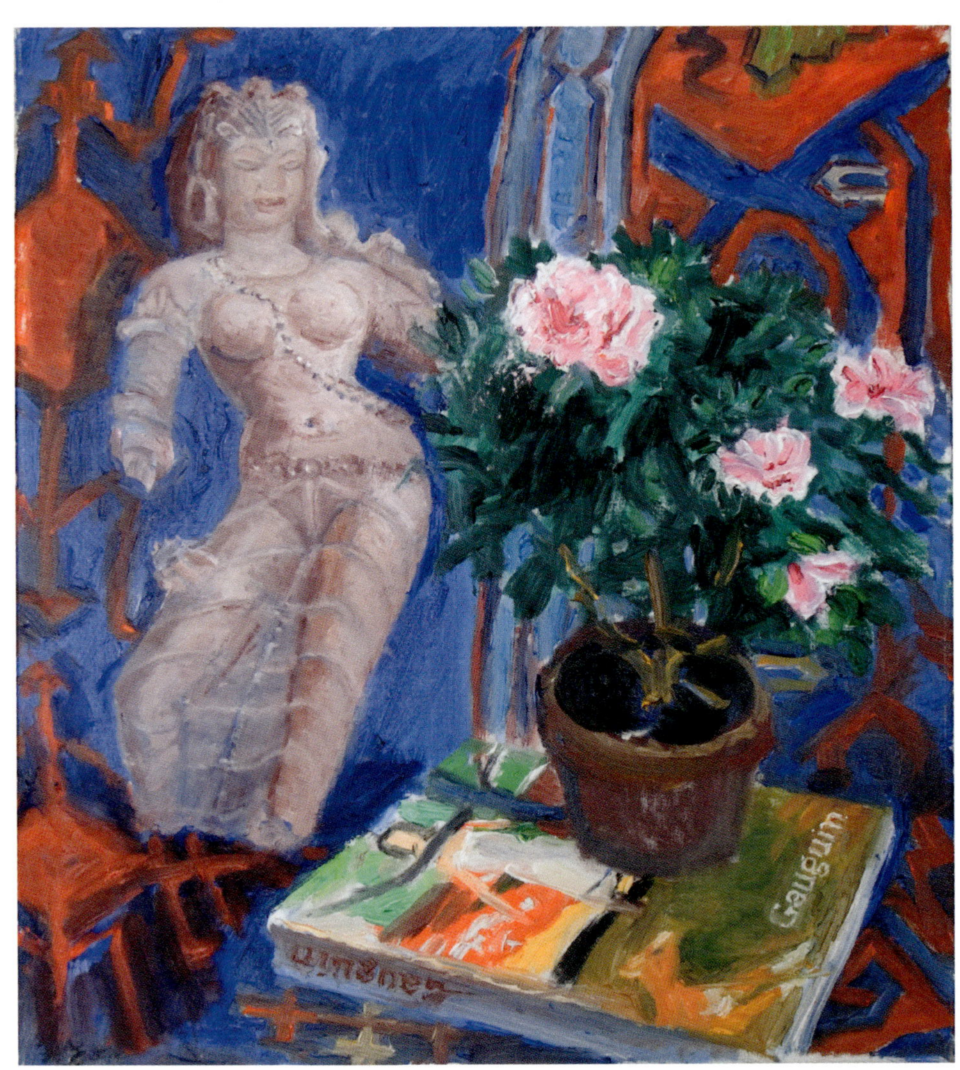

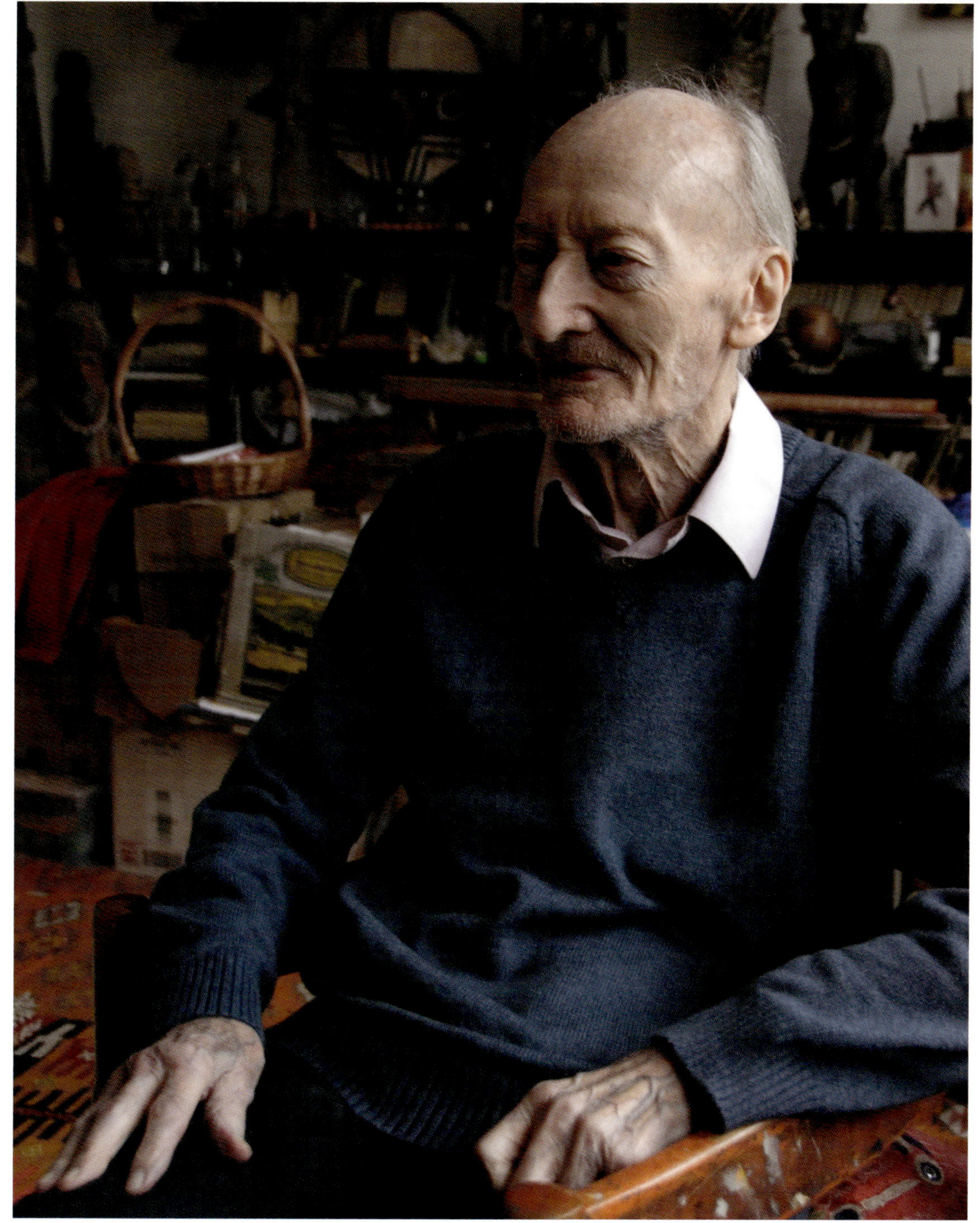

FREDERICK GORE CBE RA

ANTHONY GREEN RA

Elected ARA 23rd April 1971
Elected RA 1st March 1977

J'admire beaucoup Marcel, mais réflexion faite, je préfère ma femme (grande version finale)
1991-2006

Oil on hardboard
Courtesy of the artist
229 x 226 cm

Born 30th September 1939
Luton, Bedfordshire

Anthony Green was educated at Highgate School in London before studying at the Slade School of Art from 1956-60. In 1960 he received a French Government Scholarship to visit Paris where he lived for a year before returning to England to marry Mary Cozens-Walker. He returned to the Slade in 1964 to teach and in 1967 received a Harkness Fellowship to visit the United States, living in New Jersey and California for 2 years.
He is a very recognizable painter who in his narrative, autobiographical style mainly chronicles his family and surroundings.
The irregular shapes to which he works emphasise his view that paintings have no edges and do not have to be contained in box-like forms.

Anthony Green lives and paints in Cambridgeshire.

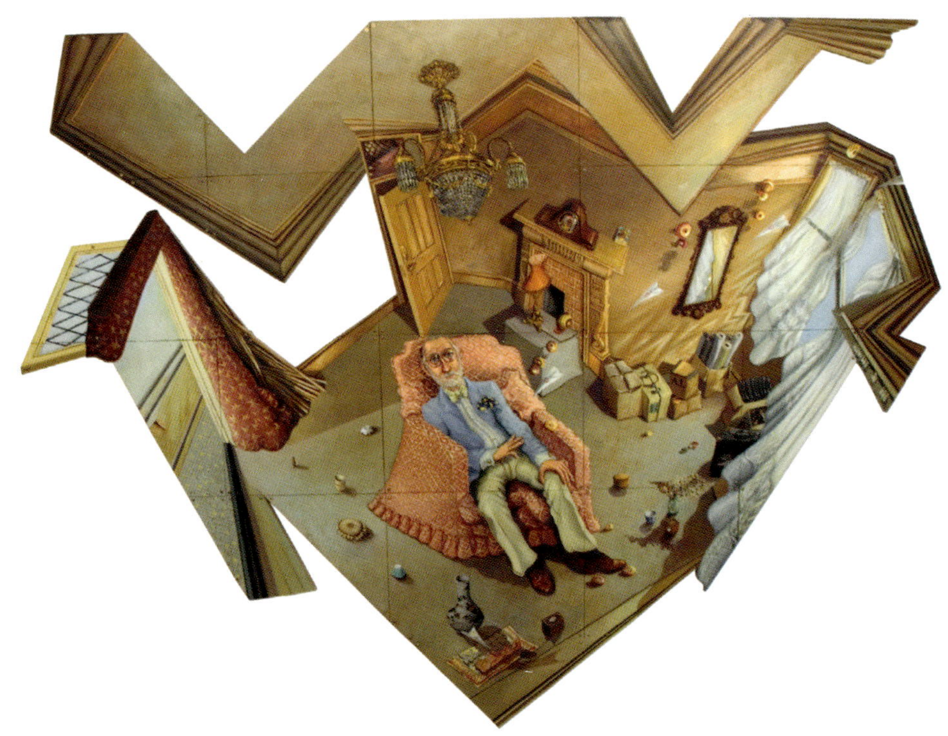

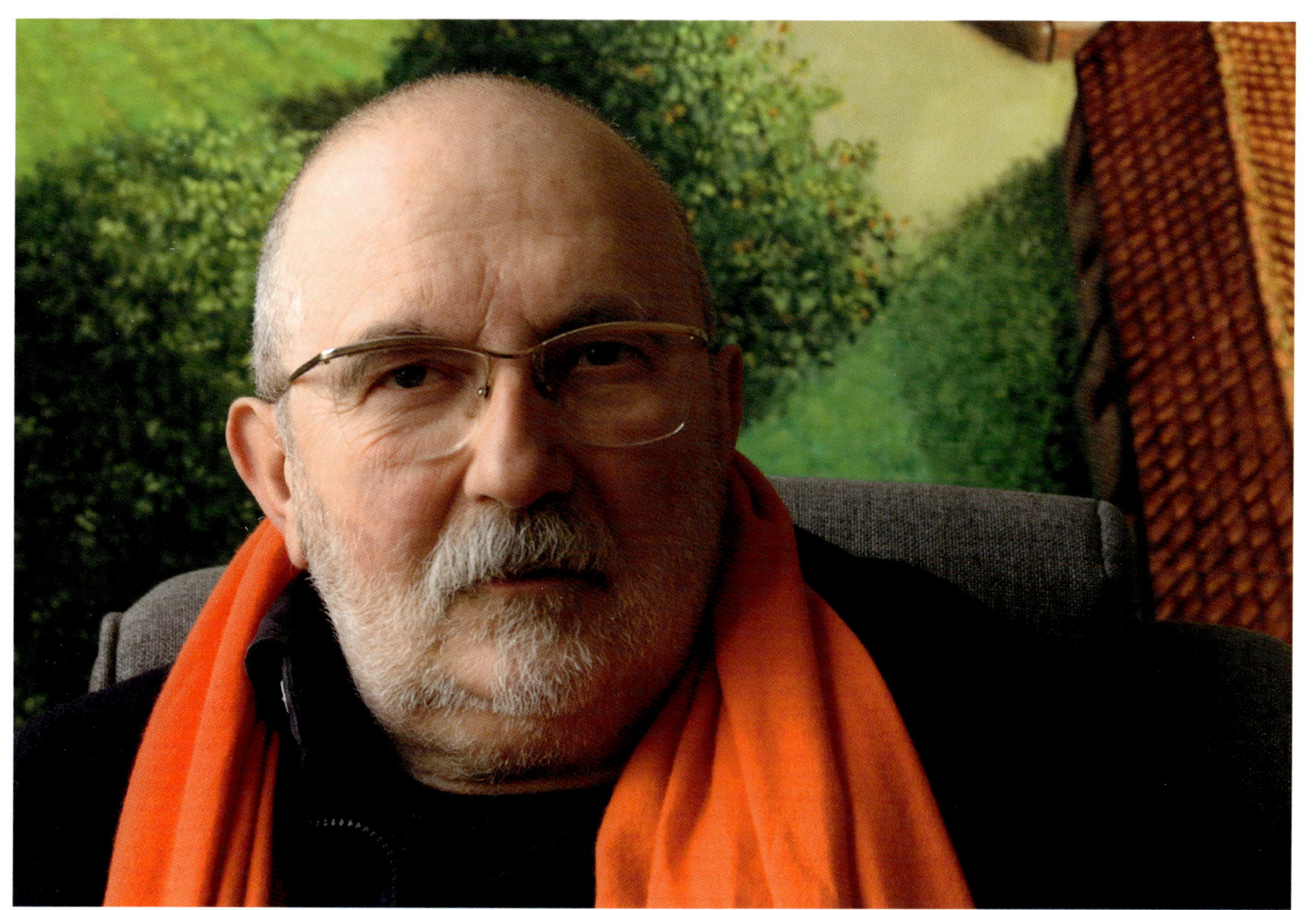

ANTHONY GREEN RA

DONALD HAMILTON FRASER RA

Elected ARA 24th April 1975
Elected RA 20th May 1985

Lindisfarne
Oil on board
Courtesy of the artist
31 x 43 cm

Born 30th July 1929
London

Donald Hamilton Fraser studied at St Martin's School of Art from 1949-52 and gained a French Government Scholarship to visit Paris in 1953 where he lived and worked for 2 years from 1953-54.

In 1957 he became Visiting Tutor at the Royal College of Art where he remained until 1983. He was a Fellow of the Royal College of Art in 1970 and an Honorary Fellow in 1983. He was made a member of the Royal Fine Art Commission from 1986-2000. He is Vice-President of the Royal Overseas League and the Artists' General Benevolent Institution. In his instantly recognisable landscapes Hamilton Fraser combines his Scottish descent and his affinity with French painting both being reflected in his style and execution. His layers of thick bright paint applied with a palette knife produce an almost collage effect, forming abstract, dream-like fields of colour. Contrasting in style and highlighting Hamilton Fraser's diversity are his beautiful chalk and wash drawings of dancers which reveal his intimate knowledge of dance.

Donald Hamilton Fraser lives and works in Henley-on-Thames.

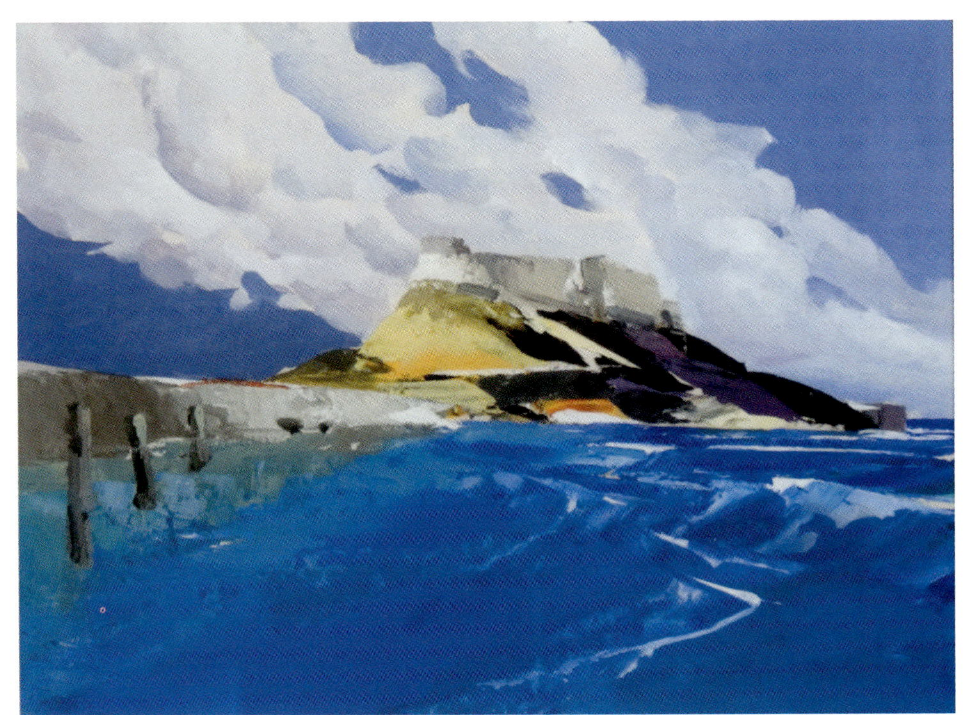

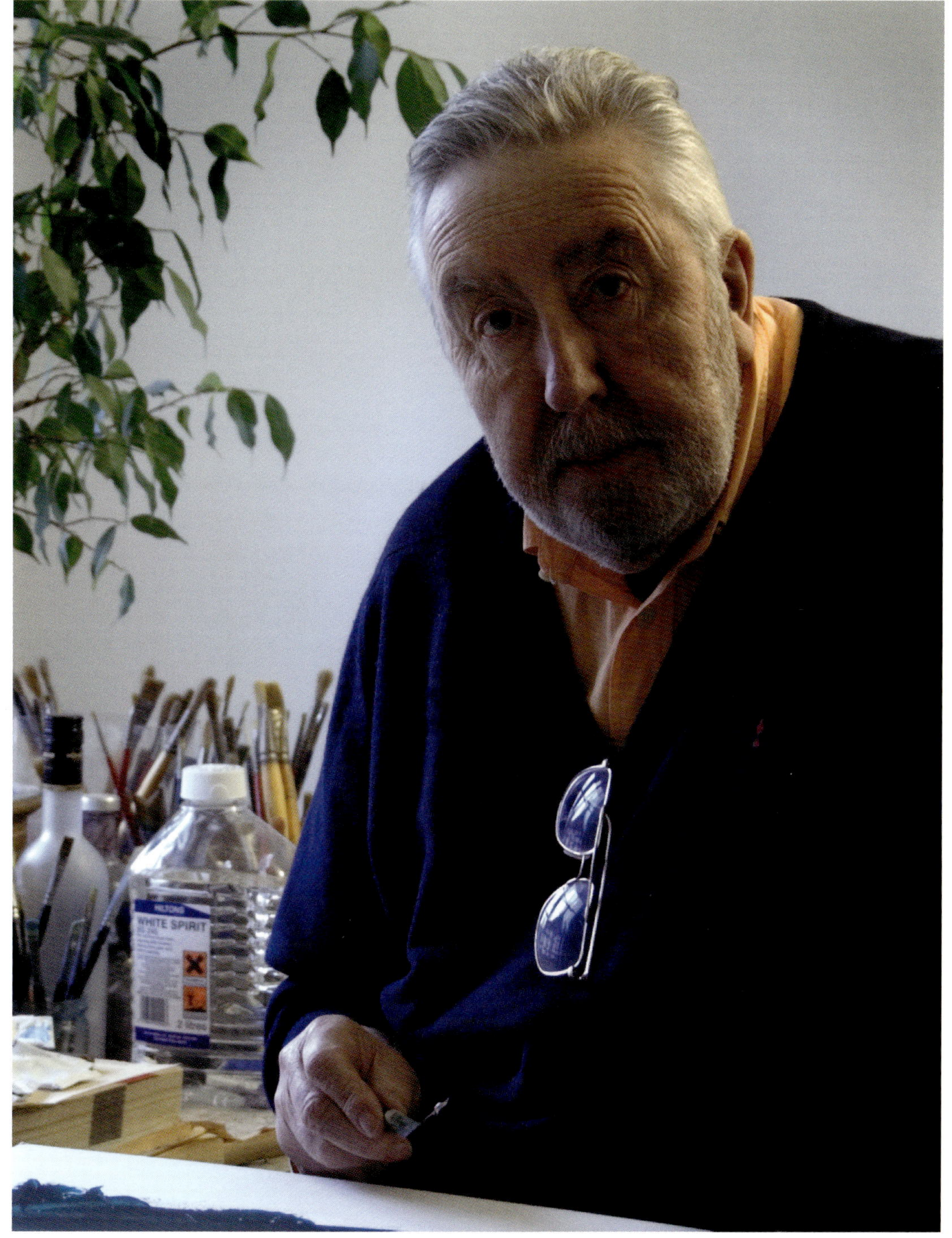

DONALD HAMILTON FRASER RA

KEN HOWARD RA

Elected ARA 19th May 1983
Elected RA 26th June 1991

Dora Dark and Light
Oil on canvas
Courtesy of the artist
102 x 122 cm

Born 26th December 1932
London

Ken Howard studied at Hornsey School of Art from 1949-53 when he did his National Service in the Royal Marines. He returned to study at the Royal College of Art from 1955-58 winning a British Council Scholarship to Florence from 1958-59. In 1973 and 1979 he was appointed Official War Artist in Northern Ireland. From 1973-82 he also worked with the British Army in Germany, Cyprus, Oman, Hong Kong, Nepal, Norway, Canada, Belize and Brunei.

Howard's much sought-after work demonstrates how everyday scenes can be brought to life and provide the viewer with points of interest he might not have noticed for himself. In London Howard lives and works in the house and studios of Sir William Orpen. He feels that in many ways he shares more than his surroundings, having been a War Artist like Orpen who died a year before his own birth.

Ken Howard also has homes and studios in Cornwall and Venice

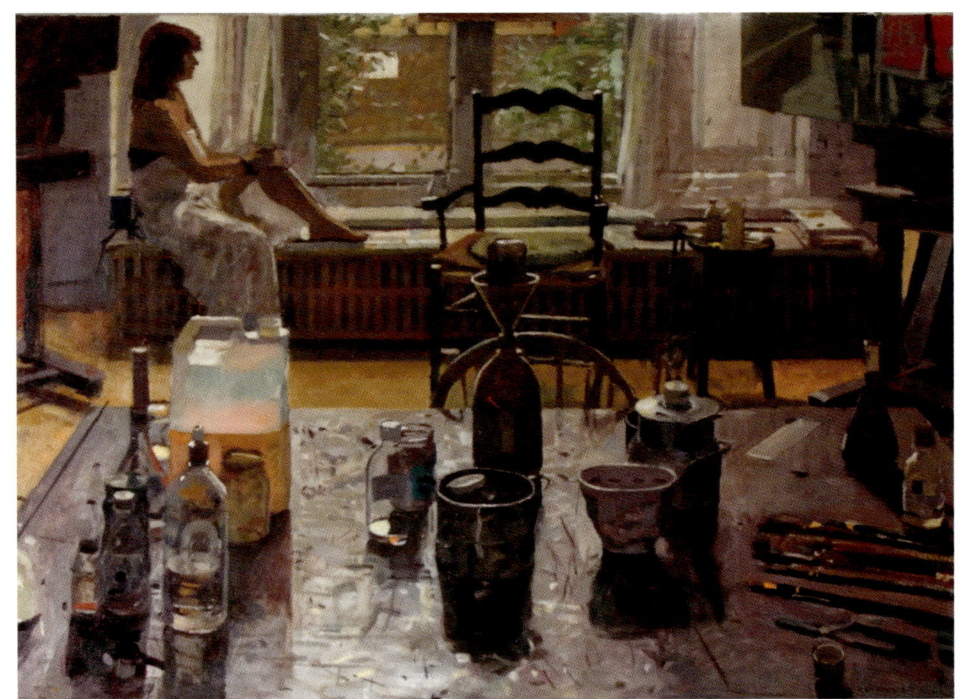

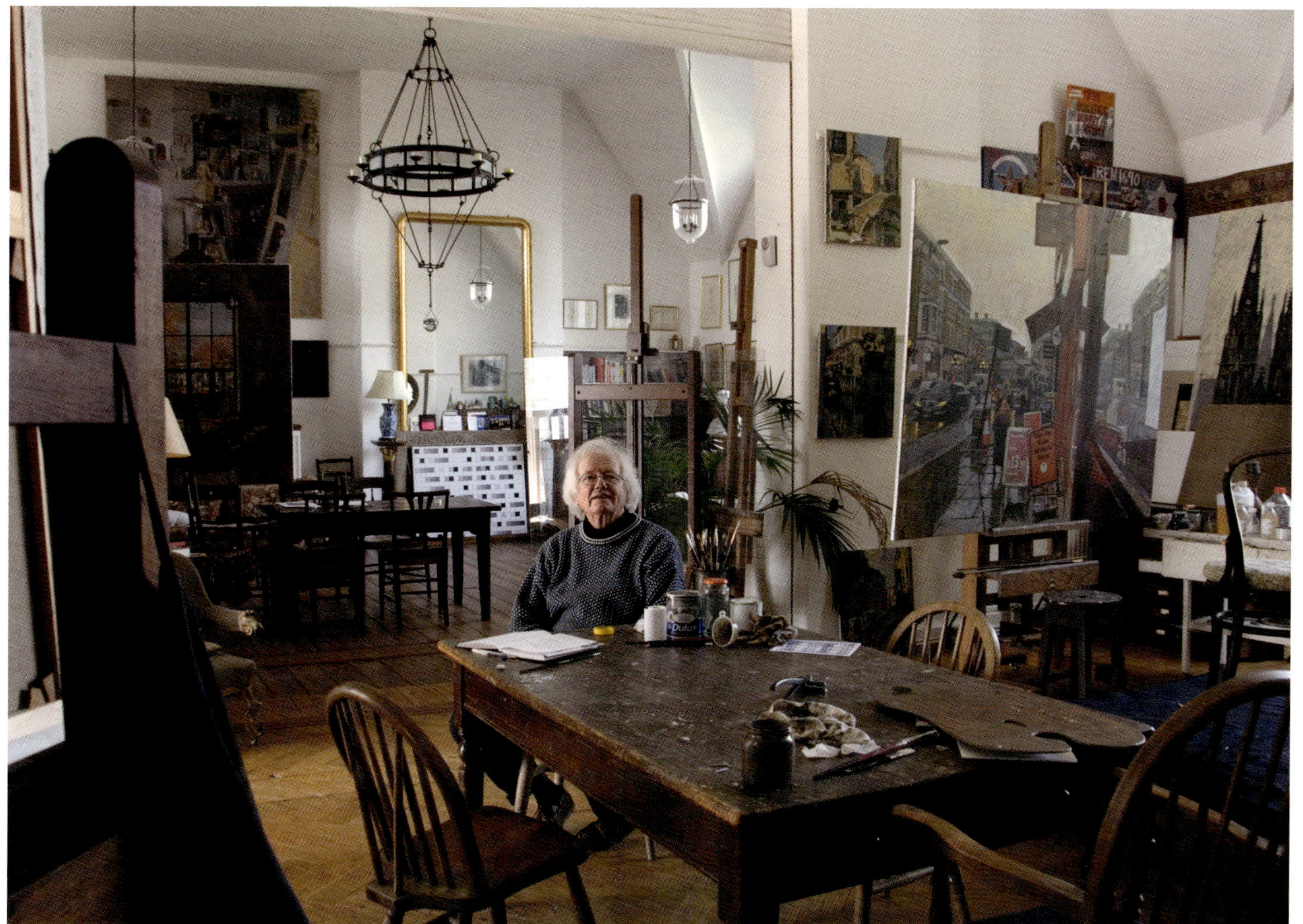

JOHN HOYLAND RA

Elected ARA 18th May 1983
Elected RA 26th June 1991

Souvenir for Patrick 2.4.06
Acrylic on canvas
Courtesy of the artist
152 x 127 cm

Born 12th October 1934
Sheffield

John Hoyland studied at Sheffield School of Art from 1951-56 and subsequently at the Royal Academy Schools from 1956-60. He then went on to teach at Hornsey College of Art from 1960-62 and at Chelsea School of Art from 1962-69 where he was also Principal Lecturer from 1965-69. From 1974-77 he taught at St Martin's School of Art and the Royal Academy Schools while teaching at the Slade School of Fine Art from 1974-89.
He had his first solo exhibition in 1964, while still a student, followed by a string of shows from 1967 and through the 1970s to today. He has received many awards and developed strong links with America, from the late 60s being appointed the Charles A. Dana Professor of Fine Art at Colgate University, Hamilton, New York in 1972. He received an Honorary Doctorate from Sheffield University in 2001.

In 1959 he came under the influence of the American Abstract Expressionist movement which decisively influenced the direction of his work. He travels widely taking with him notebooks in which he records colourful depictions of his reactions to scene or circumstance in sketches which are in themselves formidable works of art.

John Hoyland lives and works in London.

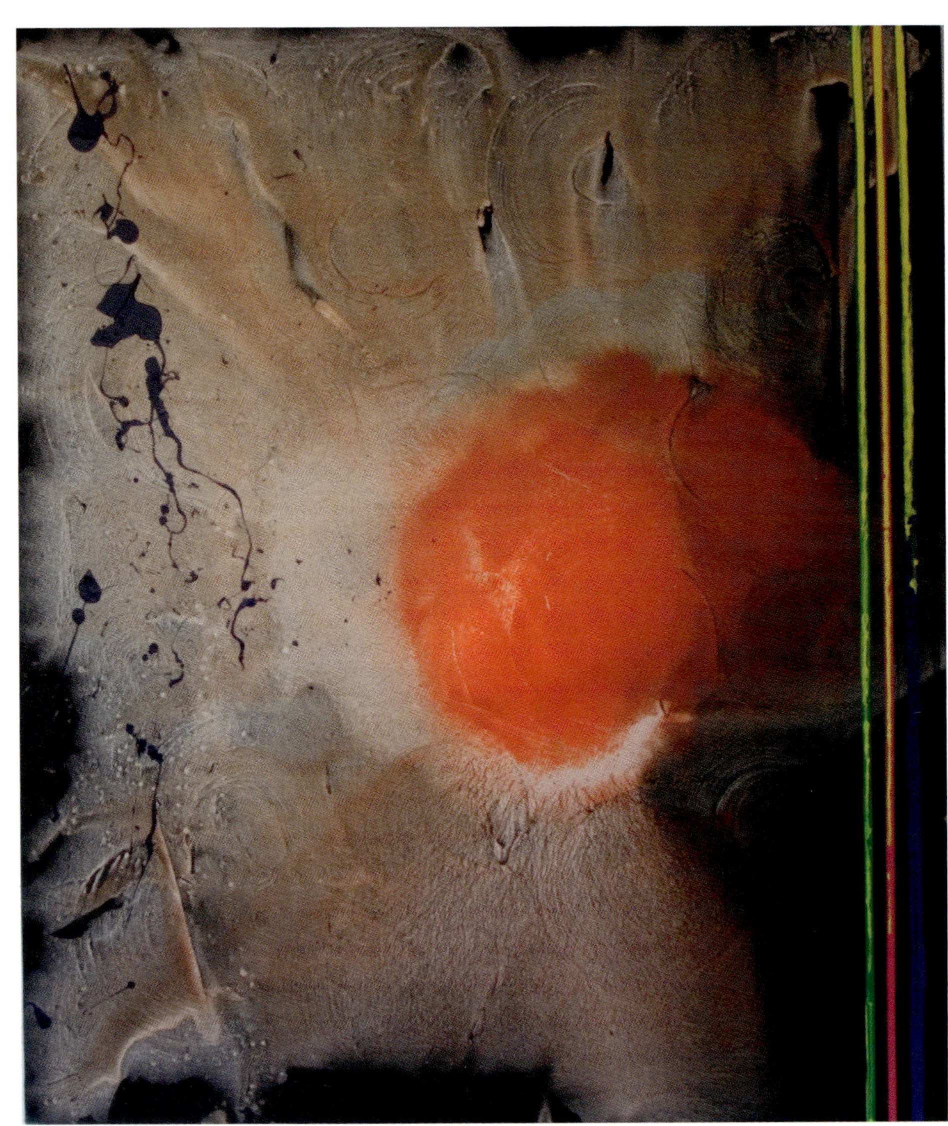

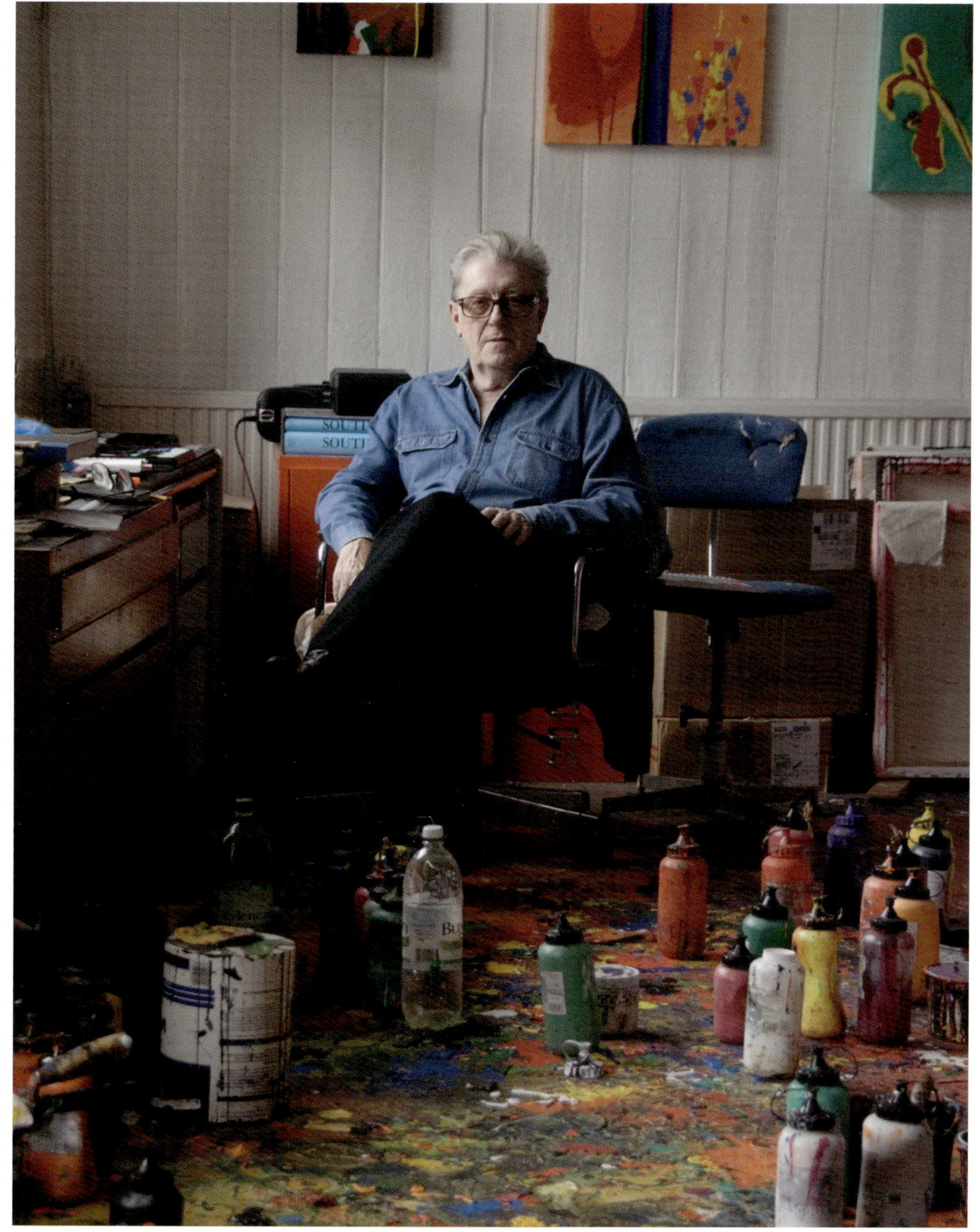

JOHN HOYLAND RA

GARY HUME RA

Elected RA 24h May 2001

American Tan no? 2007
Gloss on aluminium
Courtesy of the artist
100 x 74 cm

Born 9th May 1962
Kent

Gary Hume graduated from Goldsmiths College in London in 1988 and held his first exhibitions that year at Karsten Schubert and Frieze Part II, London, after which he rapidly established an international reputation for his 'door' paintings being shortlisted for the Turner Prize in 1995 and winning the Jerwood Painting Prize in 1997.

His minimal and abstract works painted on aluminium (because, he says, the high gloss paints he uses would crack under the movement of canvas) with their highly reflective surfaces, form a fluid and lyrical method of painting with bright colours and largely flat areas. He has described much of his work as 'beautiful'.

Gary Hume is Professor of Drawing at the RA Schools and lives and works in London and upstate New York.

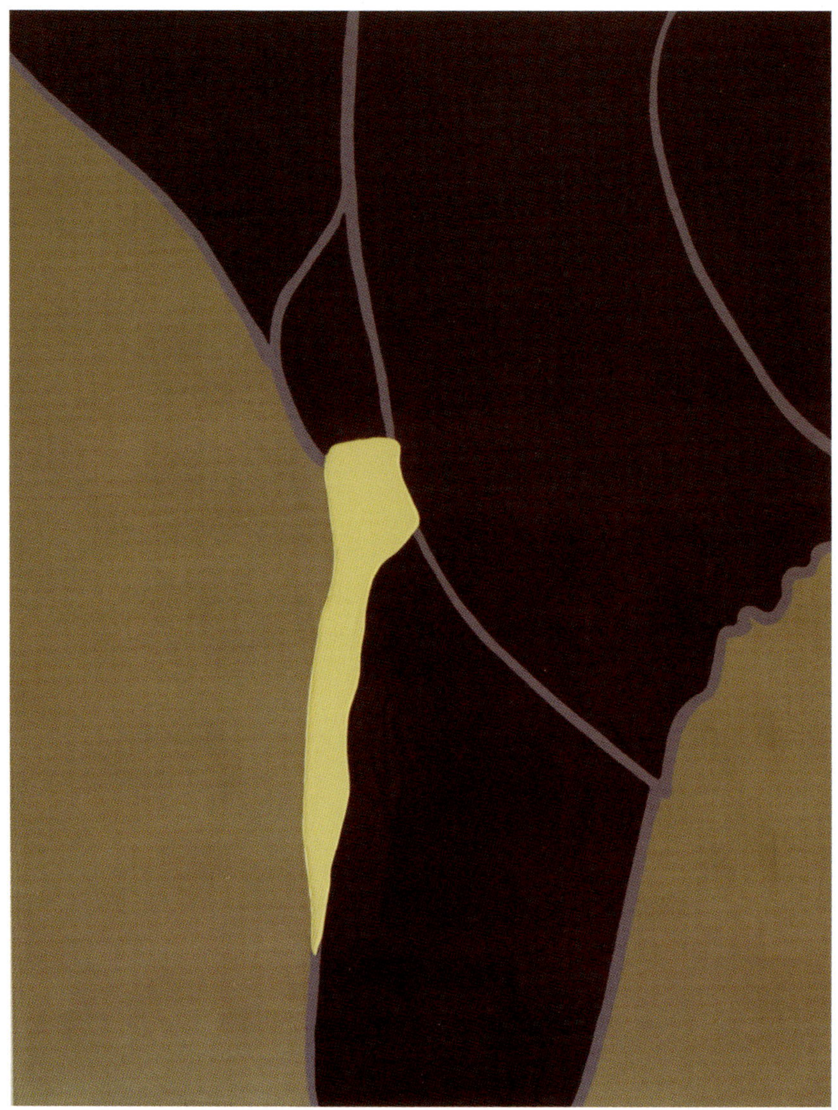

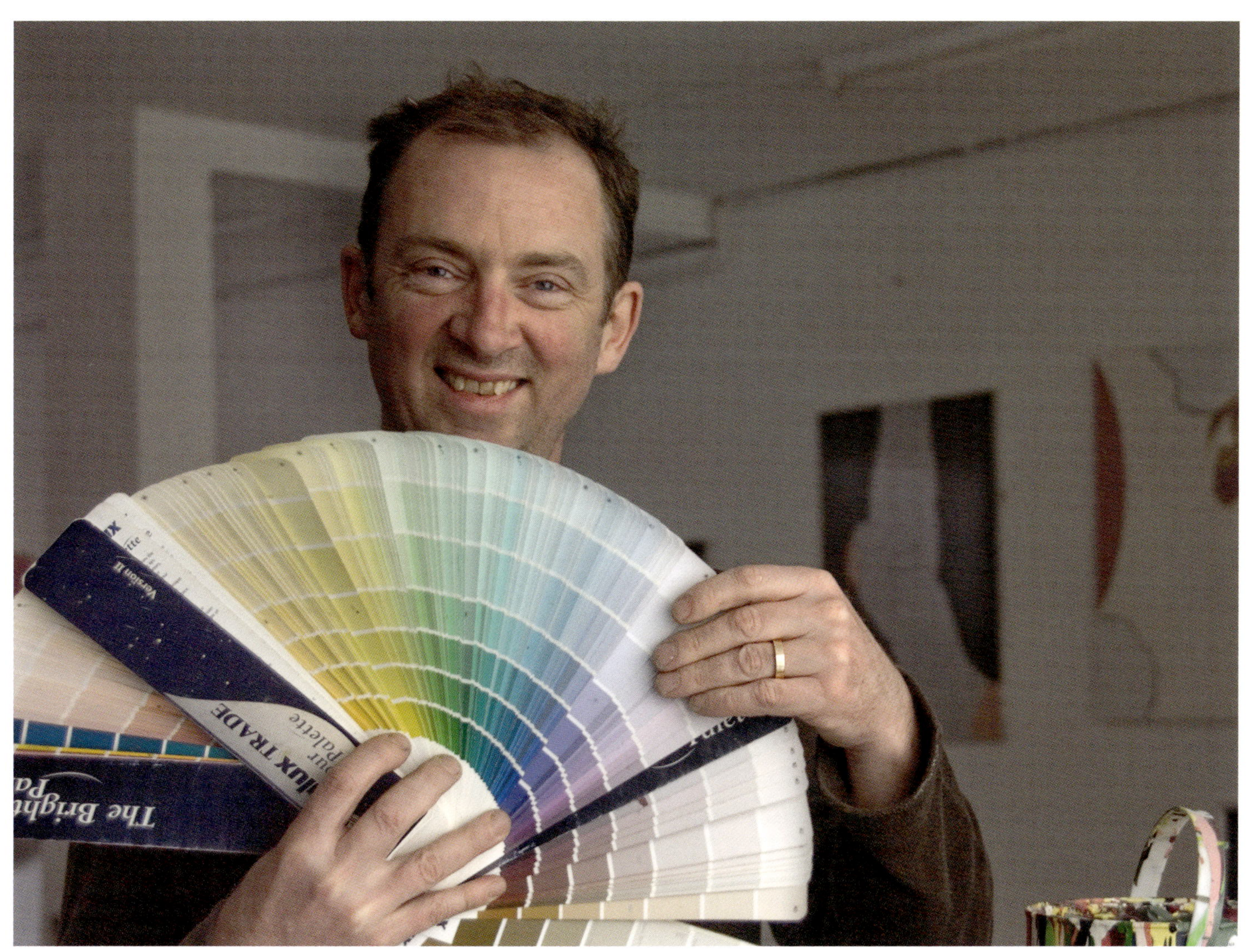
Dulux TRADE
The Brightest Pa
Version II
Colour Palette

PAUL HUXLEY RA

Elected ARA 27th May 1987
Elected RA 6th June 1991

'Rang' 2005
Acrylic on canvas
Courtesy of the artist
173 x 173 cm

Born 12th May 1938
London

Paul Huxley studied at Harrow School of Art from 1951-56 and then at the Royal Academy Schools from 1956-60. He taught at the Royal College of Art from 1976 and became Professor of Painting there from 1986-98 when he was appointed Professor Emeritus. First prize in the Stuyvesant Travel Awards took him to America in 1964. He won the Paris Biennale in 1965 the same year that he was awarded a Harkness Fellowship for a 2-year residency in New York. Among his many commissions are 22 ceramic mural designs for King's Cross Station, a wall drawing at the entrance and stairway of Pallant House Gallery in Chichester and the sets and costumes for the Rambert Dance Company in 1991.

He has been an adviser to the Arts Council and the Serpentine Gallery, a Trustee of the Tate Gallery and has been Treasurer of the RA since 2000. His work shows a concern for the formal properties of painting, often using shapes to suggest the three dimensional or to lead the eye to different levels in his paintings.

Paul Huxley lives and works in London.

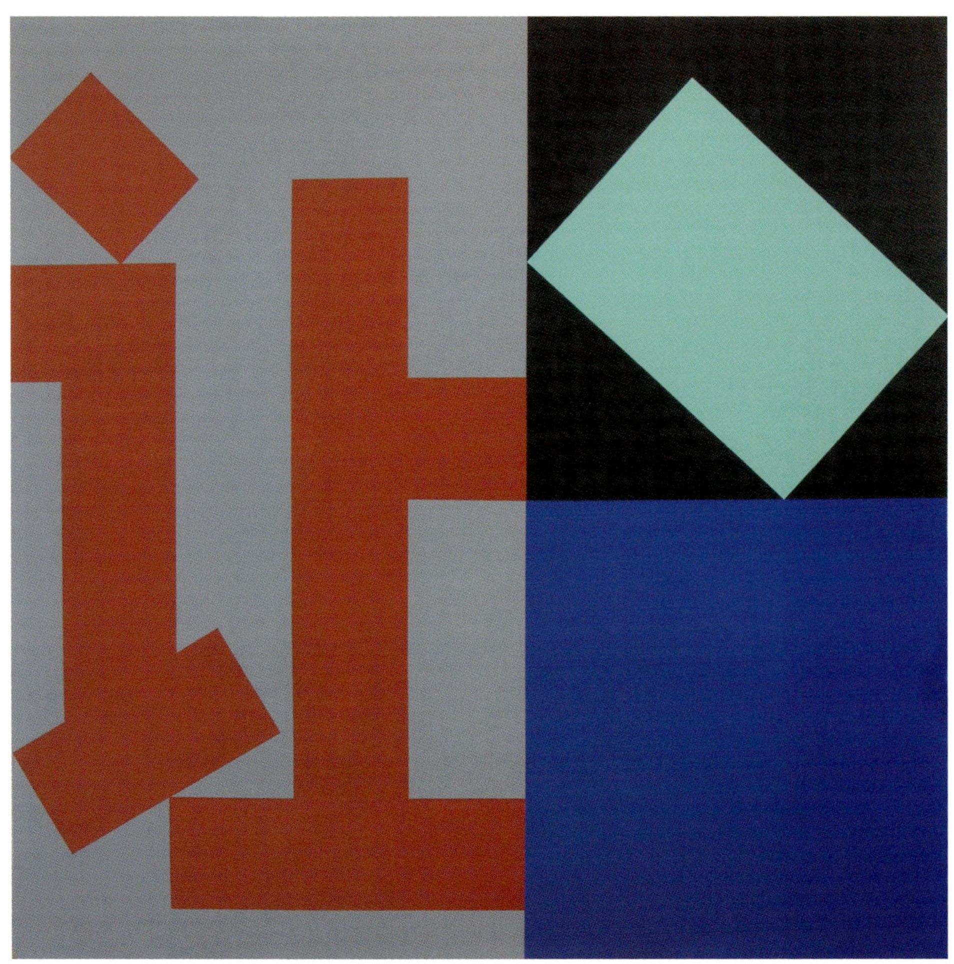

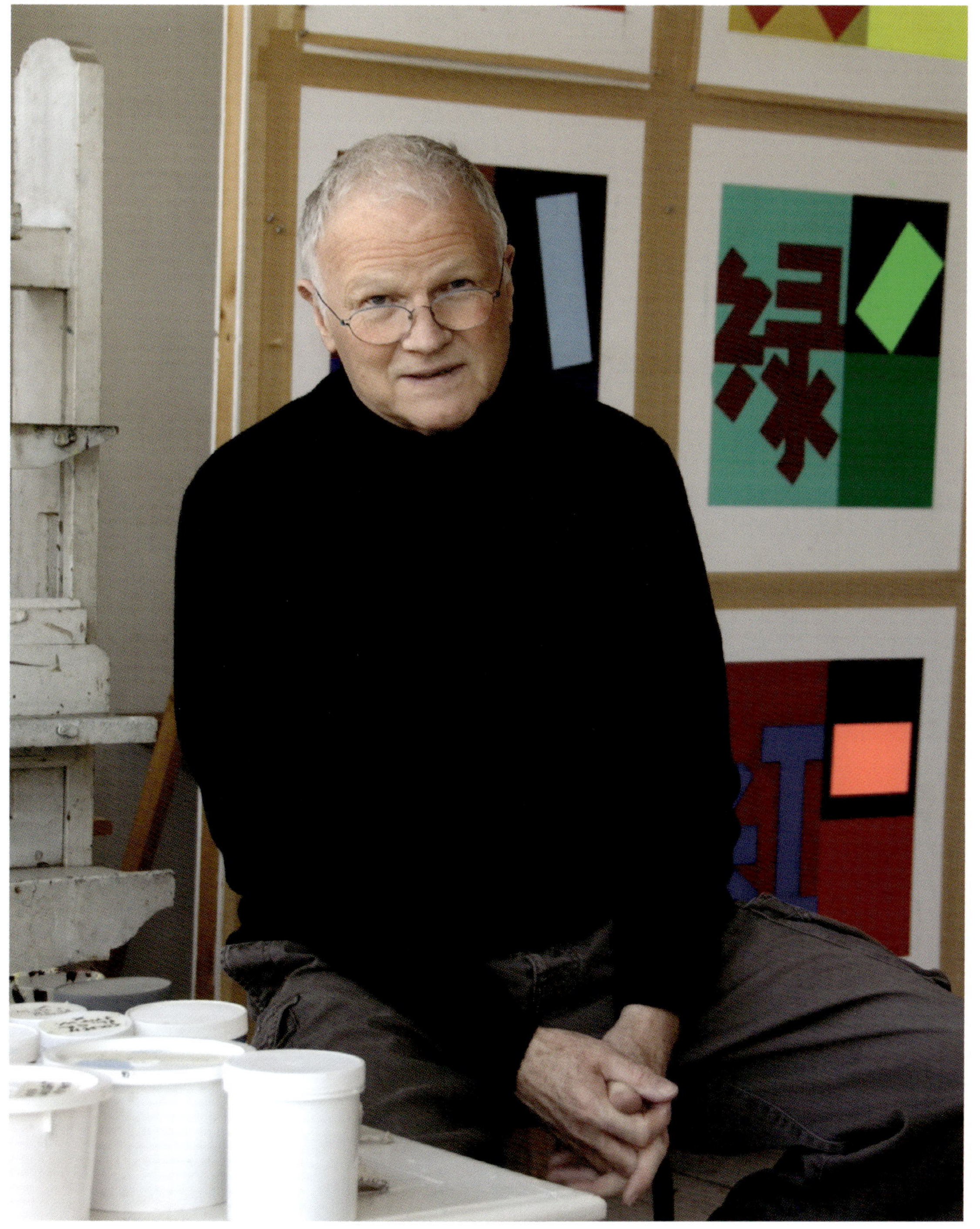

ALBERT IRVIN RA

Adventurer - 2006
Acrylic on canvas
Courtesy of the artist and Gimpel Fils
232 x 153 cm

Born 21st August 1922
London

Albert Irvin studied at the Northampton School of Art from 1940-41 before serving as a navigator in the Royal Air Force.
After the war he studied at Goldsmiths College from 1946-50 where he later returned to teach from 1962-83.

He went to America in 1968 on an Arts Council Travel Award and subsequently received an Arts Council Major Award.
Born and based in London, Irvin embraces his urban surroundings and much of his inspiration is derived from the inexhaustible energy of the city. Tate Curator Peter Moorhouse wrote of Bert Irvin: *'seeing a new painting by Irvin can be an extraordinary experience akin to discovering a young, energetic artist in the first flush of ambition'.* Irvin says, *'painting is a language you have to learn'.* His fluency with colour, form, space and light can be traced back to influences from Matisse to Rothko and beyond. As a young artist, Irvin connected to the Abstract Expressionists´ direct way of exploring experience and finding metaphors for it in paint.

Bert Irvin lives and works in London

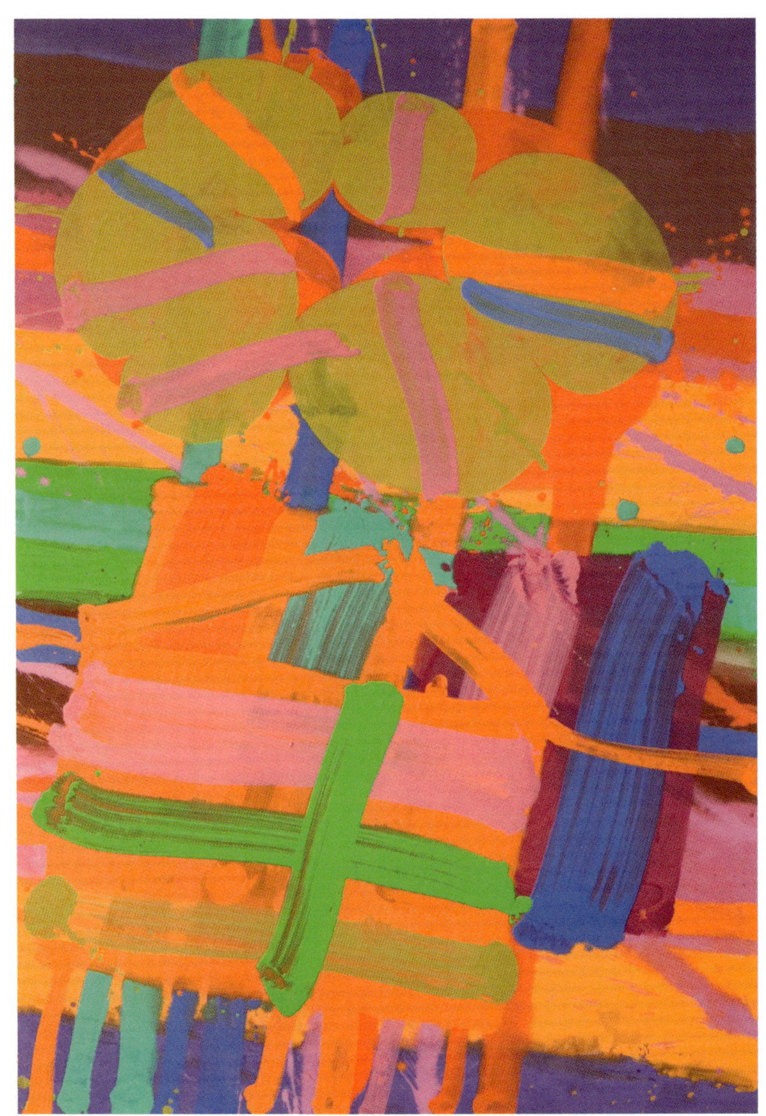

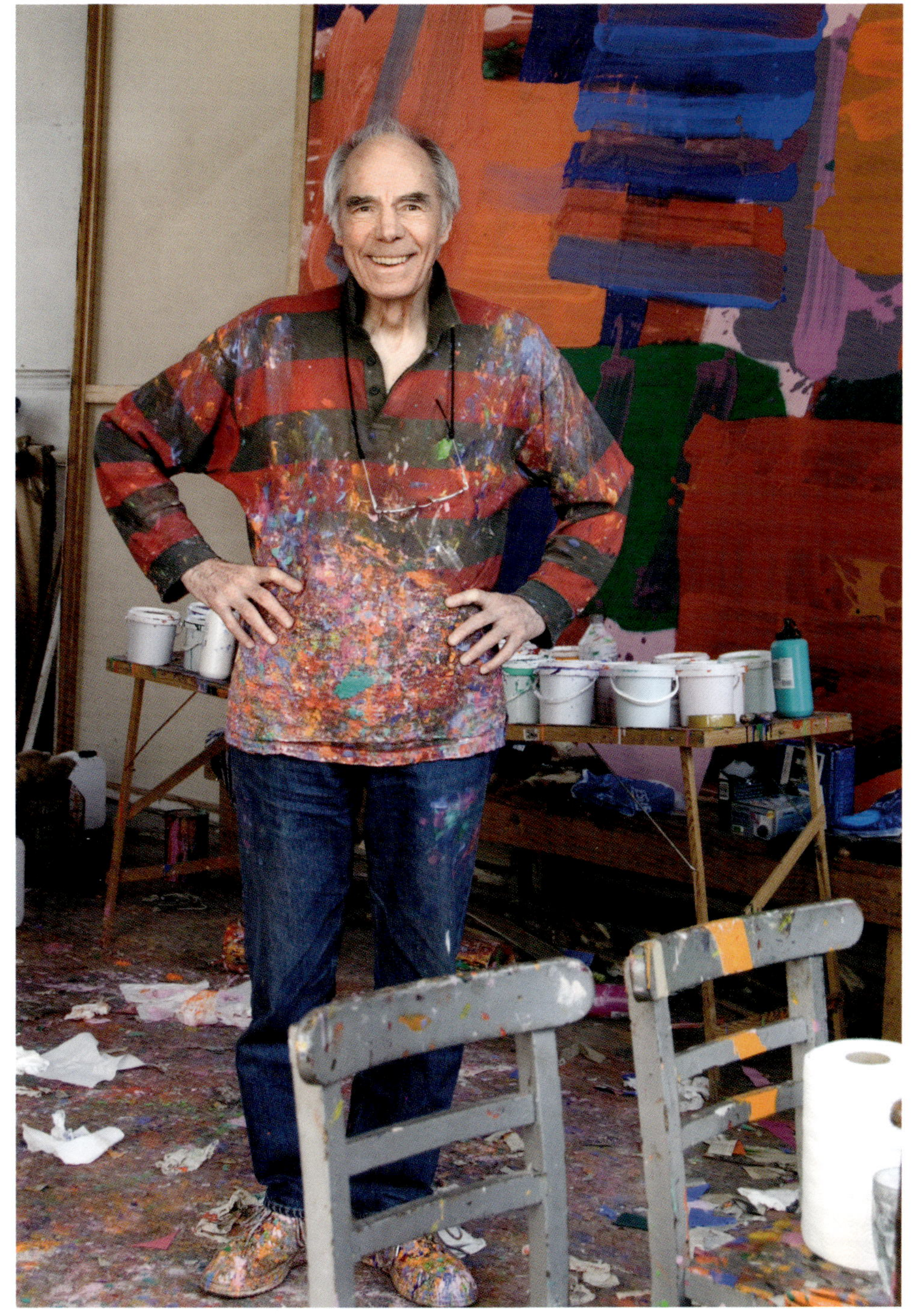

FLAVIA IRWIN RA

Elected RA 29th May 1996

Shadow Mark 2
Acrylic and pencil on canvas
Courtesy of the artist
87 x 66 cm

Born 15th December 1916
London

Flavia Irwin studied at the Chelsea School of Art under Henry Moore and Graham Sutherland and then at the Ruskin School of Art, Oxford. She taught general design at Medway College of Art from 1970-75 and was senior Tutor of Decorative Arts at City & Guilds of London Art School from 1975-97.

Flavia is an Honorary Member of the Royal West of England Academy, has exhibited widely throughout the UK and has work in many public and private Collections both here and in the USA.

She says that she *'has always held a passion for drawing but could not live without painting'* and is still, at 91, to be found every day working in her studio adjacent to the orchard in the grounds of her house. Dominant among Flavia's passions is the nature of the light entering the studio, which forms a constant theme in her paintings, and the un-primed duck canvases on which she creates her work in acrylic paints.

Flavia was married to Sir Roger de Grey who was a distinguished President of the RA from 1984-93 and who died in 1995.

Flavia Irwin lives and works in Kent.

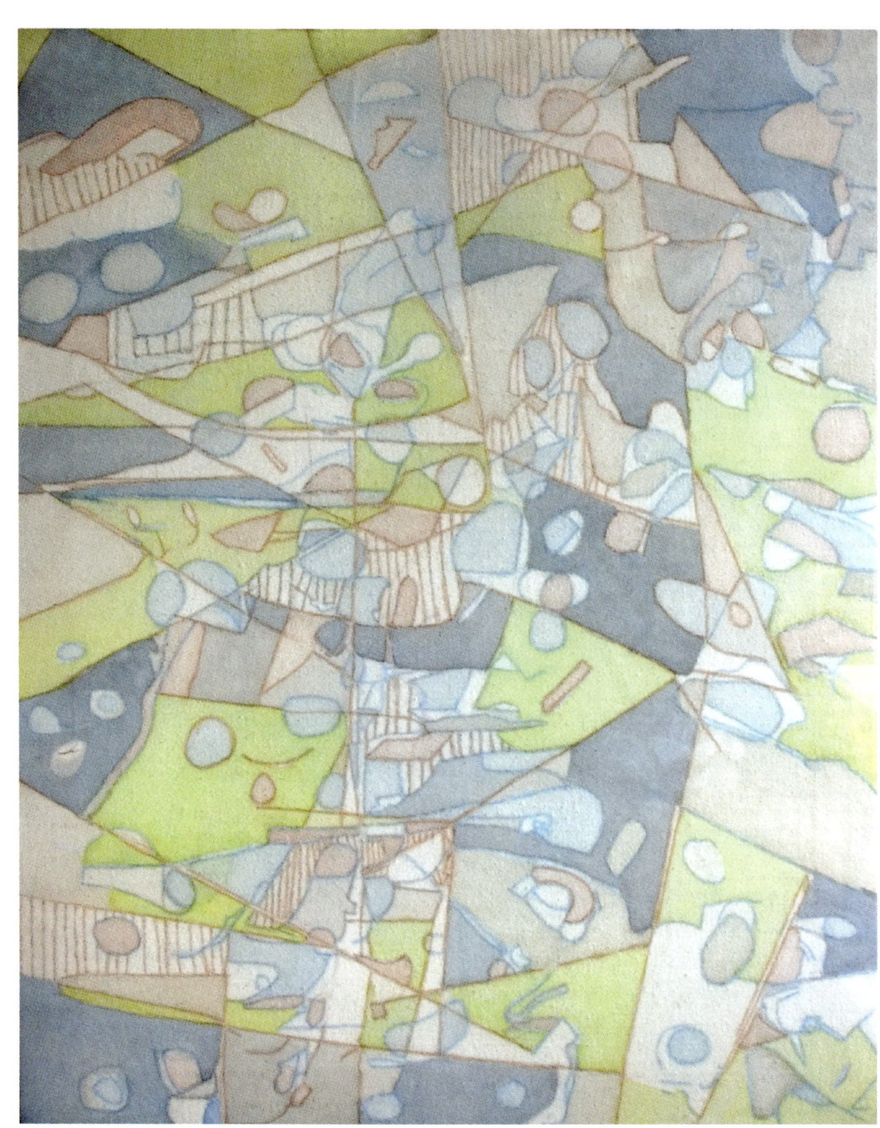

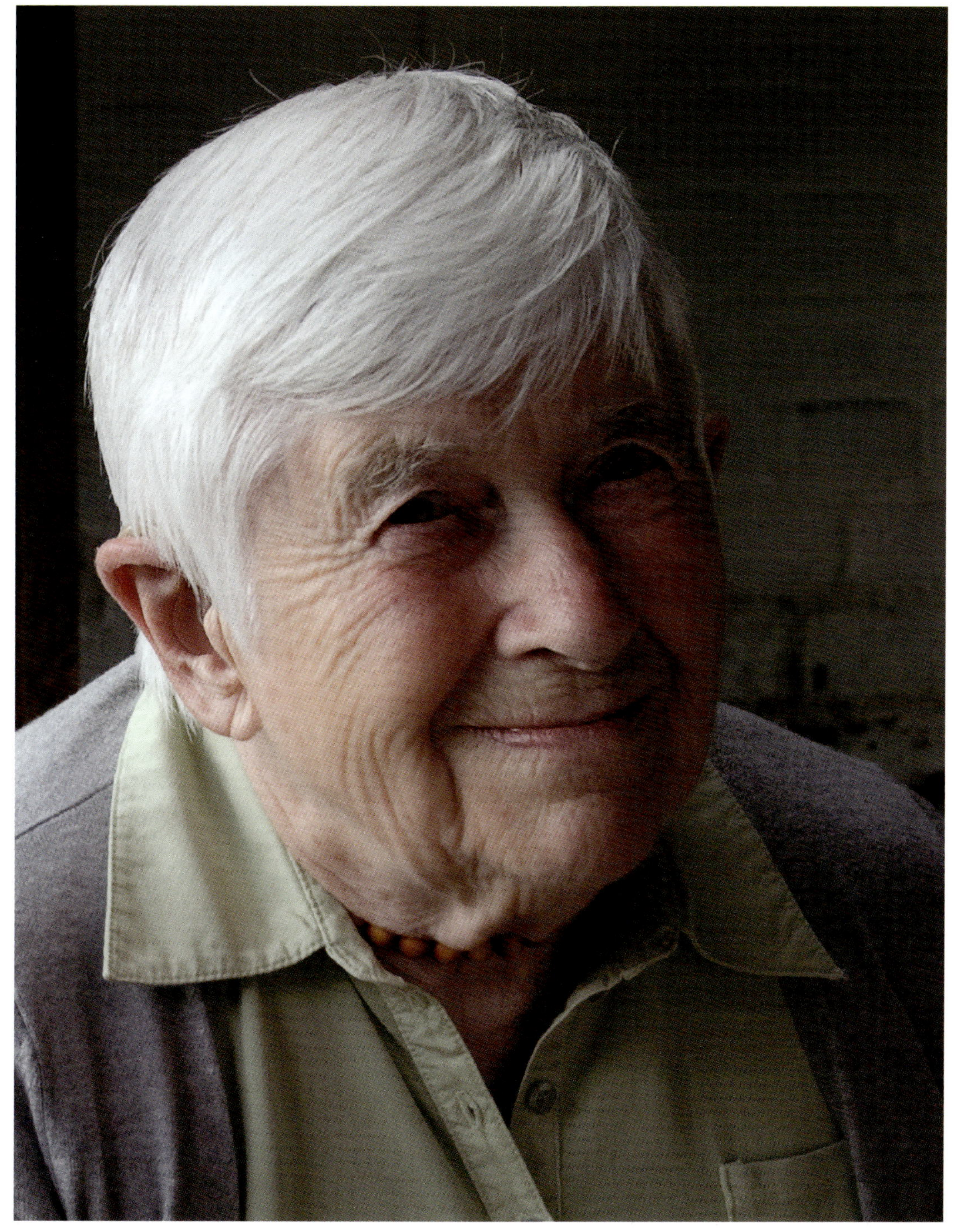

FLAVIA IRWIN RA

BILL JACKLIN RA

Elected ARA 1st June 1989
Elected RA 26th June 1991

Chance Encounter, Grand Central Station II
Oil on canvas
Courtesy of the artist
198 x 183 cm

Born 1st January 1943

Bill Jacklin studied graphics at Walthamstow School of Art, London (1960-61) before working as a graphic designer at Studio Seven in Holborn (1961-62). In 1962 he returned to Walthamstow to study painting and subsequently went on to the Royal College of Art from 1964-67. From 1967-75, Jacklin taught at Chelsea School of Art, Hornsey and the Royal College of Art and at schools in Kent and Surrey. Jacklin was awarded an Arts Council Bursary in 1975. He was Official Artist-in-Residence for the British Council in Hong Kong 1993-94.

From abstraction, his work moved to figuration in the mid 1970s, becoming preoccupied with the effects of light and movement. He has received commissions from the Bank of England, the Ivy Restaurant, De Beers and most recently from the Metropolitan Washington Airports Authority for the North Terminal of Washington National Airport.

Moving to New York in 1985, Bill Jacklin has concentrated on painting 'Urban Portraits' of 'the city' in all its guises; from large scale canvases of crowds in flux to intimate moments in Seurat-like etchings.

Bill Jacklin lives and works in New York and Rhode Island.

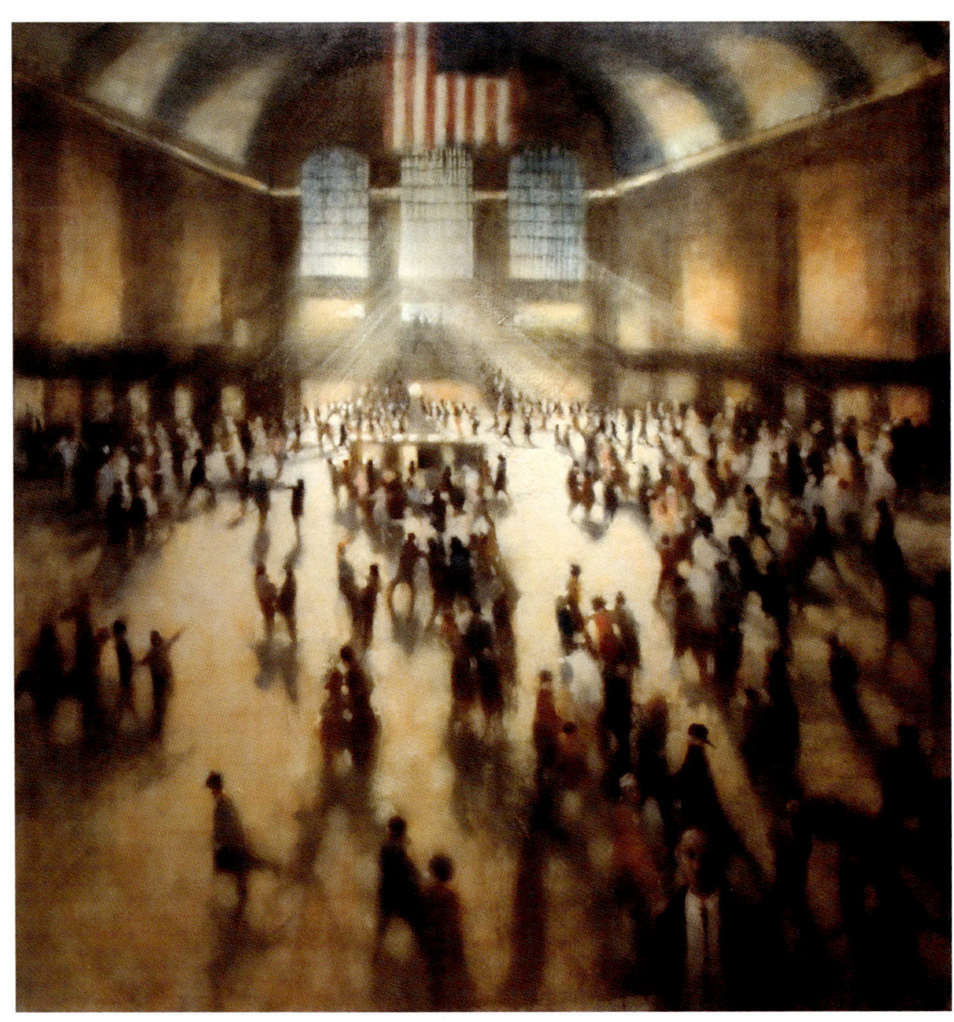

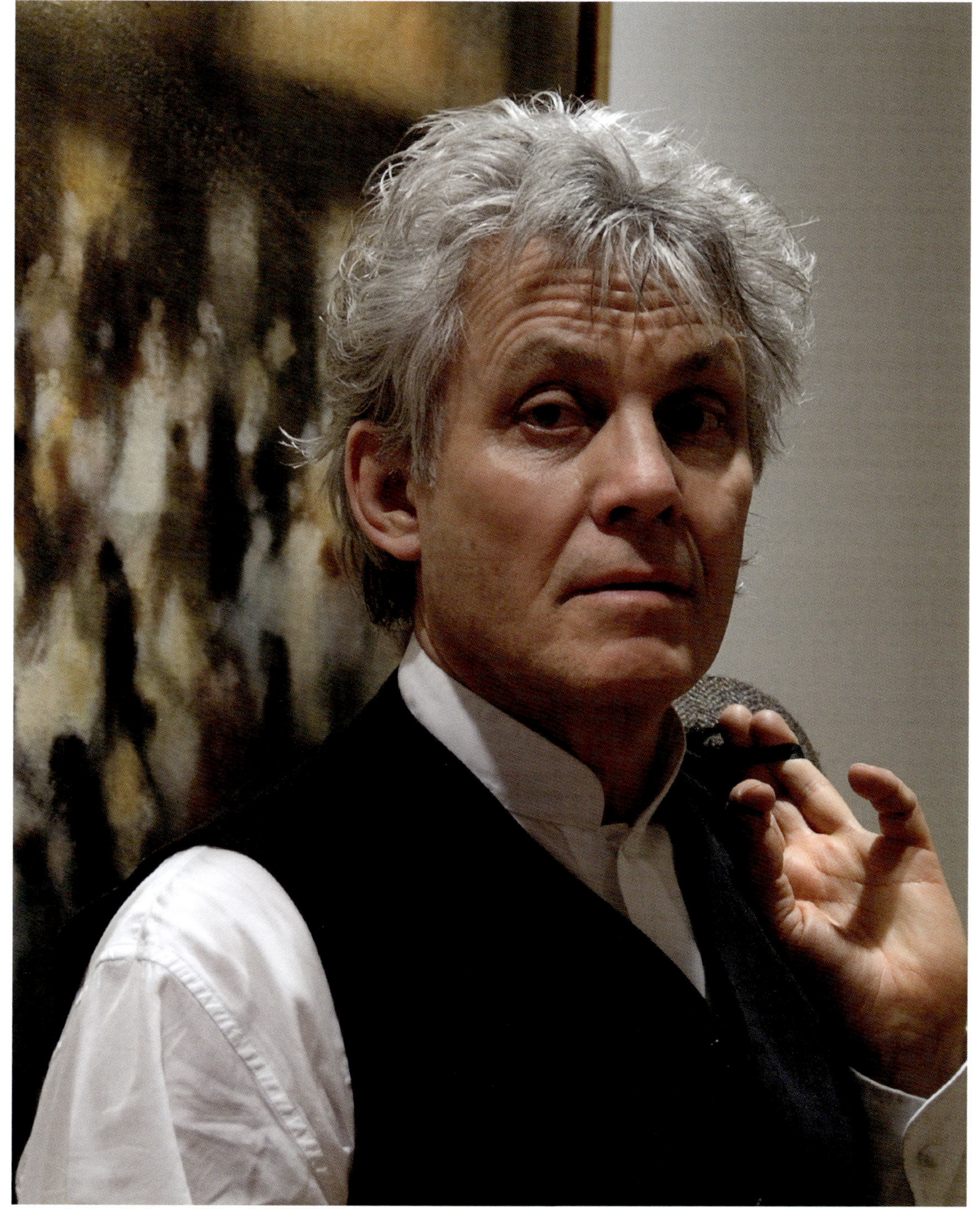

ALLEN JONES RA

Study for Temple
Oil on canvas
Courtesy of the artist
183 x 153 cm

Born 1st September 1937
Southampton

Allen Jones studied at Hornsey School of Art from 1955-59 and the Royal College of Art from 1959-61. From 1961-63 he taught at Croydon College of Art, Chelsea School of Art, University of South Florida, Hochschule für Bildenen Kunst, Hamburg, University of California, Los Angeles, University of California, Irvine and Hochschule der Kunste, Berlin. He was a Trustee of the British Museum from 1990-99.

He became associated with the rise of Pop Art while still at the Royal College of Art and like contemporaries, Hockney and Kitaj, mixed conflicting styles although drawing less from contemporary culture than from the colour abstractions of Kandinsky.

Allen Jones quickly established an international reputation and for more than 40 years his works have been exhibited on every continent. Although elected as a 'Printmaker' his reputation rests equally on his paintings and sculpture with excursions into Television and Theatre design.

Allen Jones lives and works in London and Oxfordshire.

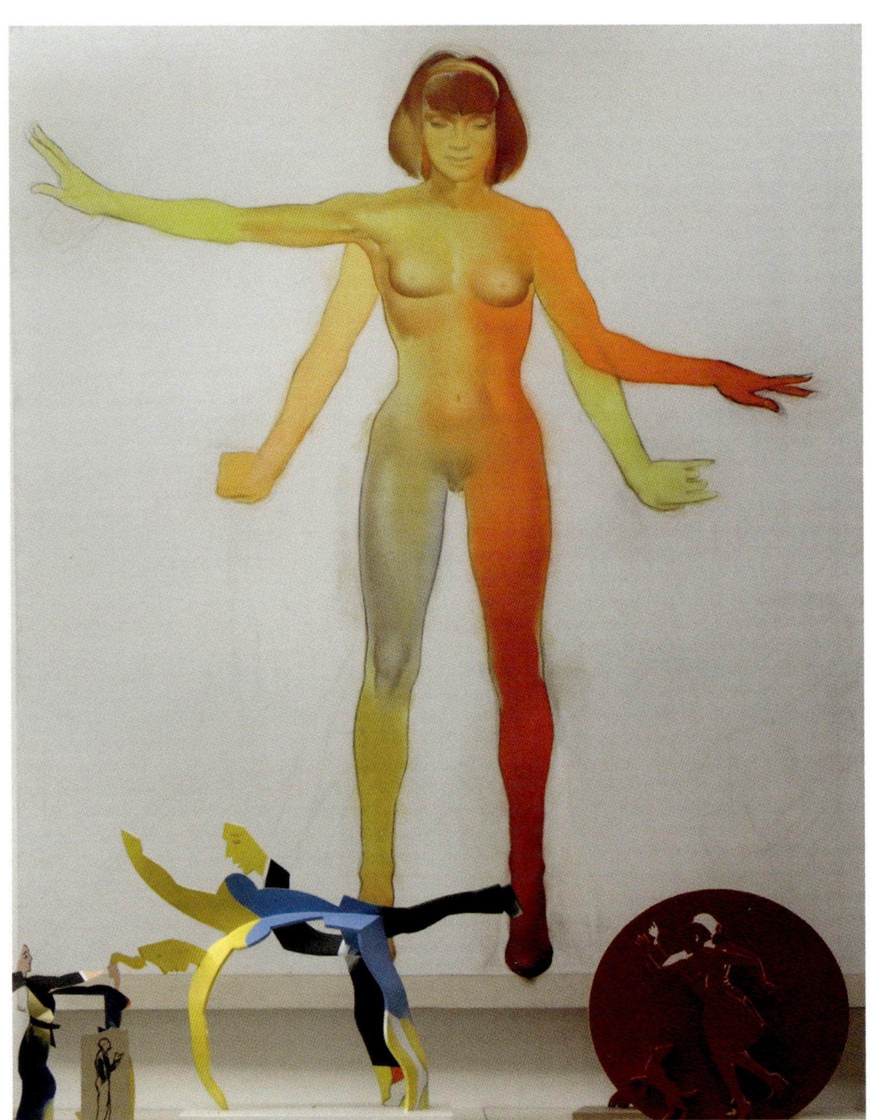

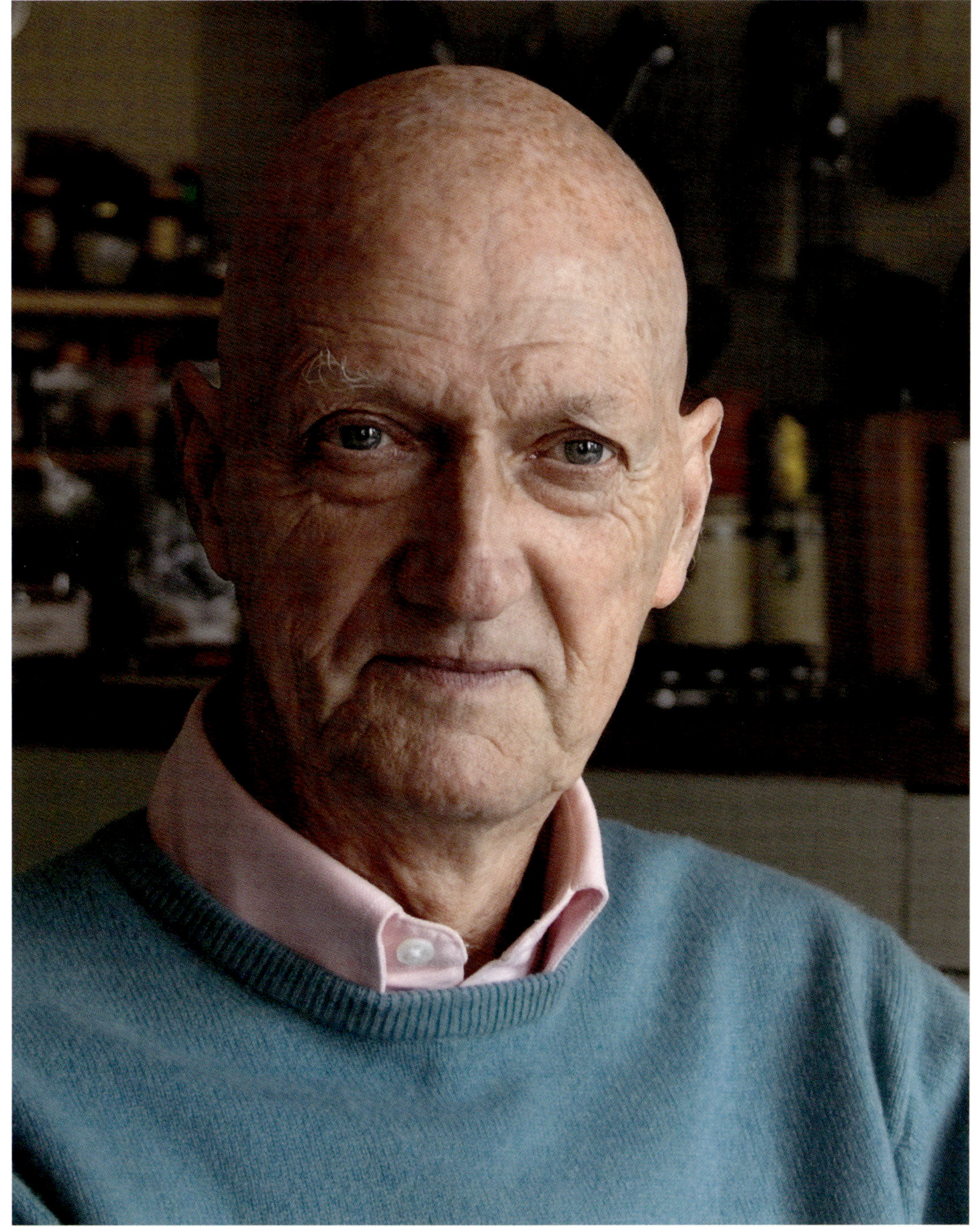

ALLEN JONES RA

MICHAEL KIDNER RA

Unpredictable Colour System
Drawing on paper
Courtesy of the artist
107 x 164 cm

Born 11th September 1917
Kettering

Michael Kidner read History and Anthropology at Cambridge before studying landscape architecture at Ohio State University from 1940-41. After spending 5 years in the Canadian Army he went to Goldsmiths College but left after a short spell as he disliked the teaching methods. Moving to Paris he trained himself as an artist and worked as a theatre designer in the early 1950s before starting to paint full-time in 1953. His first solo exhibition at St Hilda's College, Oxford brought him to prominence. Coming under the influence of the Bauhaus and in particular Johannes Itten he formed his distinctive style and became a pioneer in the 'Op Art' movement.

His work, though strongly founded in a rigorous intellectual approach to colour and form, resonates emotionally. As a master colourist his distinguished career has included many honours, influential teaching posts, group shows all over the world and one man exhibitions in Britain, Eastern Europe, Brazil, Austria and Scandinavia.

Michael Kidner lives and works in London.

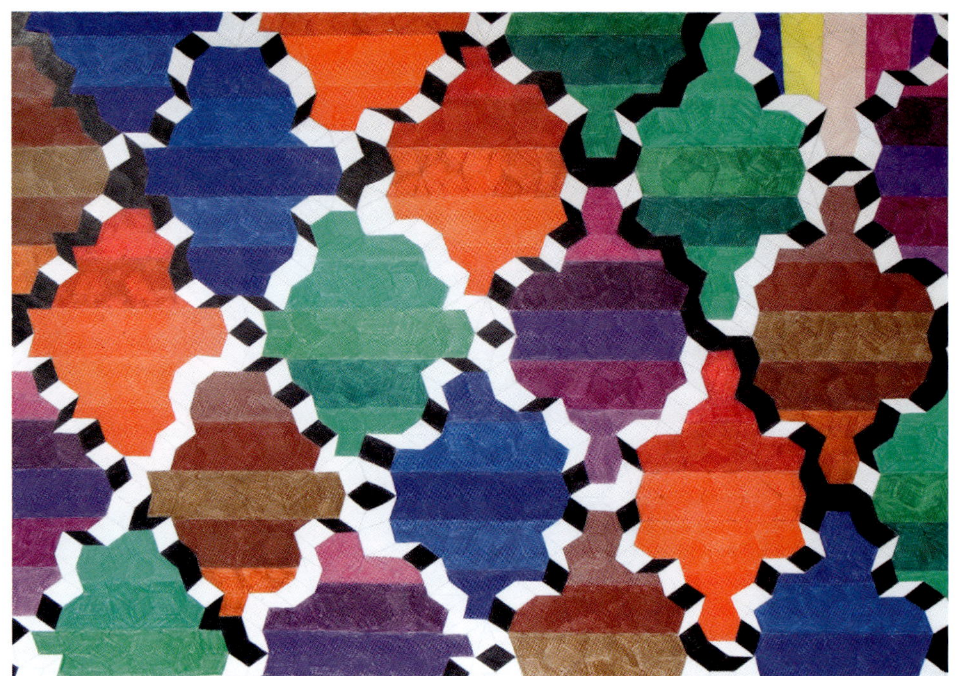

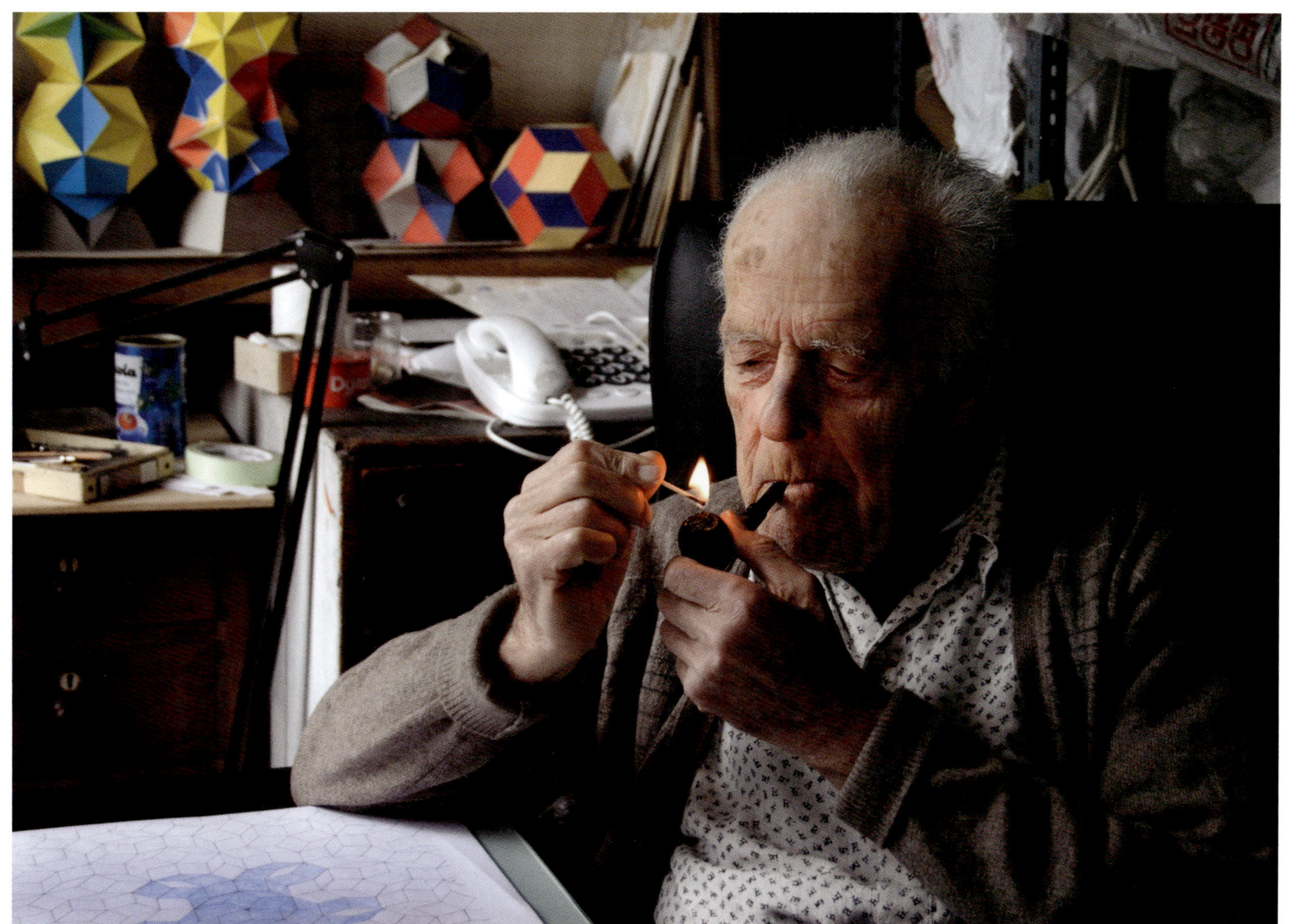

SONIA LAWSON RA

Elected ARA 6th May 1982
Elected RA 26th June 1991

History Book (detail)
Oil and raw pigment on canvas
Courtesy of the artist
203 x 165 cm

Born 2nd June 1934
Darlington

Sonia Lawson studied at Doncaster School of Art and the Royal College of Art from 1956-60 where she gained First Class Honours and was awarded a Post-graduate year and a travelling scholarship to France. She then taught at Harrow School of Art and Central St Martin's School of Art in the 1960s, West Surrey College of Art from the 1960s to the early 1970s, and briefly at the Royal College of Art during the 1980s. She was Visiting Lecturer at the Royal Academy Schools 1985 – 2001 when she gave up teaching. Commissions have included recording the preparations for 'Exercise Lionheart' BAOR Western Germany for the Imperial War Museum in 1984 and a work presented by the Archbishop of Canterbury to Pope John Paul II in 1989 which is now in the Vatican Collection. Lawson's work is in the collections of the Arts Council and municipal galleries throughout the UK. She believes in the importance of good drawing as a foundation transcending other forms of visual expression and being about discovery, awareness and articulacy, the core of creativity. Her work deals with personal truths and experiences challenging the viewer on several levels.

Sonia Lawson lives and works in Bedfordshire and Wensleydale.
www.sonialawson.co.uk

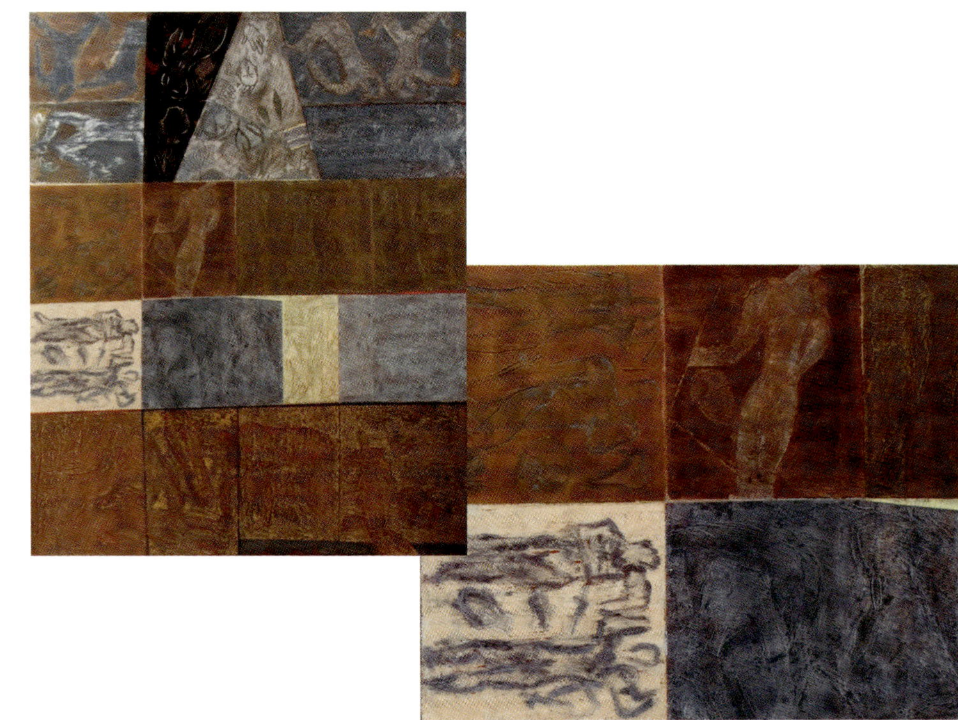

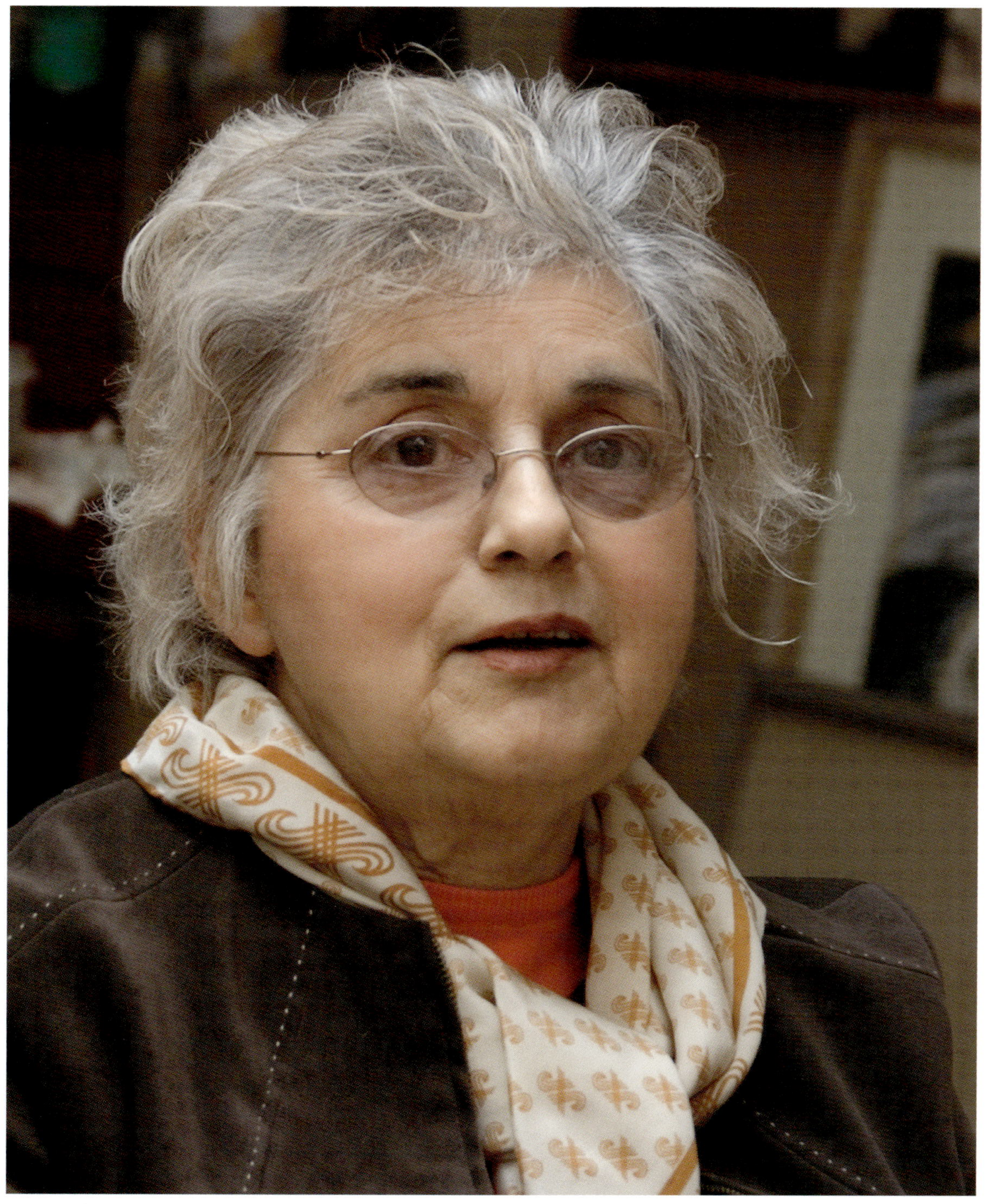

SONIA LAWSON RA

CHRISTOPHER LE BRUN RA

Elected RA 12th December 1996

Etching 25 from Fifty Etchings 2006
Courtesy of the artist
19 x 17 cm

Born 20th December 1951
Portsmouth

Christopher Le Brun studied at the Slade
School of Fine Art from 1970-74 and at the
Chelsea School of Art from 1974-75.
Le Brun has exhibited in many significant
surveys of International art, from Zeitgeist,
Berlin in 1982, to Contemporary Voices, at the
Museum of Modern Art New York in 2005.
From 1987-88 he received the D.A.A.D.
award from the German government, living
and working in Berlin for a year. In 2000 he
became the Royal Academy's first Professor of
Drawing. Le Brun is a former trustee of the
Tate, the National Gallery, and Dulwich Picture
Gallery. He is currently a trustee of the
Prince's Drawing School. His commissions
include paintings for the choir of Liverpool
Cathedral and a portrait of George Steiner for
the National Portrait Gallery. His work
represents an eloquent fusion of abstract and
figurative impulses, enriching painting by
building from the art of the past and
invigorating subject matter through recourse
to mythology.

Christopher Le Brun lives and works in
London and Suffolk.
www.christopherlebrun.co.uk

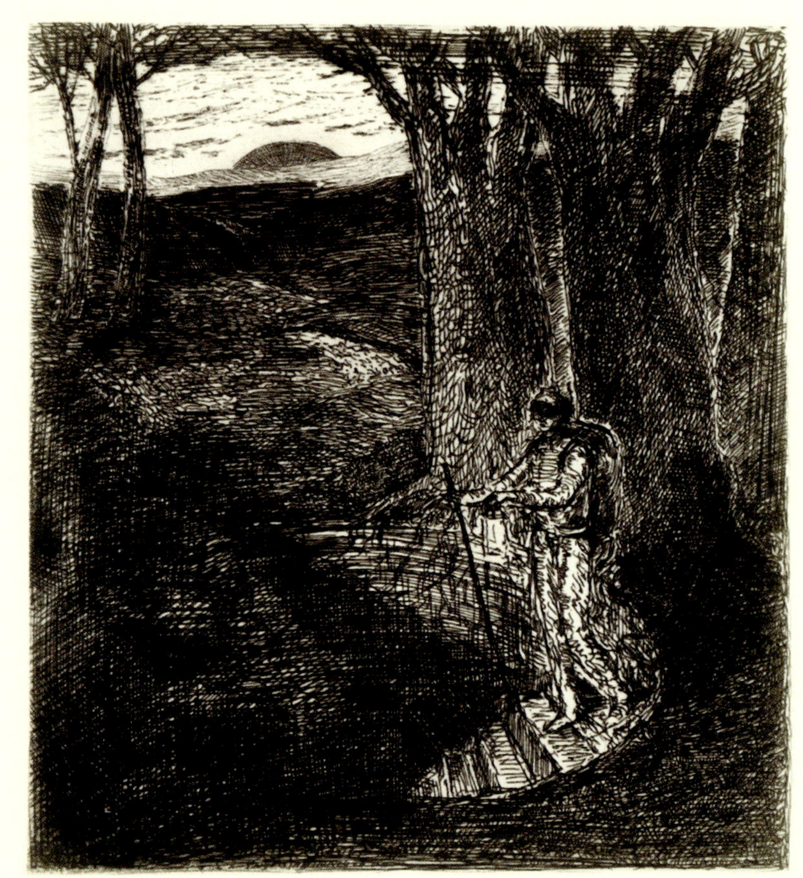

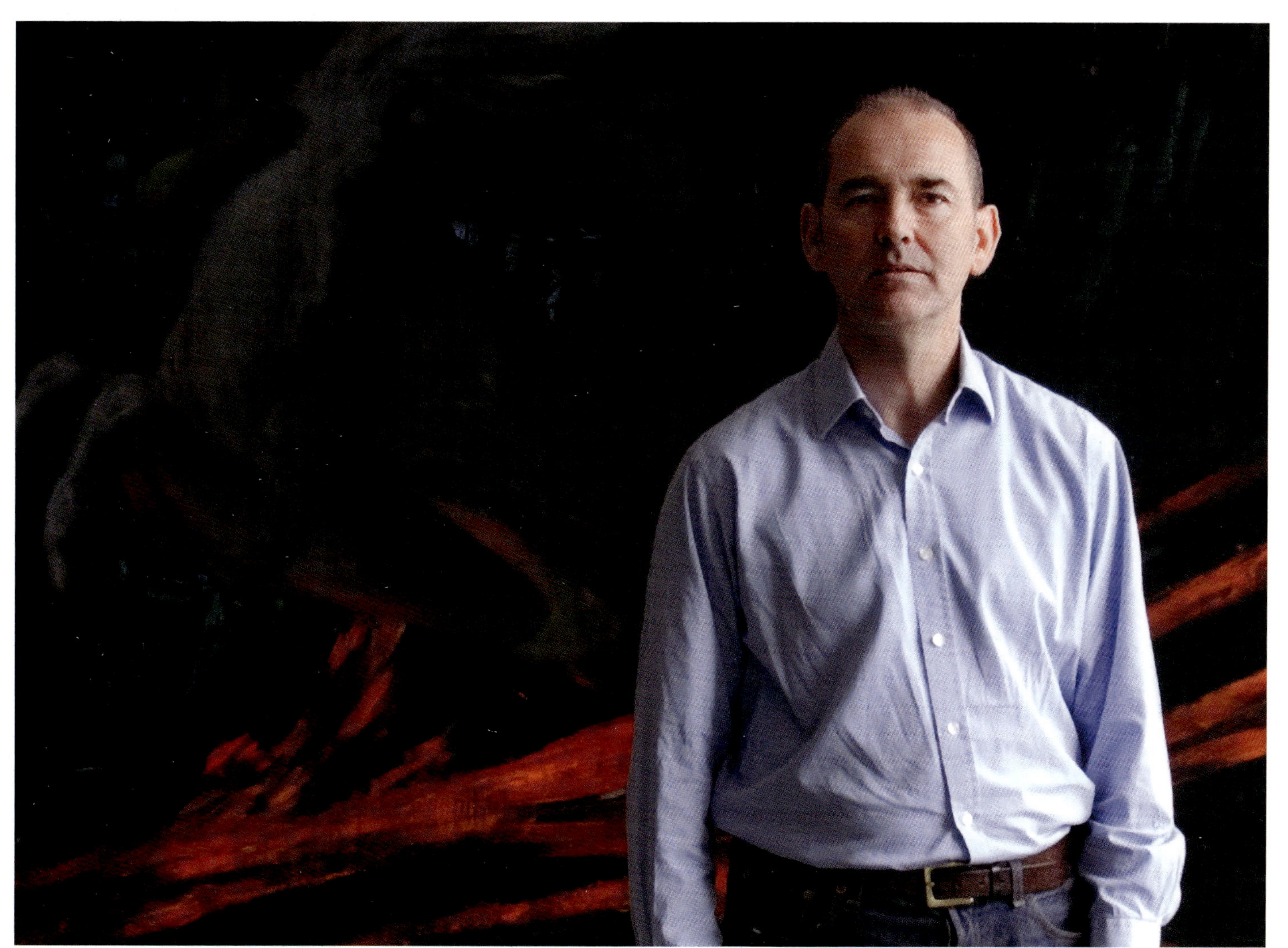
CHRISTOPHER LE BRUN RA

BEN LEVENE RA

Elected ARA 25th April 1975
Elected RA 20th November 1986

Snow Scene
Oil on board
Courtesy of the artist
42 x 41 cm

Born 23rd December 1938
London

Ben Levene studied under Claude Rogers and William Coldstream at the Slade School of Fine Art from 1956-61 gaining a Boise Scholarship which enabled him to live in Spain from 1961-62.

He began an extensive teaching career as Visiting Lecturer and teacher of painting and drawing at Camberwell School of Art from 1963-89 and as Visiting Tutor at the Royal Academy Schools from 1980-95. He was also Visiting Tutor at the City and Guilds of London Art School from 1990-95 and in the latter year was appointed Curator at the Royal Academy Schools until 1998. His work has been widely exhibited and collected.

Levene says: *'My philosophy is that I like one foot in the unknown and one foot in reality. The familiarity of the real helps the viewer to access my pictures, but I always take liberties with the subject, depending on my own perceptions'.*

Ben Levene lives and works in London in a studio commanding exceptional views of the city which often feature in his paintings.

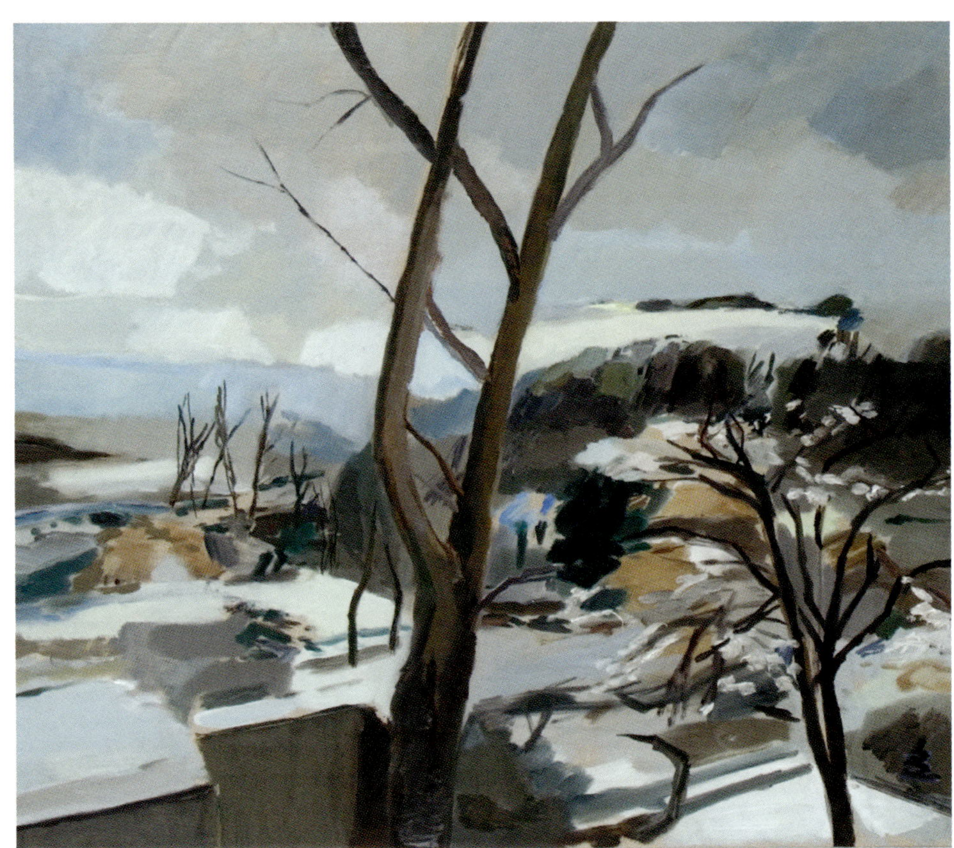

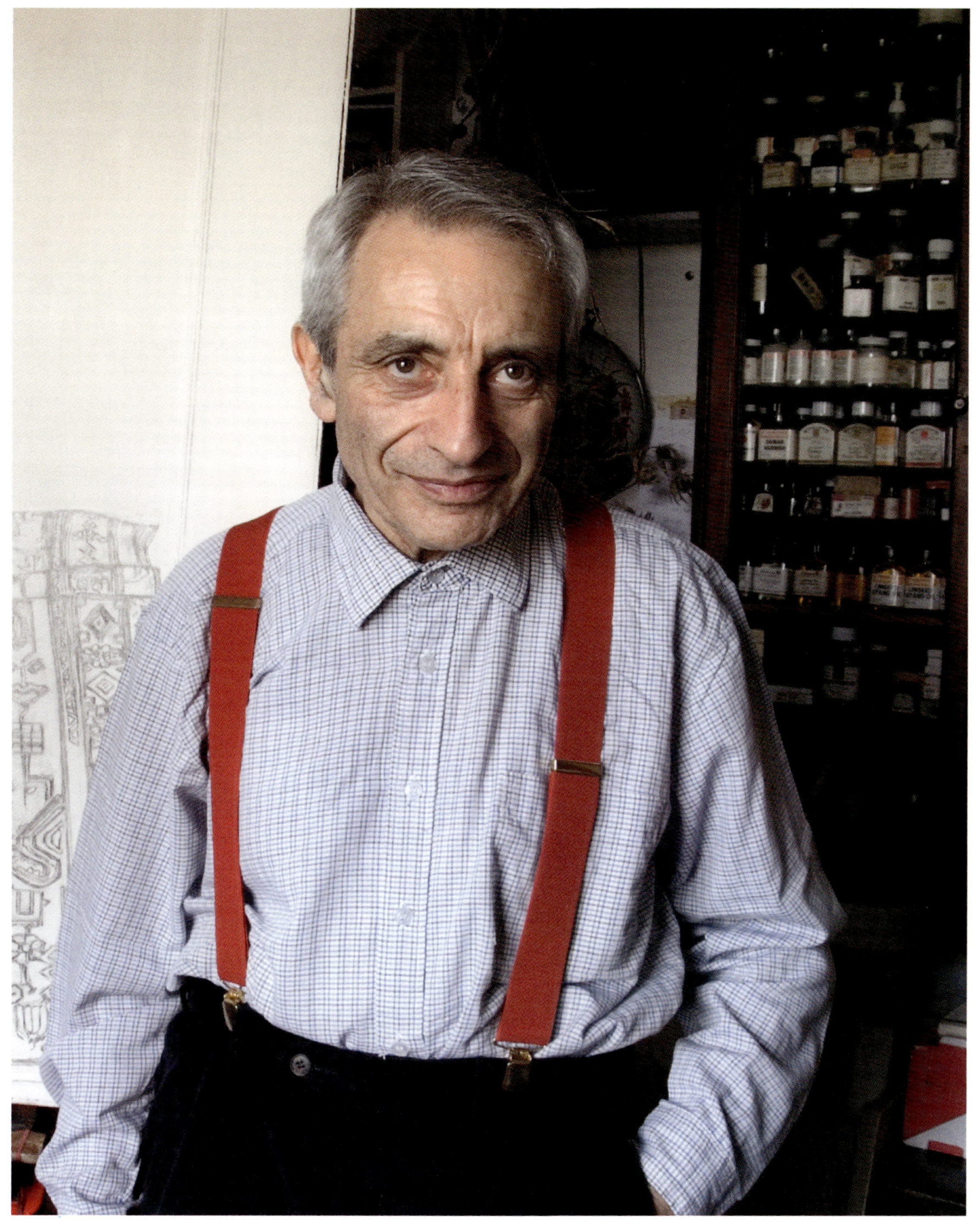

LEONARD McCOMB RA

Elected ARA 27th May 1987
Elected RA 26th June 1991

Cartoon for proposed mosaic lunette of 'St Francis of Assisi' for Westminster Cathedral
Courtesy of the artist
190 x 305 cm

Born 3rd August 1930
Glasgow

Leonard McComb studied at Manchester School of Art, 1954-56 and the Slade School of Fine Art 1956-59 followed by a post-graduate year in Sculpture 1959-60 at the Slade. He then taught at various art Schools including Oxford Brookes University, St John Cass School, London, Goldsmiths College, The Slade, the Royal College of Art and the Royal Academy Schools. In 1974 he founded Sunningwell School of Art, Oxford. He was elected Keeper of the Royal Academy Schools from 1995-98. He has won many awards and, despite having destroyed most of his early works, is represented in a large number of collections both public and private. His work, carefully constructed with great detail, has almost meditative qualities which transcribe his perceived World. He has described them as *'visual abstractions after nature'*

McComb is probably unique in being the single contemporary artist who has sculpture, oil painting, watercolours and prints in the Tate collections.

Leonard McComb lives and works in London

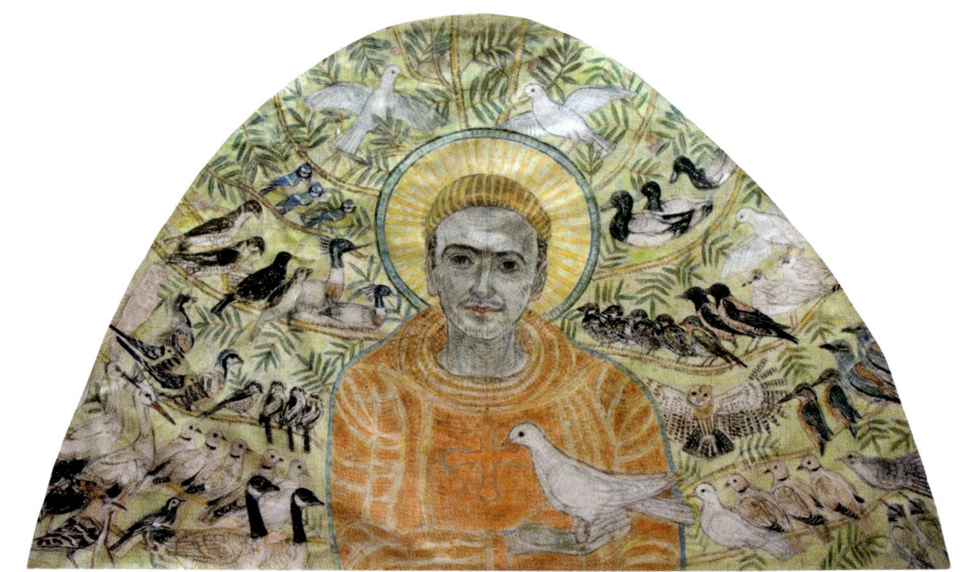

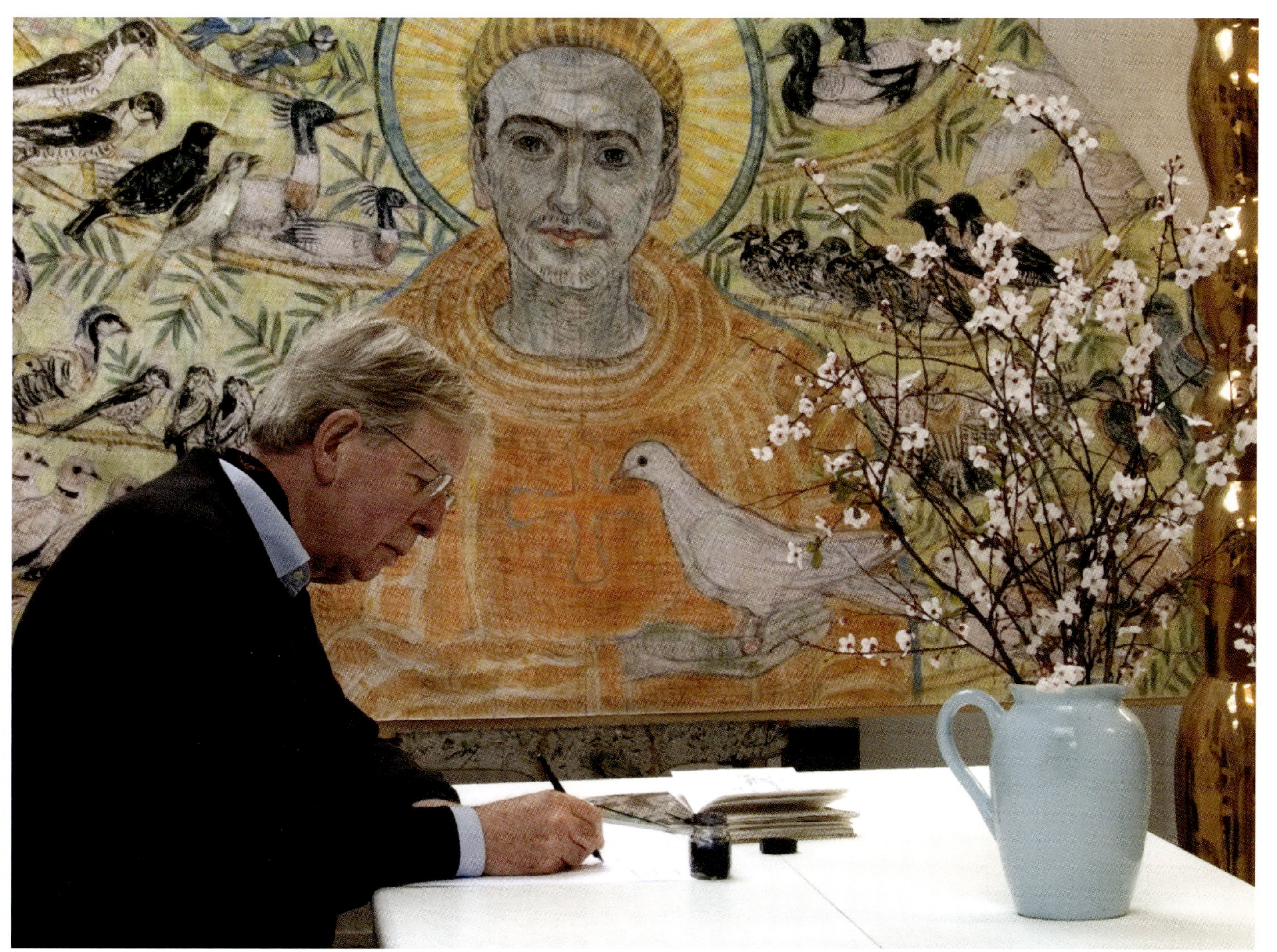

IAN McKEEVER RA

Elected RA 23rd May 2003

Here Painting VI
Acrylic and oil on canvas
Courtesy of the artist
220 x 360 cm

Born 30th November 1946
Withernsea, East Yorkshire

Ian McKeever is a self-taught painter who began to paint in 1969 when he rented space in an Artists' Collective Studio in St Katherine's Dock in East London. He had his first exhibition in 1971 in Berlin with colleagues from the Collective, following which he started to teach at the Slade School of Fine Art. Since that time he has had his work exhibited widely in the UK, Europe, Scandinavia and the United States and is represented in many public and private collections. In 1989 he received a D.A.A.D (German Academic Exchange Serrice) scholarship enabling him to work in Berlin. He was Professor at the Stadel Academy der Kunst in Frankfurt, has taught in the UK, Europe and the USA and is currently Visiting Professor in Painting at the University of Brighton and Professor of Drawing at the Royal Academy Schools. Originally his work followed an interest in the landscapes of places as diverse as Greenland and Papua New Guinea, subsequently changing in the mid 1980s and becoming more abstract, although this is a description he rejects. His interest in light and physical presence was explored in his writings 'In Praise of Painting'.

Ian McKeever lives and works in Dorset
www.ianmckeever.com

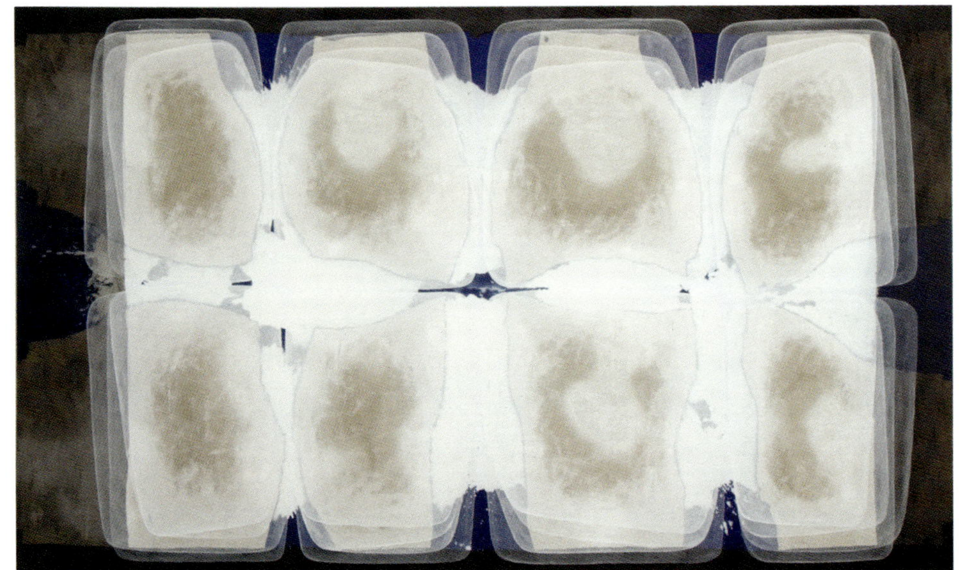

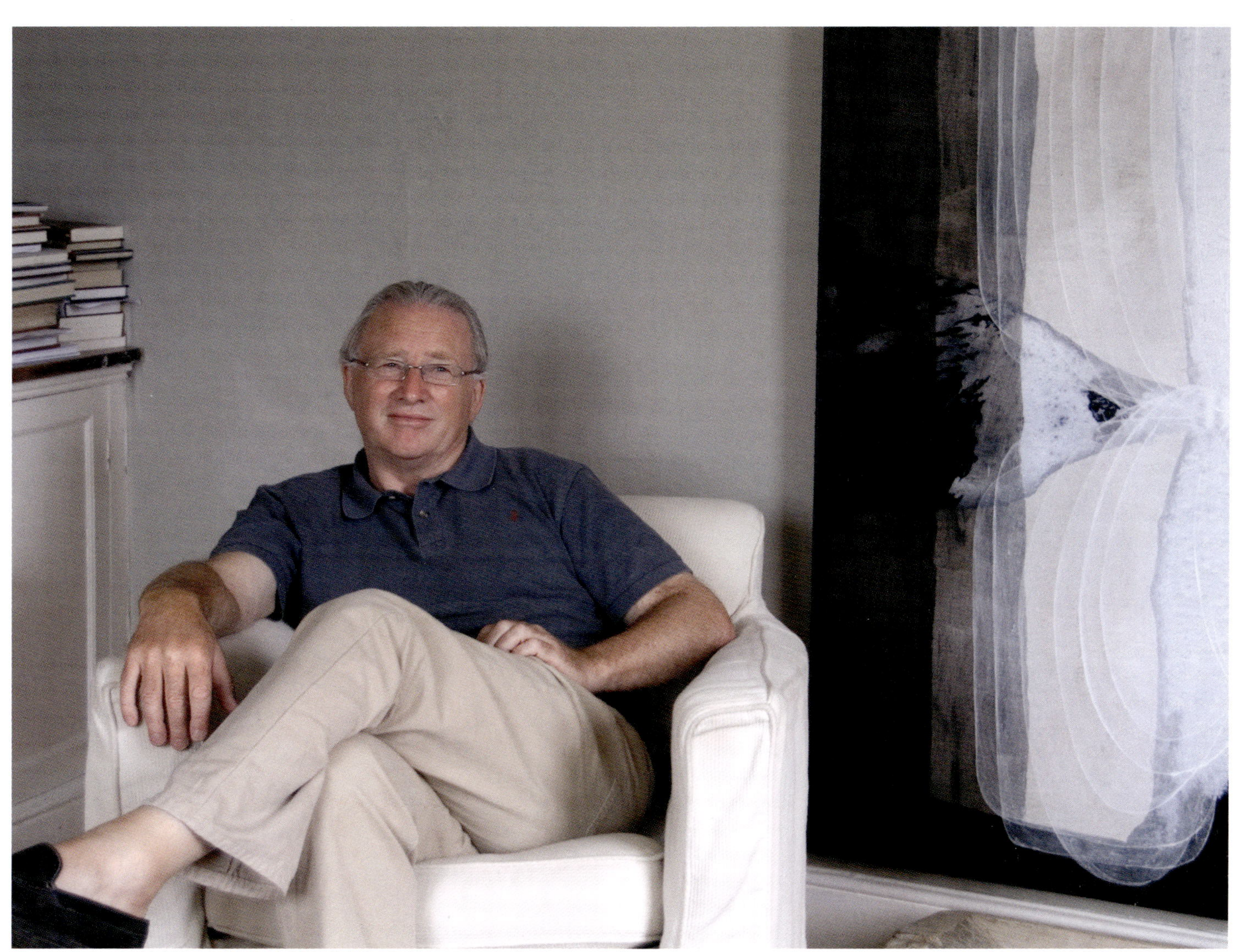

IAN McKEEVER RA

MICK MOON RA

Path, 2007
Mixed media on paper mounted on board
Courtesy of the artist
60 x 60 cm

Born 9th November 1937
Edinburgh

Mick Moon studied at Chelsea School of Art
from 1958-62 and the Royal College of Art
from 1962-63. He was Senior Lecturer at the
Slade School of Fine Art from 1973-90 and
Artist in Residence at the Phahran School of
Art and Design in Melbourne, Australia in
1982.

Mick Moon's paintings hide a lot of nostalgia
which is revealed by careful scrutiny.

Mick Moon lives and works in London

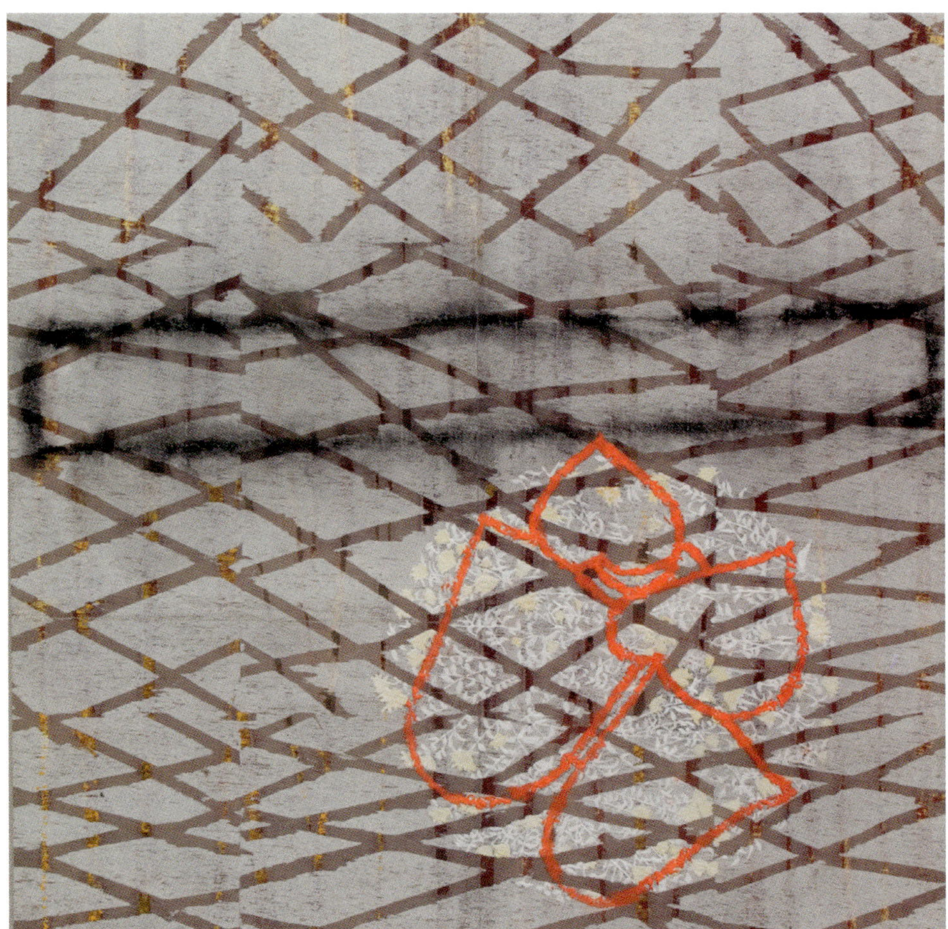

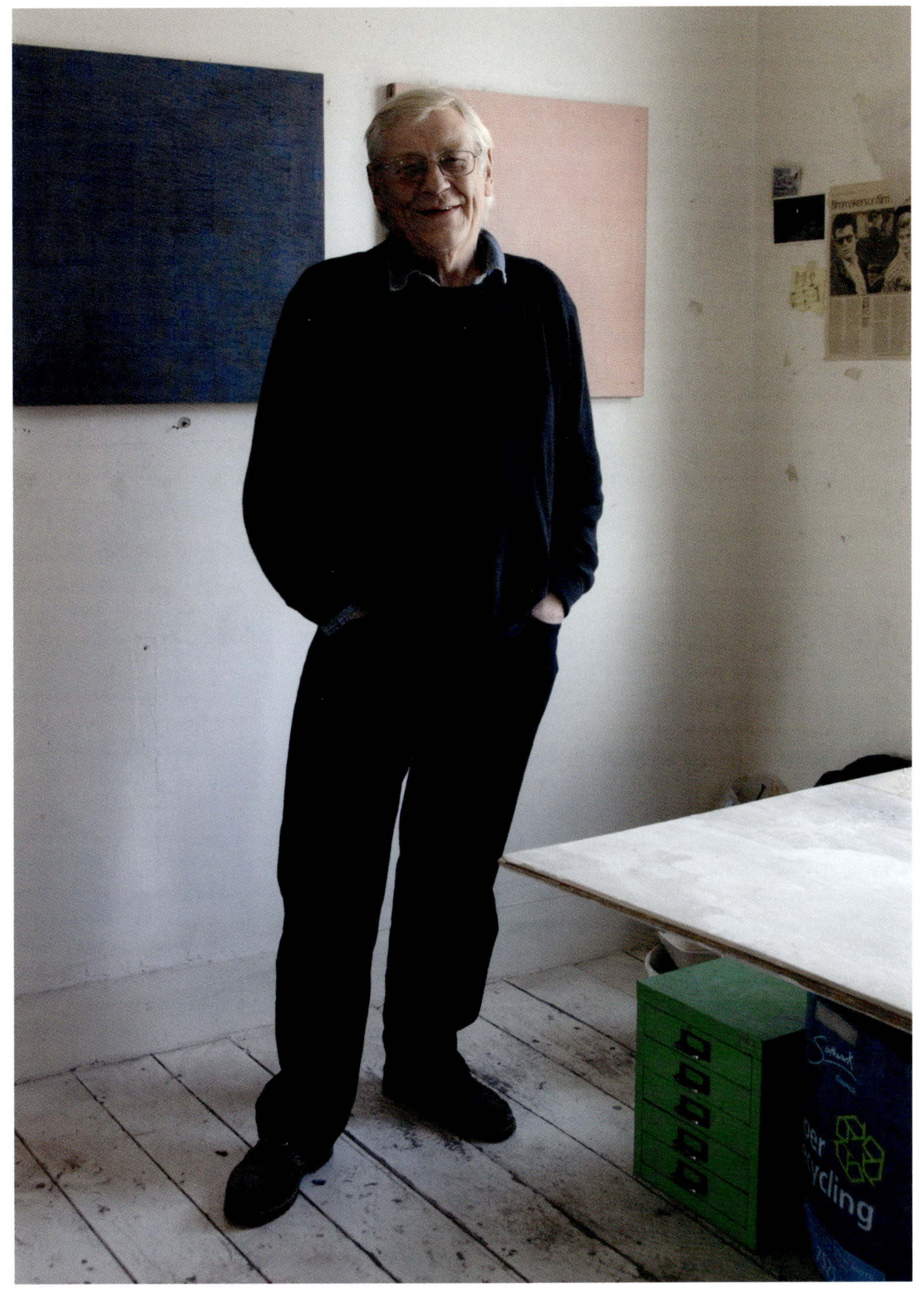

CHRIS ORR RA

Topless in Battersea
Etching and lithograph
Courtesy of the artist
69 x 63 cm

Born 8th April 1943
London

Chris Orr studied at the Ravensbourne College of Art from 1959-62, Hornsey College of Art from 1963-64 and the Royal College of Art from 1964-67.

He then taught part-time at Cardiff College of Art, Central School of Art and the Royal College of Art where he has been Professor of Printmaking since 1998. Orr was made Fellow of the Royal College of Art in 1985 and a Fellow of the Royal Society of Printmakers in 1988.

Many of Orr's works depict his interpretations of cities visited and include Hiroshima, Nagasaki, Santiago de Compostella and the background to this portrait, 'Moo Cow Farm, the Somme' in which he has also placed one of his grandfathers who fought there in World War I and lived to tell the tale.

Chris Orr lives and works in Buckingham and London
www.chrisorr-ra.com

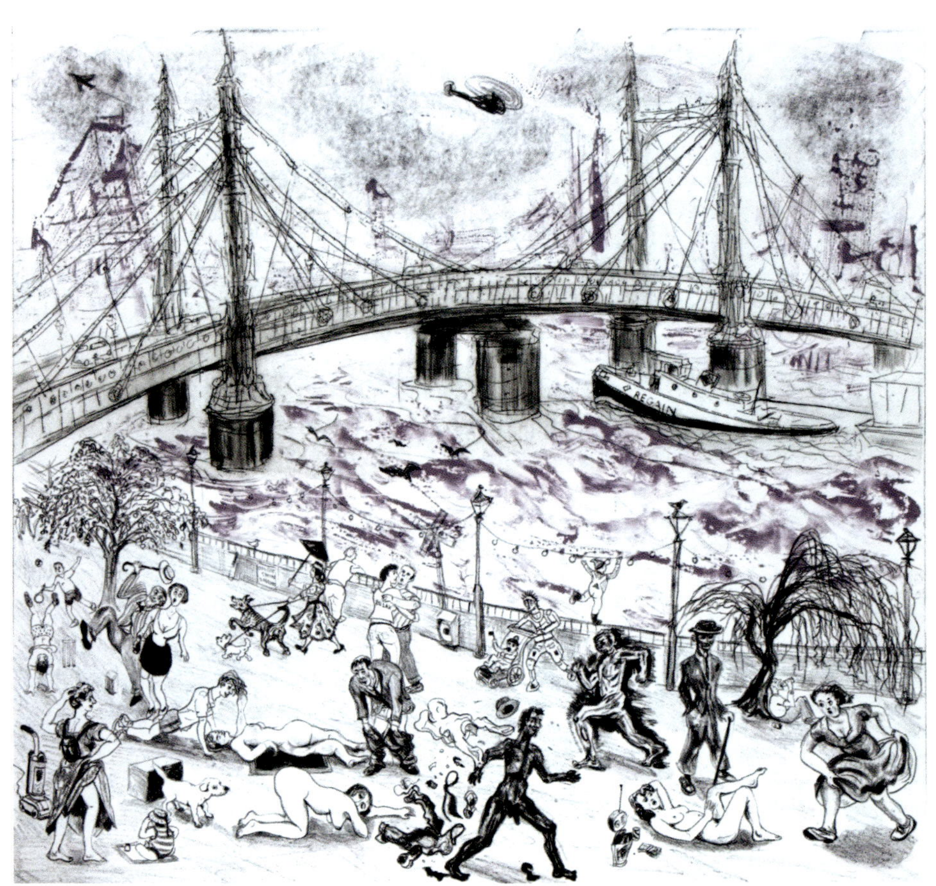

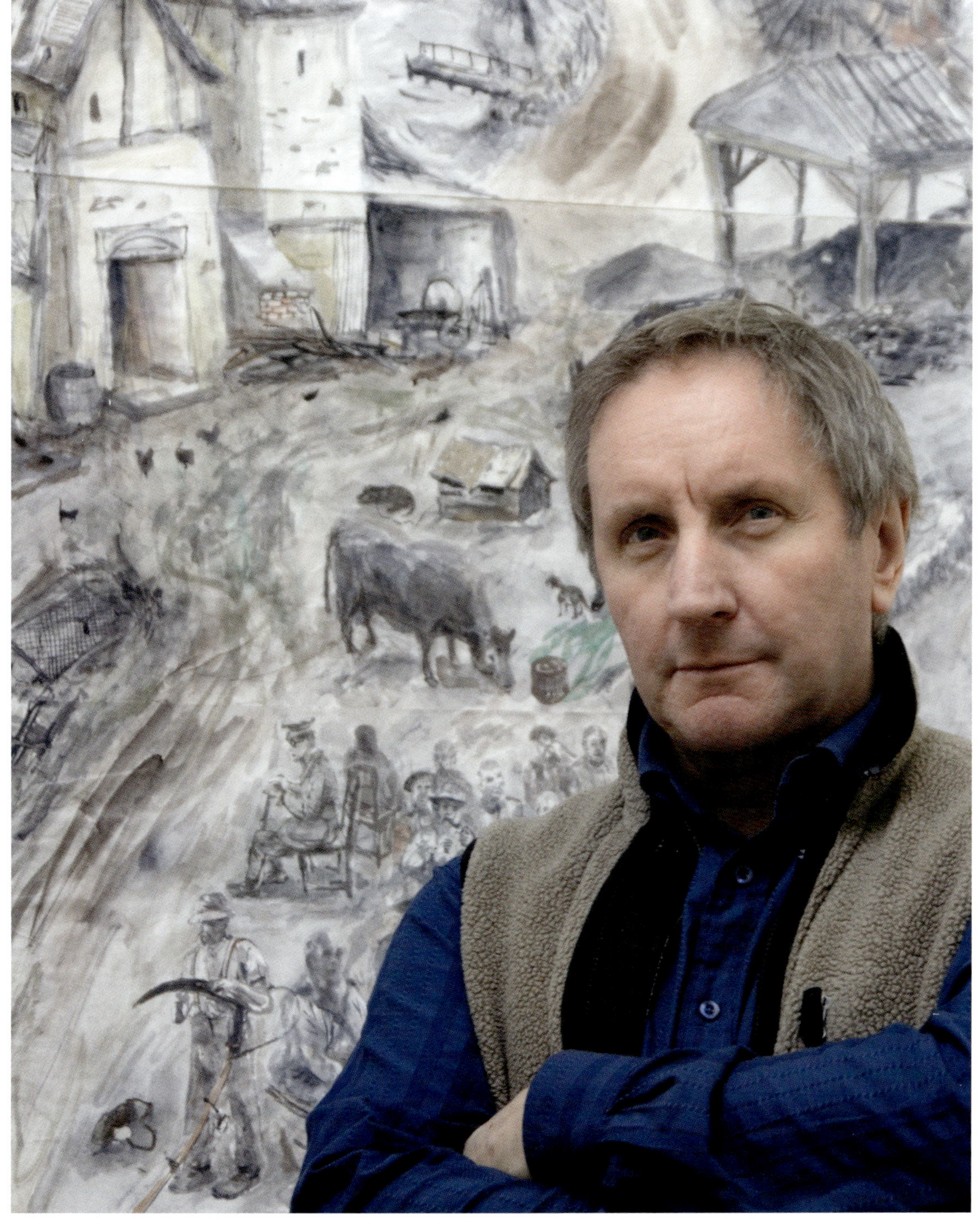

TOM PHILLIPS CBE RA

Elected ARA 9th May 1984
Elected RA 7th December 1989

Concerto Grosso
Pastel on paper
Courtesy of the artist
166 x 203 cm

Born 24th May 1937
London

After reading English at St Catherine's College, Oxford and at the same time studying drawing at the Ruskin School, Tom Phillips went to Camberwell School of Art in 1961 where Frank Auerbach was his main source of inspiration. He went on to teach at Bath Academy of Art, Ipswich School of Art and Wolverhampton Art College between 1965 and 1972. He has held many positions including Vice-Chair of the Copyright Council, Chairman of the Royal Academy Library and Exhibitions Committee. He is an Honorary Fellow of St Catherine's College, Oxford, Fellow of Leeds University and Slade Professor of Art History at the University of Oxford 2006. As an Internationally established artist and prominent Royal Academician he is represented in museum collections worldwide. Tom Phillips is well known for his pioneering artist's book 'A Humument' and his work on Dante's Inferno which he translated and illustrated (as co-director of the TV version which won the Italia Prize). Major retrospectives of his paintings have been held on both sides of the Atlantic.

Tom Philips was born in South London and still lives and works there.
www.tomphillips.co.uk

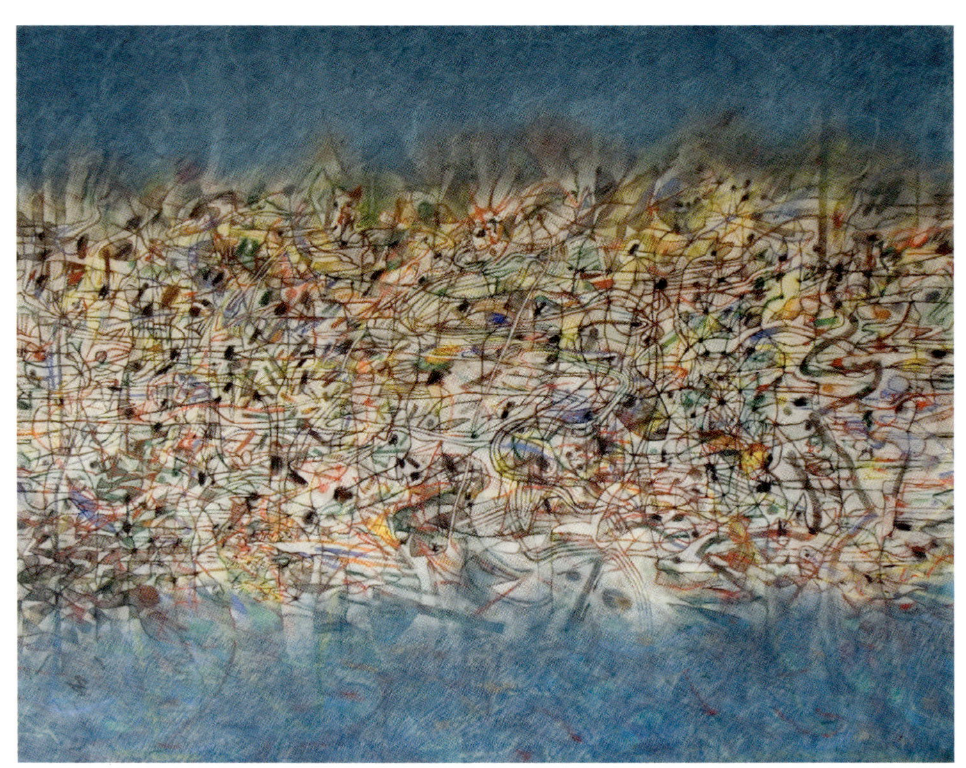

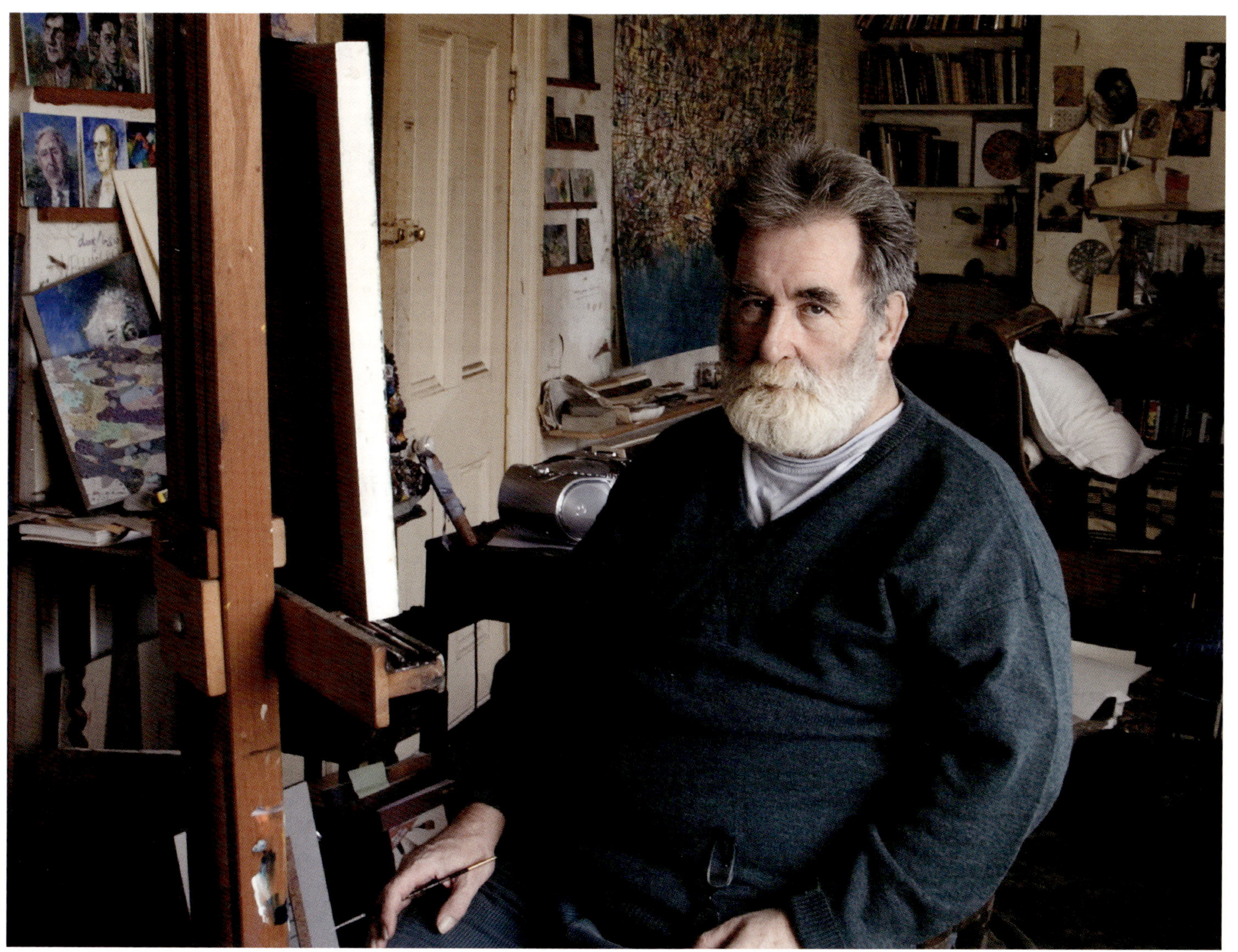

TOM PHILLIPS CBE RA

BARBARA RAE CBE RA RSA

Elected RA 29th May 1996

Siena Farm
Mixed media
Courtesy of the artist
105 x 86 cm

Born 10th December 1943
Falkirk

Barbara Rae studied at Edinburgh College of
Art from 1961-65 where she was awarded a
Travelling Scholarship which, in 1966, took
her to France and Spain.
She attended Moray House College of
Education and taught in Edinburgh until
1972. She then lectured in drawing, painting
and printmaking at Edinburgh College of
Education from 1972-74.

From 1975-96 she lectured in drawing and
painting at Glasgow School of Art. Barbara
Rae was made a Member of the Royal
Scottish Academy in 1962 and is, with Dame
Elizabeth Blackadder, one of the only two
women to be members both of the RA and
RSA. She has held many positions including
President of the Society of Scottish Artists,
member of the Royal Art Commission for
Scotland, member of the Board of the British
School in Rome and, in 1999 was made a
CBE and received an Honorary Doctorate from
Napier University, Edinburgh in 2000. In 2003
she received an Honorary Doctorate from
Aberdeen University and in the same year
was made an Honorary Fellow of the Royal
College of Art.

Barbara Rae lives and works in Edinburgh
and Los Angeles.
www.barbararae.com

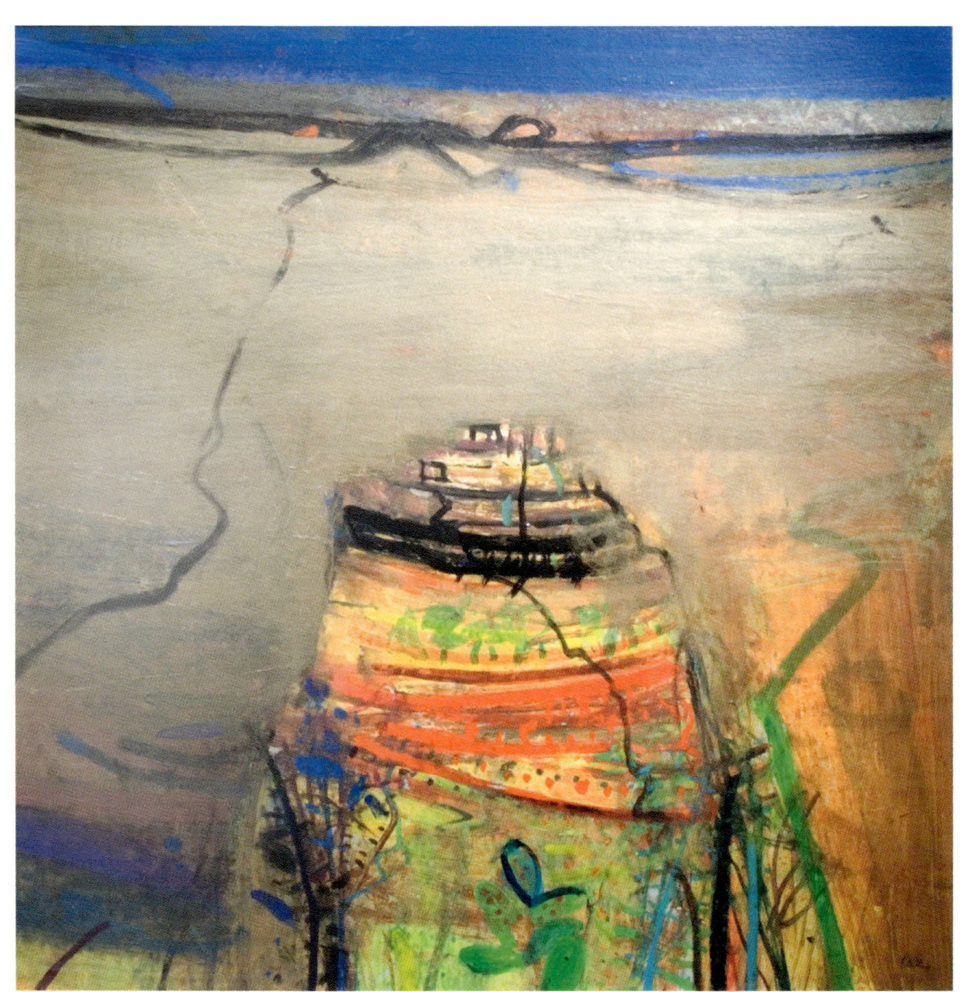

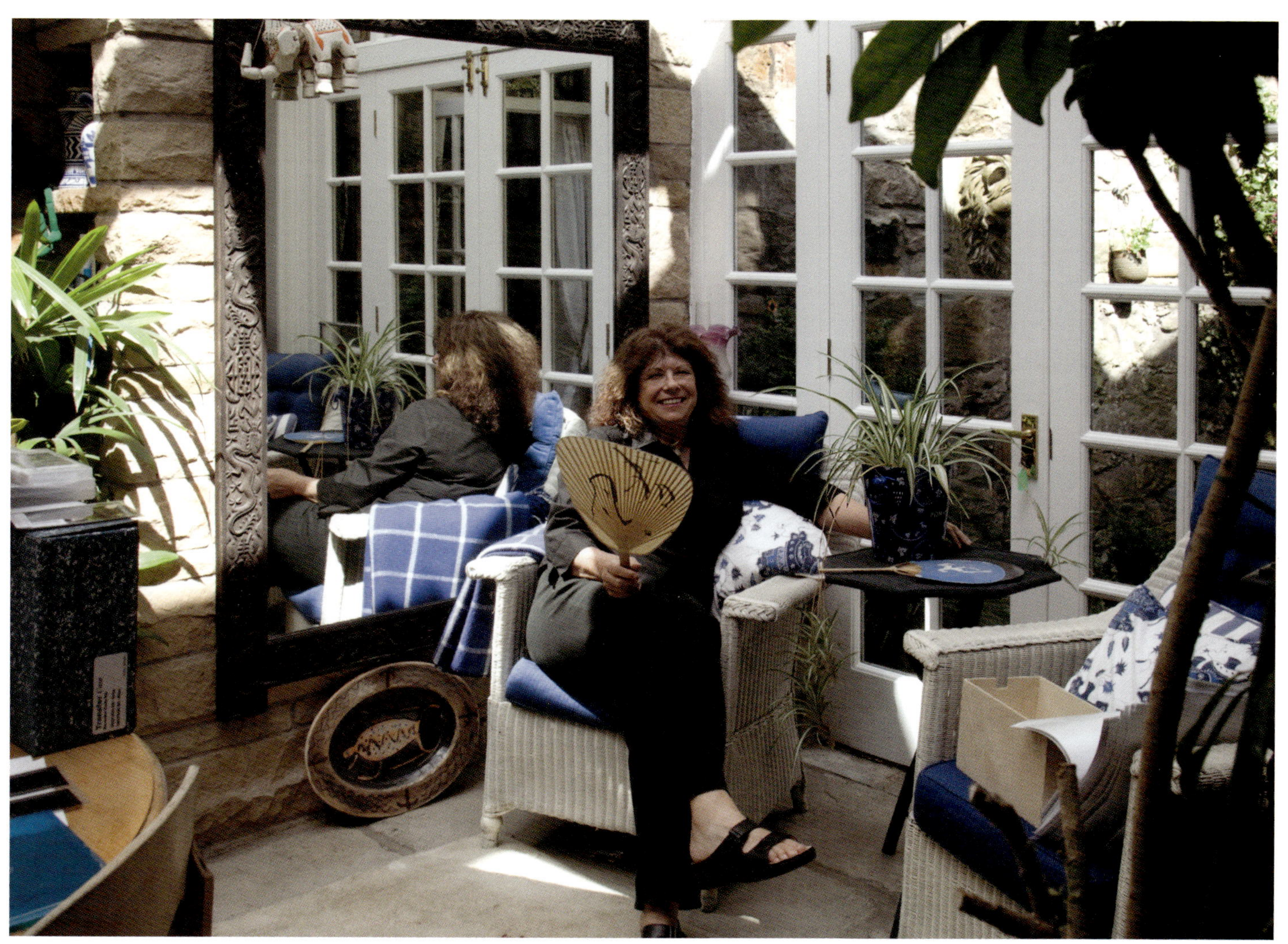

FIONA RAE RA

Elected RA 28th May 2002

'Life is full of pleasant gifts and surprises, you know!' 2007
Oil and acrylic on canvas
Copyright the artist;
Courtesy Timothy Taylor Gallery, London
183 x 150 cm

Born 10th October 1963
Hong Kong

Fiona Rae studied at Croydon College of Art from 1983-84, and Goldsmiths College from 1984-87.

Rae participated in the seminal exhibitions 'Freeze', 1988, curated by Damien Hirst, and 'Sensation: Young British Artists from the Saatchi Collection' at the Royal Academy of Arts, London, then Berlin and New York, 1997-2000. She was shortlisted for the Turner Prize in 1991 and appointed a Tate Artist Trustee in 2005, the same year that she completed a Master Artist residency at the Atlantic Center for the Arts in Florida, USA. Fiona Rae has exhibited widely throughout Europe, the Americas and Asia, and her work is represented in many museum collections. She has written of her work: *'I want to suggest unusual places where different kinds of things can coexist to create something new, like telling a story using half-remembered words and glimpses of unnameable or unexpected imagery to create a vivid world in someone else's imagination…'*

Fiona Rae lives and works in London

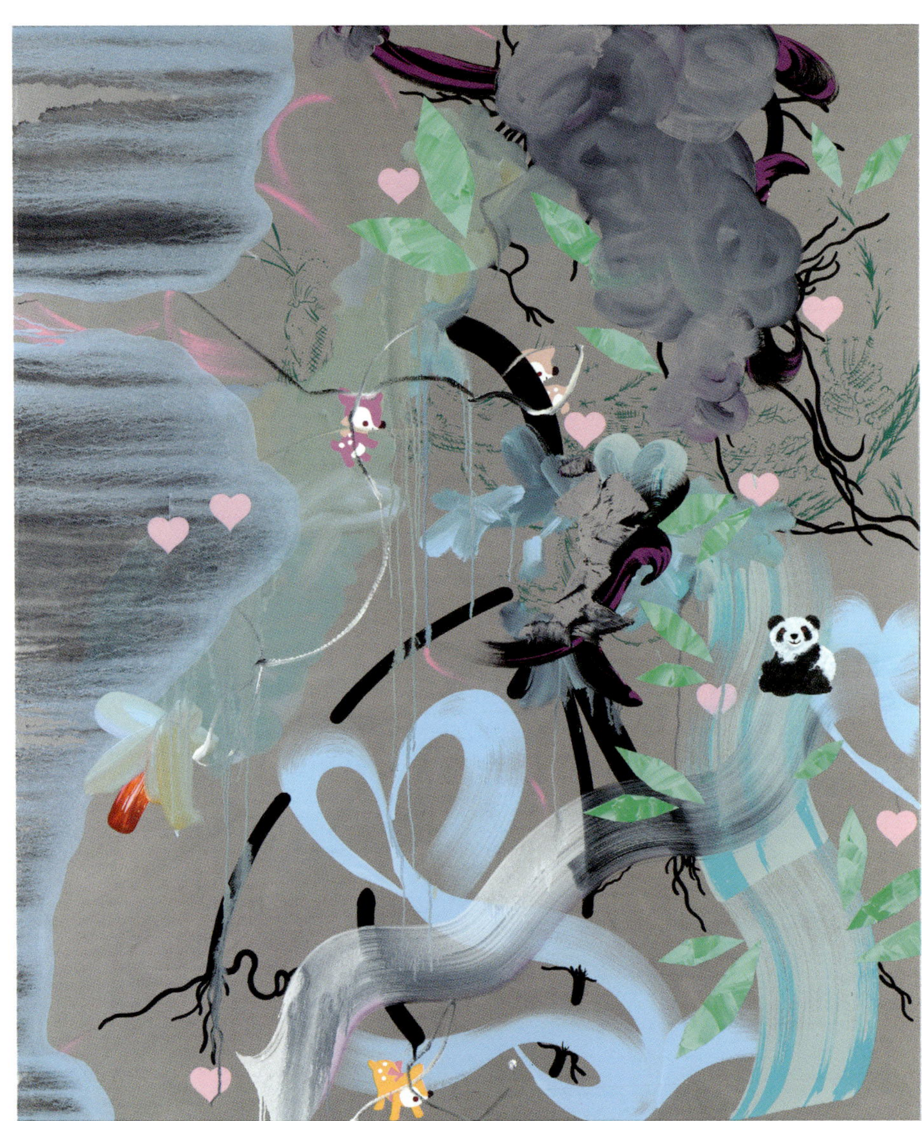

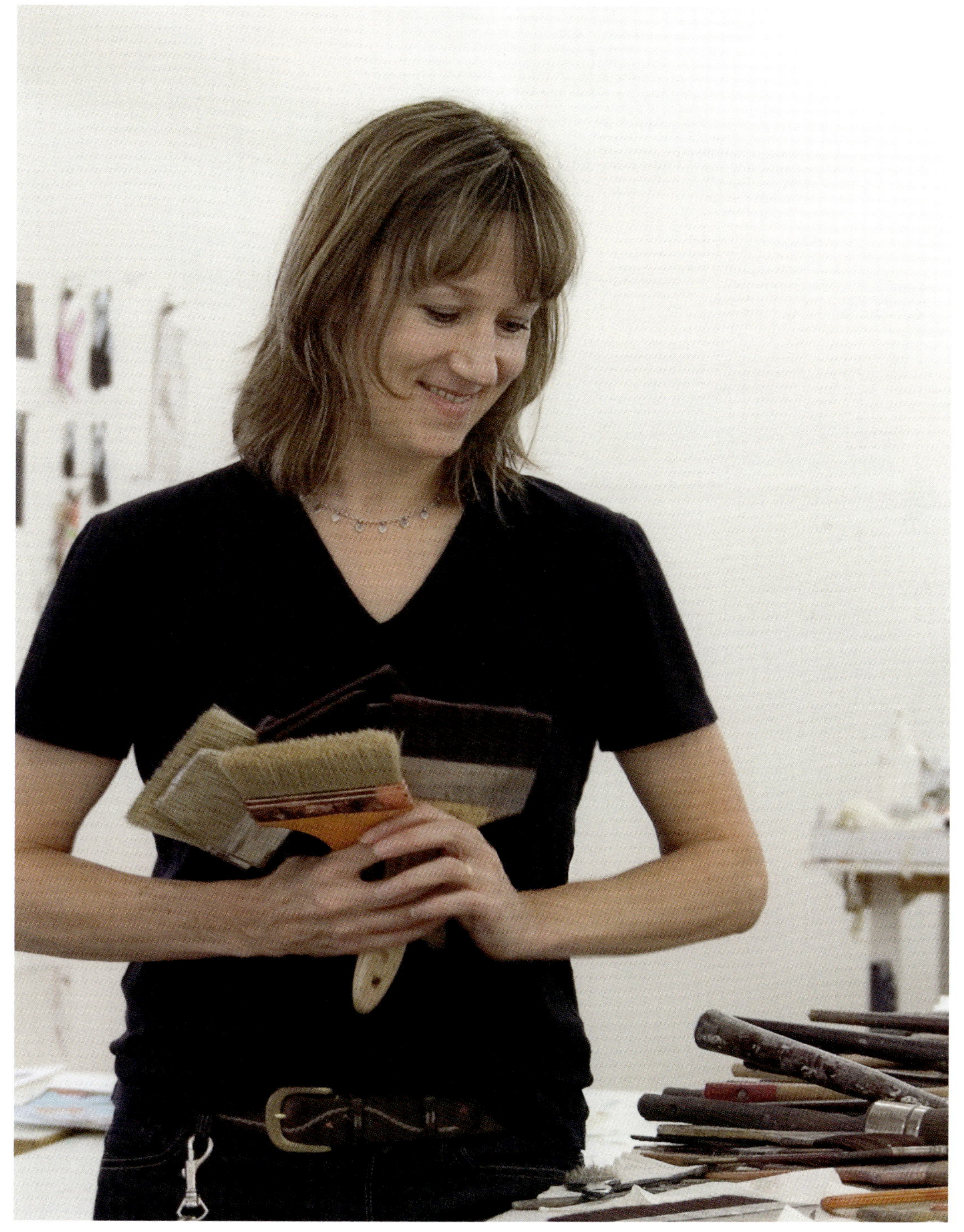

FIONA RAE RA

DAVID REMFRY MBE RA

Elected RA 2nd June 2006

Untitled
Watercolour on paper
Courtesy of the artist
152 x 76 cm

Born 30th July 1942
Sussex

David Remfry studied at Hull College of Art from 1959-64. He started to exhibit in London in 1973 and since then has had more than 50 solo exhibitions worldwide, predominantly in the USA but also extensively in the UK, Holland and Germany. Remfry was awarded an MBE in 2001 for his services to British Art in America.

Although he has portraits in the National Portrait Gallery Collection, he is well-known for his large watercolour paintings of people dancing in which he captures the extraordinary expressions and poses of the dancers. He invites people into his studio at the top of the famous Chelsea Hotel in New York where they dance in a corner in front of a large window which looks out over the rooftops of central Manhattan dominated by the nearby Empire State Building. *I'm fascinated by the human predicament, I am obsessed with how people behave together – how we embrace as we dance, how we 'distract ourselves' '* says Remfry.

David Remfry lives and works in London and New York.
www.davidremfry.com

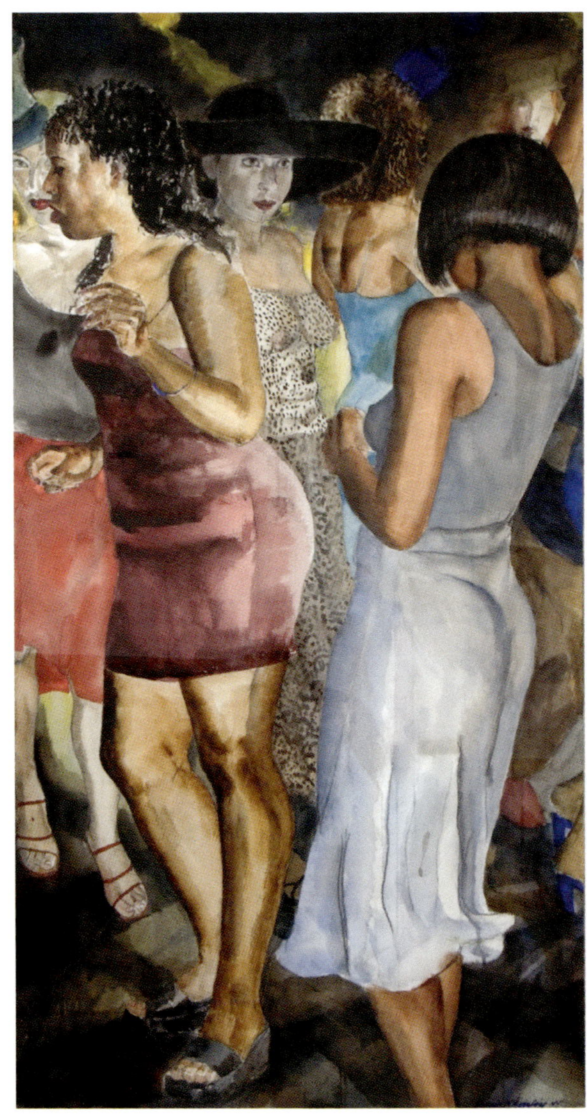

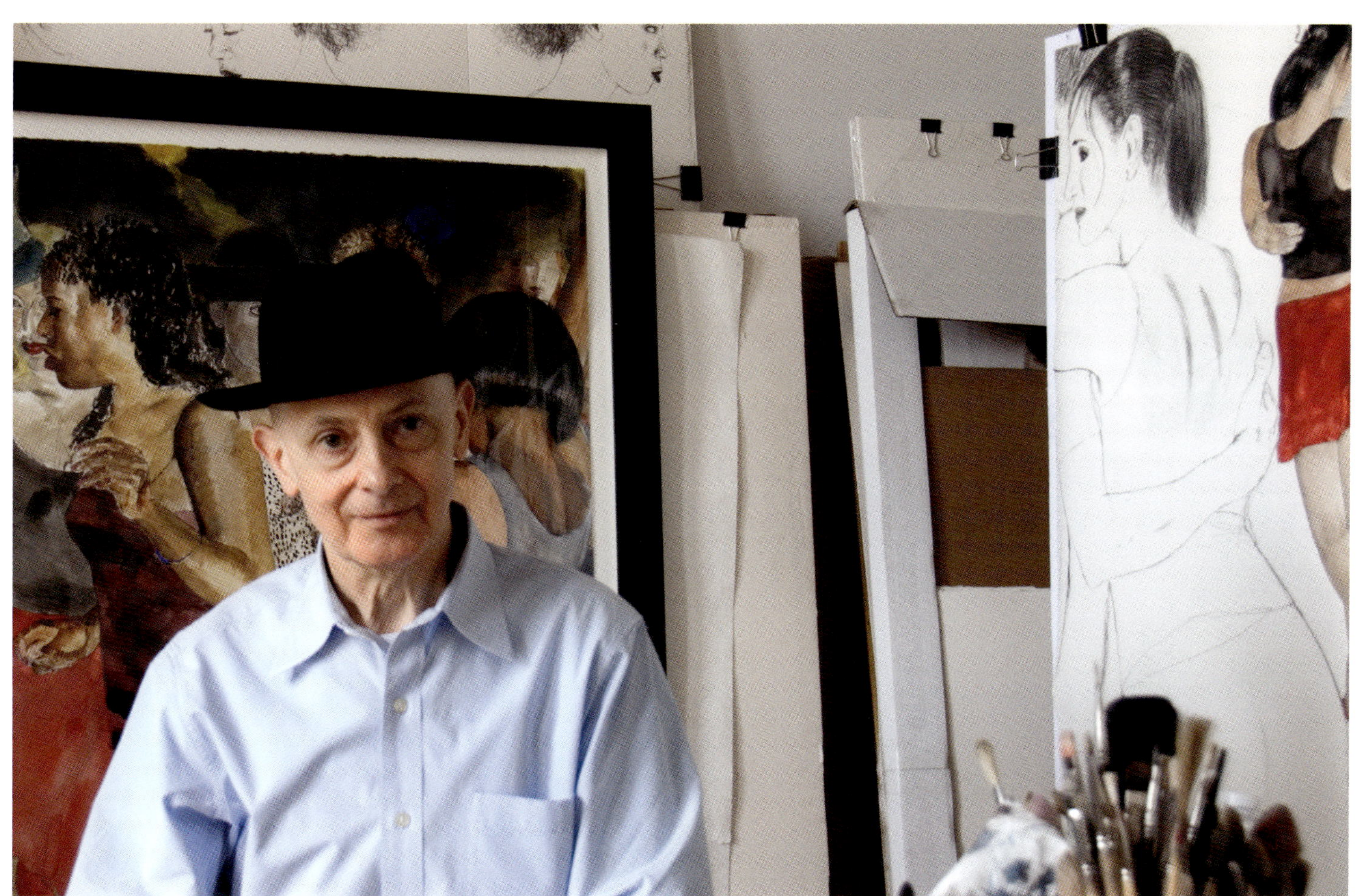

DAVID REMFRY MBE RA

MICHAEL ROONEY RA

Elected ARA 1st May 1990
Elected RA 26th June 1991

Artist Approaching his Model
Gouache on paper
Courtesy of the artist
18 x 28 cm diptych

Born 5th March 1944
Epsom

Michael Rooney studied at Sutton School of Art from 1959-62, Wimbledon School of Art from 1962-64 and subsequently at the Royal College of Art from 1964-67 where he was awarded the Austin Abbey Major Scholarship to study at the British School at Rome from 1967-68. There he was commissioned by the Franciscan Order to create a wall mosaic for a new Basilica in Nazareth, Israel. From 1968-82 he taught part-time at various art colleges

He says that his work mostly attempts to focus on describing in traditional, graphic, narrative and poetic terms, what is (perhaps overly) called 'The Human Condition'. Music, world literature, poetry and travel are, and have always been, crucial to reinforce the subject matter.

Paul Theroux said of his work – *'I respond to his work as to few other people's. For one thing, he is interested in 'difference', in happiness, in loss, in alienation. There is no faking and always a sort of wit and humour'.*

Michael Rooney lives and works in London and Oxfordshire.

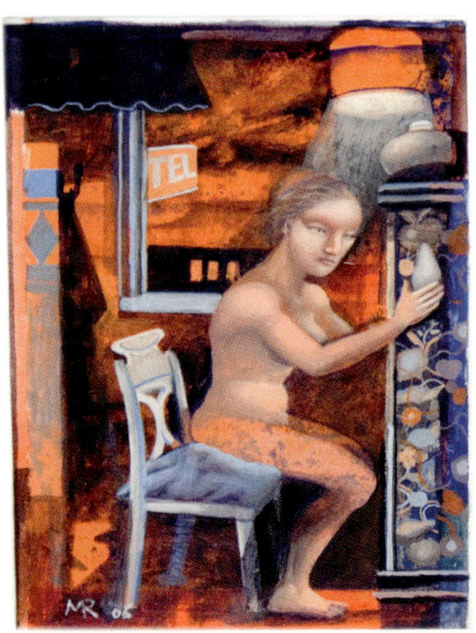
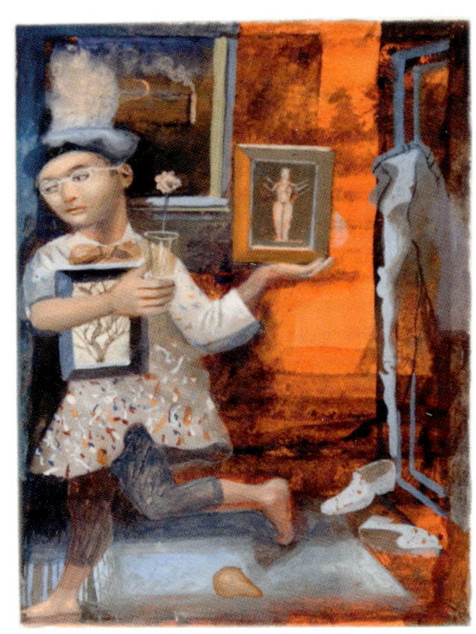

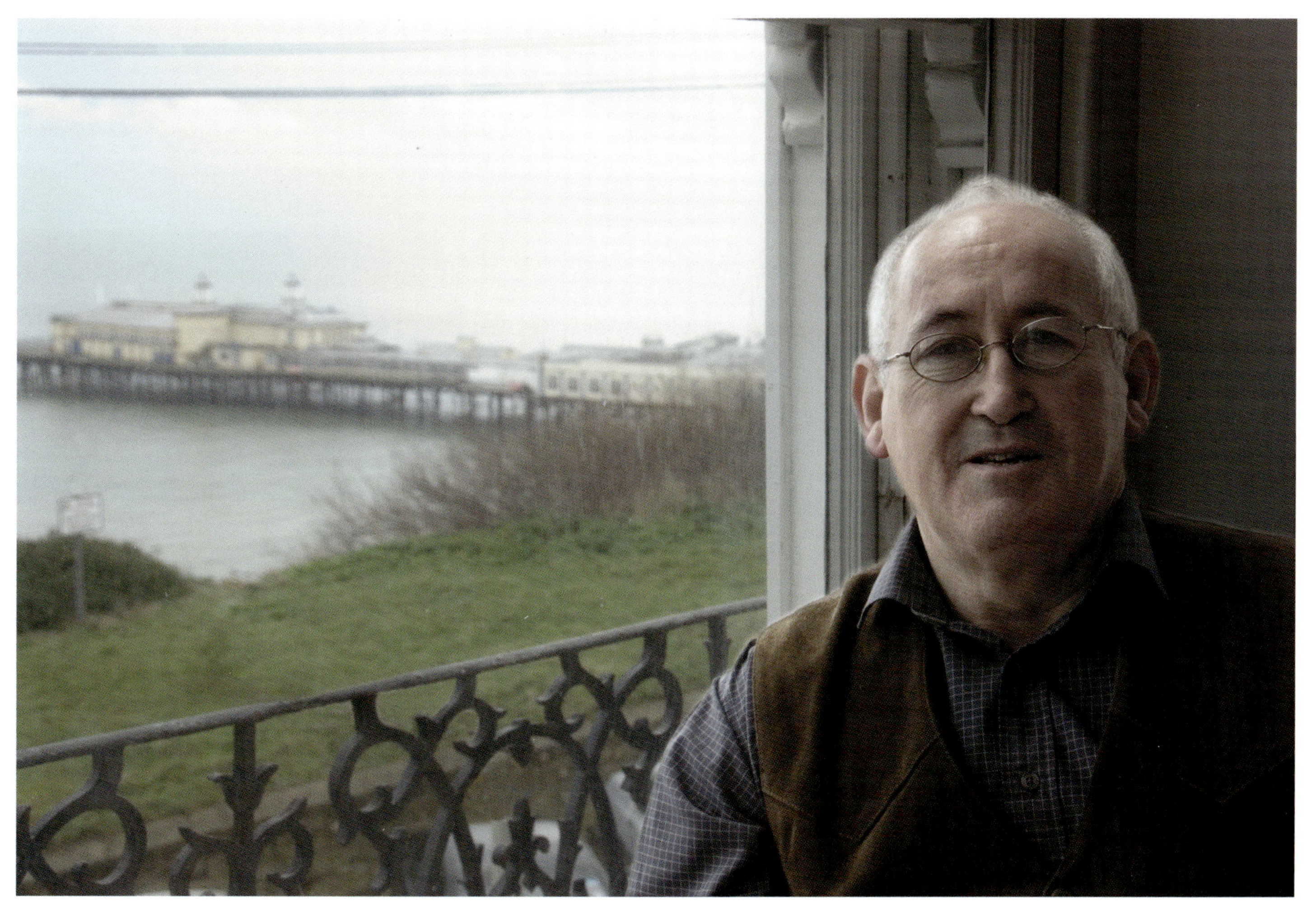

MICHAEL ROONEY RA

Elected RA 25th February 1969

… and the tree fell slowly forward
Watercolour on paper
Courtesy of the artist
83 x 59 cm

Born 27th October 1913
London

Leonard Rosoman studied at King Edward VII School of Art, University of Durham from 1930-35, the Royal Academy Schools from 1935-36 and the Central School of Arts and Crafts from 1936-37. Rosoman was appointed Official War Artist to the Admiralty in 1943 working with the Pacific Fleet. The work from this period was not exhibited until 1989, in a 'War Retrospective' at the Imperial War Museum. 'The Falling Wall', painted when he was a Fireman Artist, has become an icon of the Blitz.

Rosoman taught at Reiman School of Art, London 1937-39, Camberwell School of Art from 1946-47, Edinburgh College of Art from 1948-56, Chelsea School of Art 1956-57 and the Royal College of Art 1957-78. He was made an OBE in 1981 and an Honorary Fellow of Edinburgh College of Art in 2005. His work has been widely exhibited in both the UK and USA and is in a number of public and private collections which include many murals for which he is well known. John McEwen wrote of Leonard Rosoman that *'…quirkiness both in subject matter and form enables Rosoman to move from intimate watercolours to public murals without his hand betraying any loss of spirit or enjoyment'*

Leonard Rosoman lives and works in London.

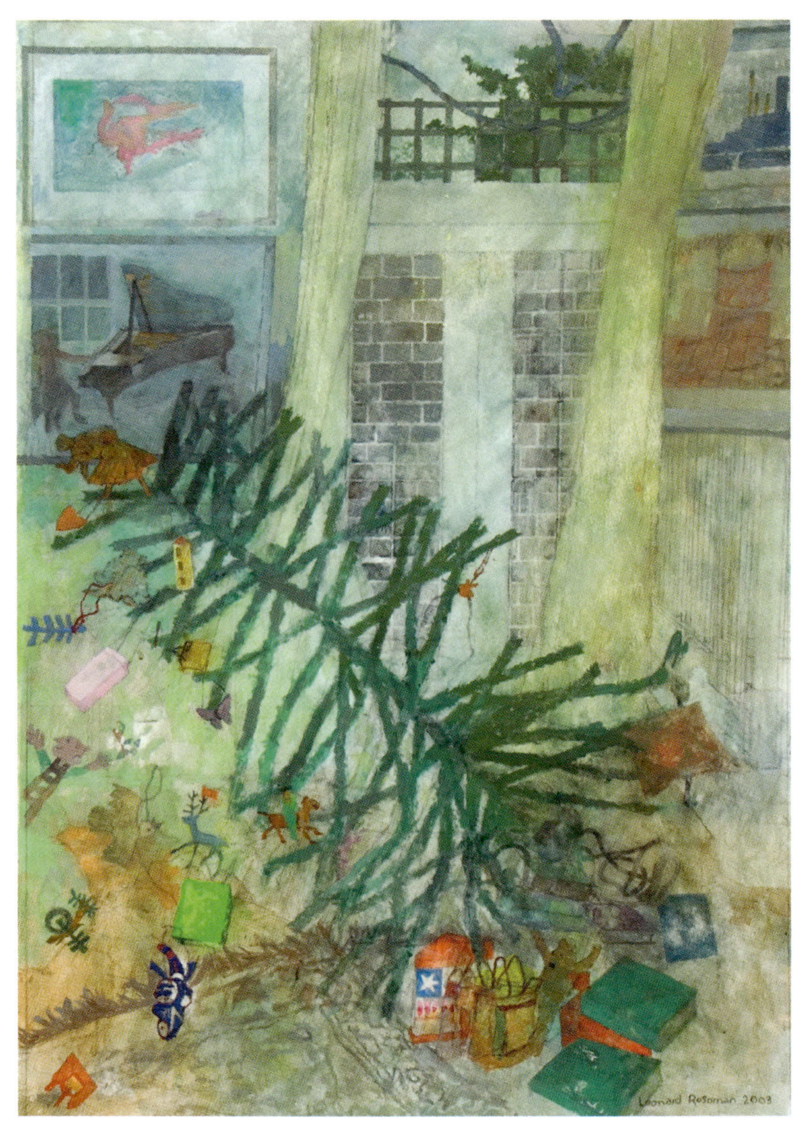

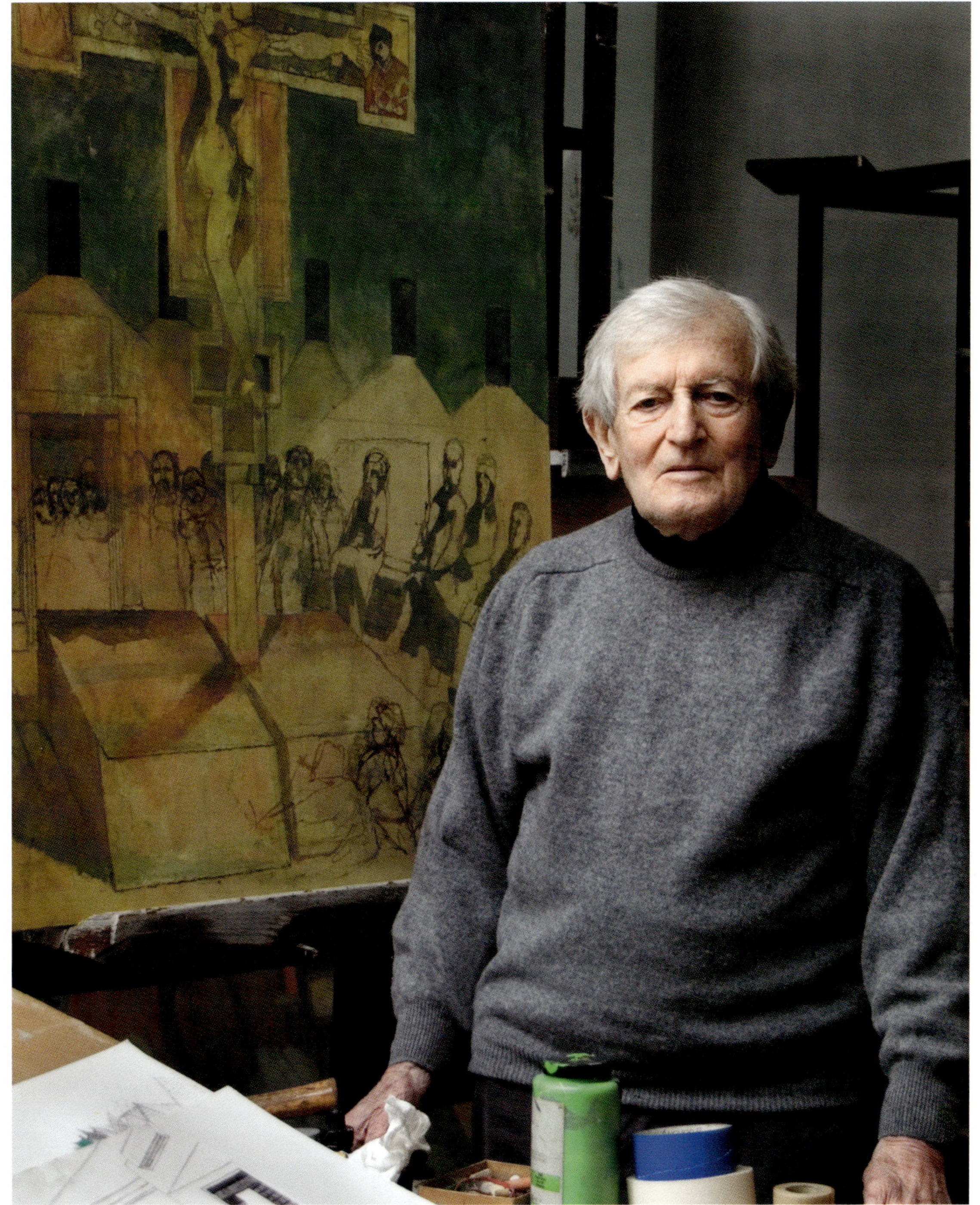

Elected RA 31st May 2007

Rosetta 2, 2005–2006
Oil on watercolour paper mounted on board
© Jenny Saville, courtesy of Gagosian Gallery
252 x 188 cm

Born 7th May 1970
Cambridge

At her graduation show every one of her paintings was sold. Charles Saatchi tracked down and purchased all the works in the show and offered her an 18 month contract to produce work which was then shown in his Saatchi Gallery launching a remarkable career. Her large canvases of exaggerated nudes often represent the disparity between the way women are perceived and the way they feel about their bodies. They appear violent, fleshy, physically deformed or bruised. They are thought-provoking, technically accomplished and challenging convention. Interviewed by Simon Schama she said: *'I have to really work at the tension between getting the paint to have the sensory quality that I want and be constructive in terms of building the form of a stomach, for example, or creating the inner crevice of a thigh. The more I do it, the more the space between abstraction and figuration becomes interesting – I want a painting realism.'*

In 2003 Saville discovered Palermo and a world that she had carried in her head since childhood. Did she find the reputed raw brutality of Sicilian life which she has moulded into her paintings?

Jenny Saville lives and works in Sicily.

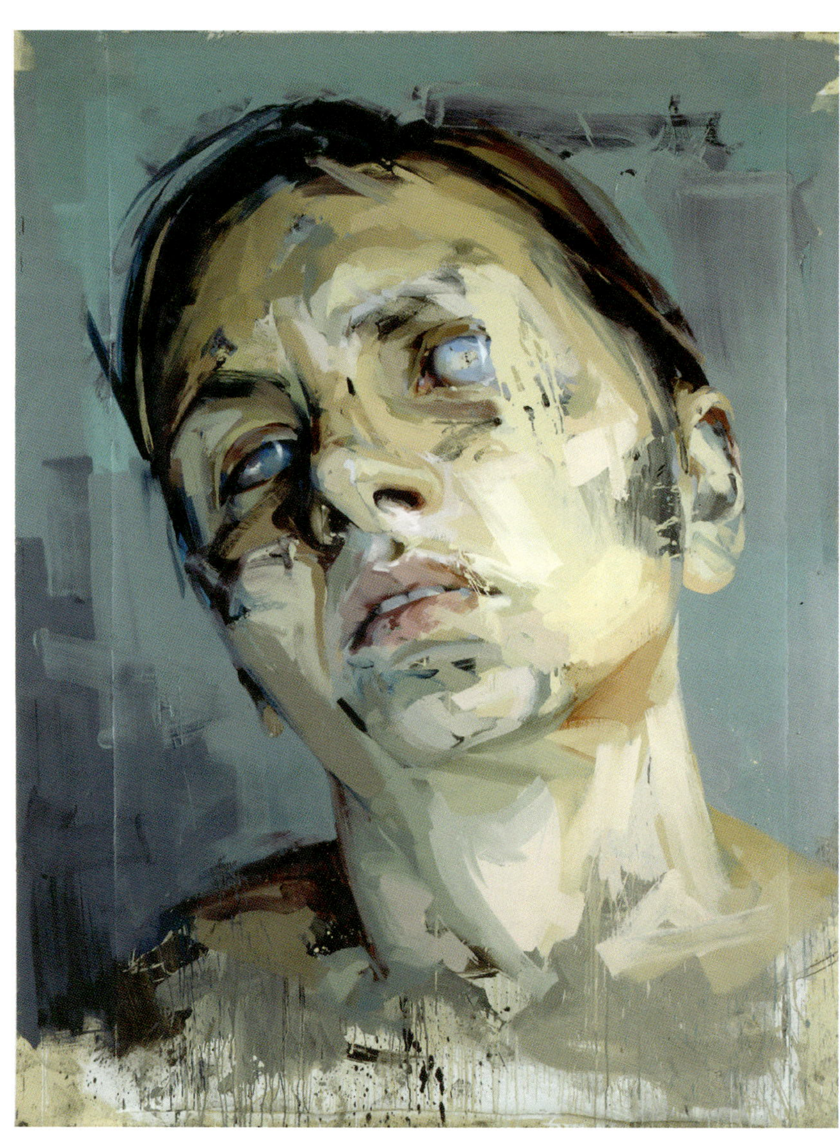

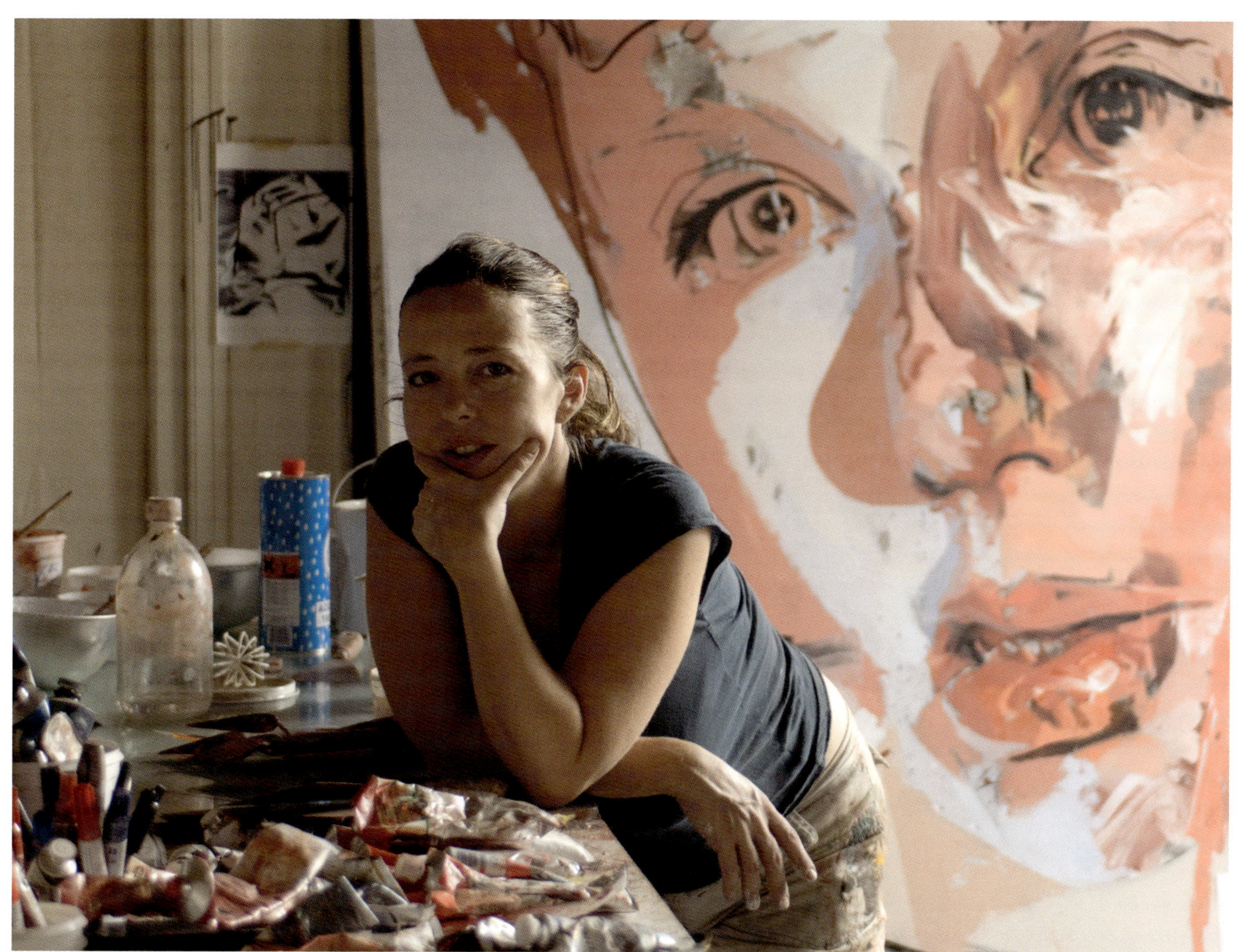

JENNY SAVILLE RA

PHILIP SUTTON RA

Elected ARA 13th May 1977
Elected RA 8th December 1988

Seabirds with Morning Dew
Oil on canvas
Courtesy of the artist
67 x 67 cm

Born 20th October 1928
Poole, Dorset

Philip Sutton studied under William Coldstream at the Slade School of Fine Art from 1948-53. He won the Summer Composition Prize and travelled to Spain, France and Italy on scholarships before returning to teach at the Slade School of Fine Art from 1954-88.

Sutton has travelled extensively to paint. In 1963 he took his family to Australia and Fiji and returned the following year with a wealth of tropical landscapes. After a return visit to Australia in 1980 he brought back large paintings of the Great Barrier Reef which were exhibited at the Royal Academy in 1982. While engaging in many forms of visual art, Sutton is best known for his sizeable and highly coloured paintings of landscape, flowers and people. He says that *'for me colour is all about invention, having the freedom to choose from a kaleidoscope of options rather than matching reality. I feel like a wild musician running through an orchestra playing any instrument I wish'.*

Philip Sutton lives and works in Pembrokeshire

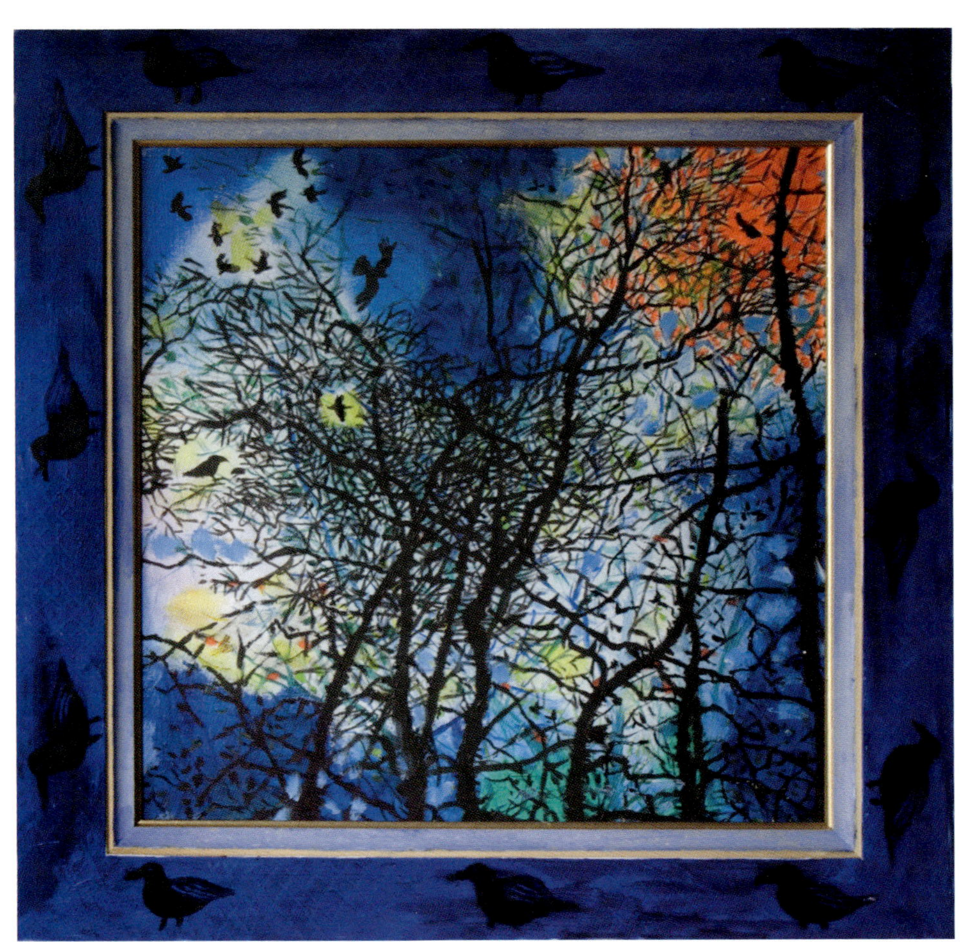

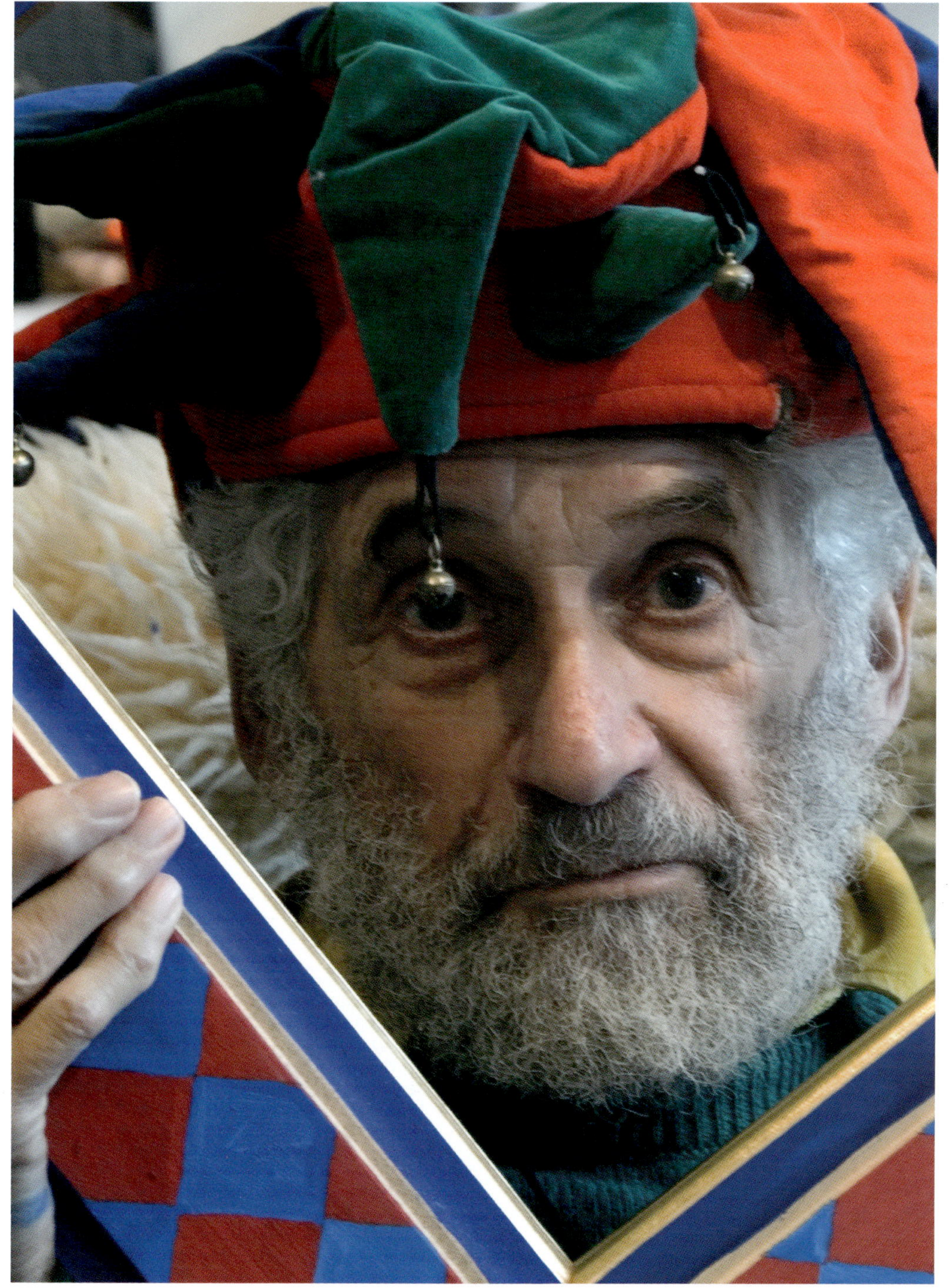

JOE TILSON RA

Elected ARA 20th May 1985
Elected RA 26th June 1991

Conjunction-Sangiovese, Notte (VI), 2003
Mixed media on paper
Courtesy of the artist
122 x 114 cm

Born 24th August 1928
London

Joe Tilson worked as a carpenter and joiner from 1944-46 before serving in the Royal Air Force from 1946-49. After his National Service he studied at St Martin's School of Art and, in 1952, at the Royal College of Art. In 1955 he won the Rome Prize taking him to Italy where he met his wife, Joslyn Morton, who was studying in Milan. After marrying in Venice and some time in Catalonia, they returned to London where Tilson taught at St Martin's School of Art from 1958-63, the Slade School of Art, University College London, King's College Newcastle upon Tyne, the School of Visual Arts New York and the Hochschule für Bildende Kunste Hamburg. One of the original 'Pop' artists with Peter Blake, David Hockney, the late Ron Kitaj and Allen Jones, he was soon led away by his deep dissatisfaction with industrial progress and the consumer society of the 1960s. His paintings, constructions, reliefs, prints and multiples have been widely exhibited and internationally collected. Attempt to enquire into the aesthetics of his work and Tilson will quote Barnett Newman who said: *'I have never met an ornithologist who thought that ornithology was for the birds'.*

Joe Tilson lives and works in London, Tuscany and Venice.

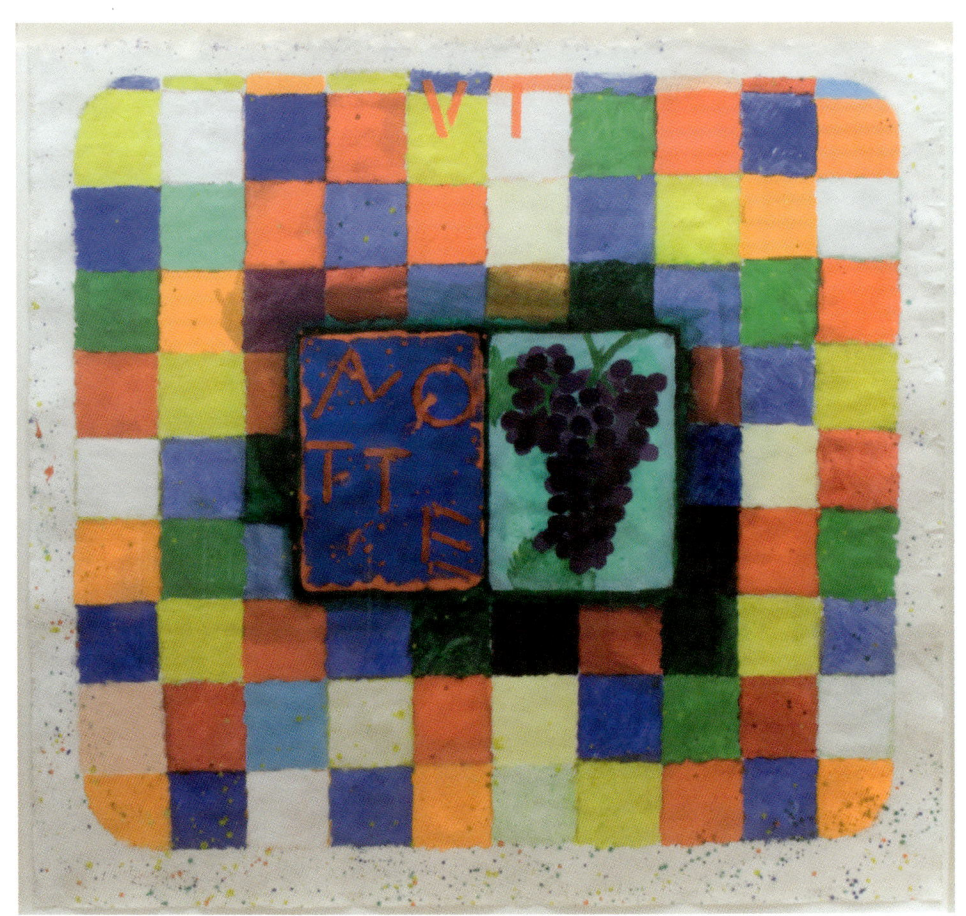

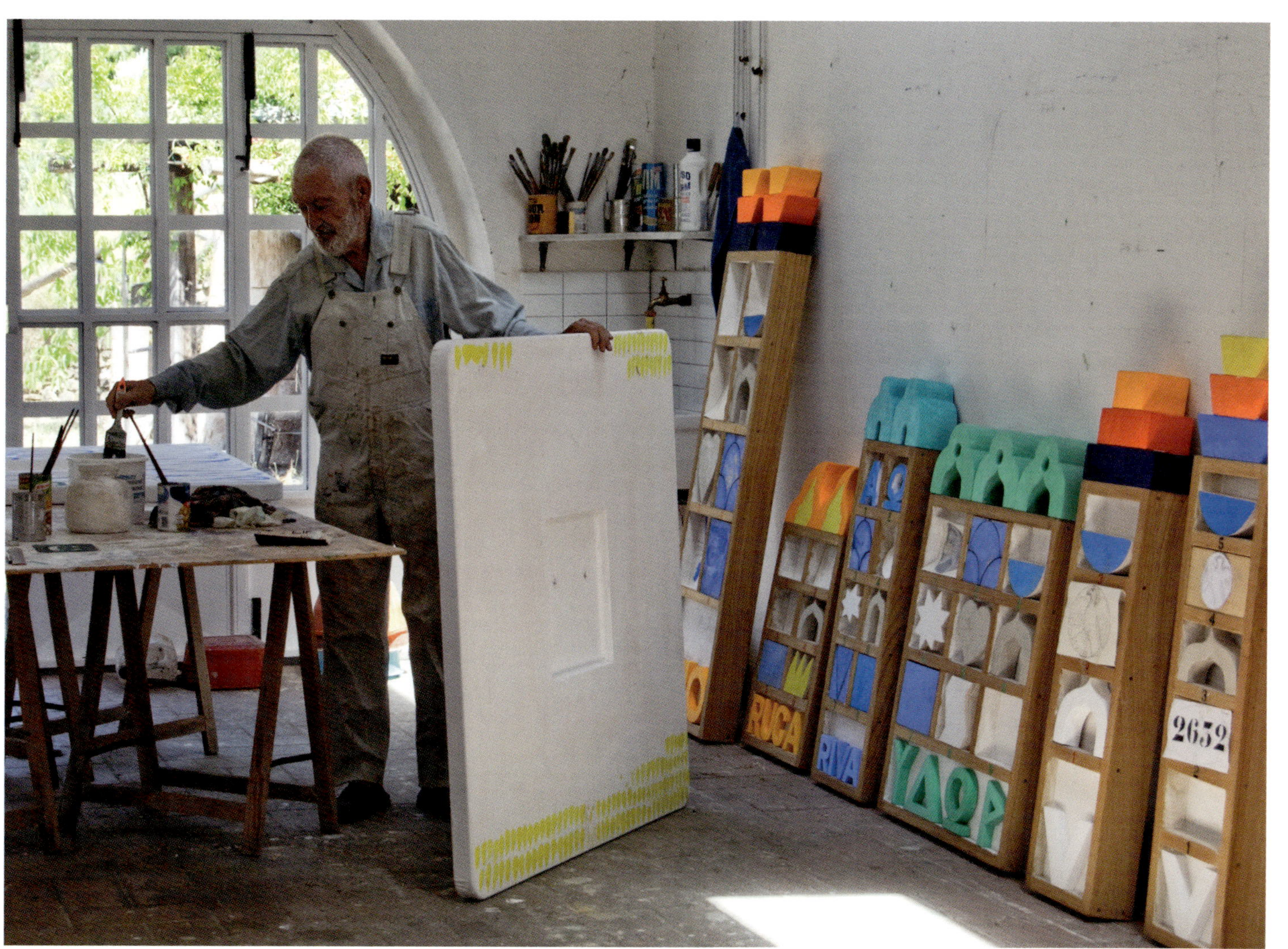

DAVID TINDLE RA

Elected ARA 27th April 1973
Elected RA 9th May 1979

Cueda's Daydreams, 2005-6
Egg tempera on canvas on board
Courtesy of the artist
50 x 70 cm

Born 29th April 1932
Huddersfield

David Tindle studied at the Coventry School of Art from 1945-47. He taught at Hornsey College of Art and Byam Shaw School of Art from 1959-74 and in 1972 was appointed visiting tutor at the Royal College of Art where he remained until 1983 being made a Fellow in 1981 and Honorary Fellow in 1984.
He went on to be made Ruskin Master of Drawing at Oxford from 1985-87.
His first solo exhibition was at the Piccadilly Gallery in 1954 moving to Fischer Fine Art in 1985 and the Redfern Gallery in 1994 where he has had a solo exhibition every other year since. His work has been shown widely throughout Europe and the UK and is in many public and private collections. Commissions include portraits of Sir Dirk Bogarde, Lord Sainsbury and the stage design for Tchaikovsky's opera 'Yolanta' at the Aldeburgh Festival. David Tindle's meticulous egg tempera paintings reflect his romanticism and imaginative sensitivity – somewhere between figurative and abstract sometimes brushed by surrealism and rendered in gentle tones which radiate an almost luminous glow.
Tindle says *'I am no longer content to use the ever ready window-scape, it does not satisfy my many interests neither does it fulfil the vision of my inner eye'*.

David Tindle lives and works in Tuscany.

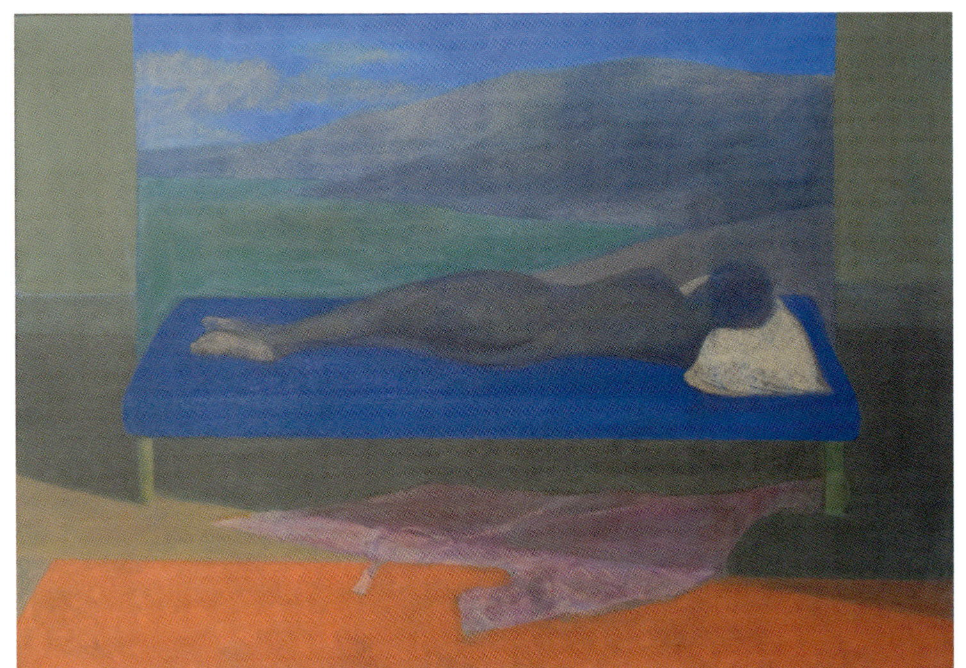

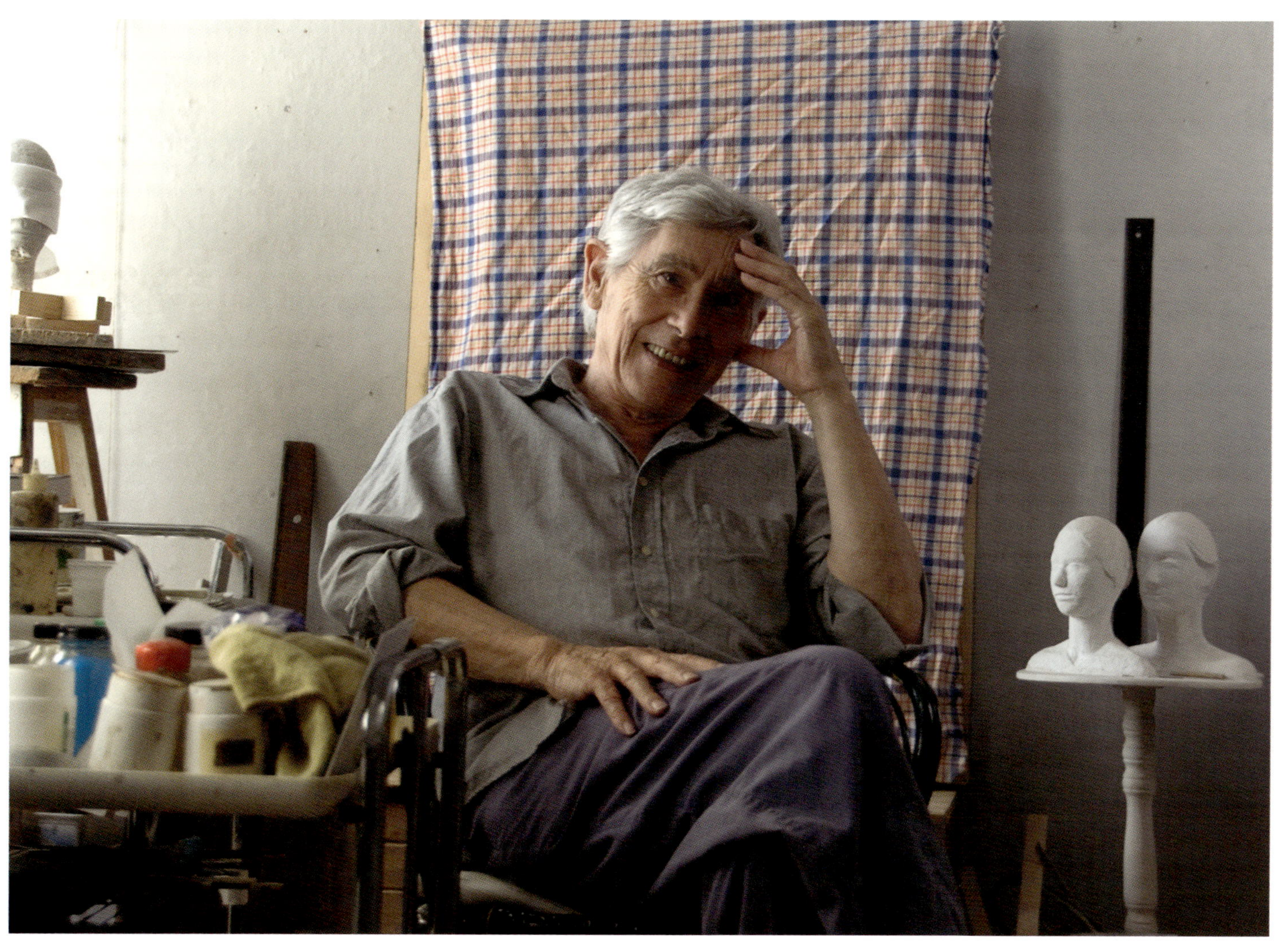

DAVID TINDLE RA

ANTHONY WHISHAW RA

Elected RA 7th December 1989

Shaped interior 2004/7
Acrylic/collage/board
Courtesy of the artist
35 x 67 cm

Born 22nd May 1930
London

Anthony Whishaw studied at Chelsea School of Art from 1948-52 and at the Royal College of Art from 1952-55 during which time he gained an Art Travelling Scholarship, a Royal College of Art Drawing Prize, an Abbey Minor Scholarship and a Spanish Government Scholarship. He was elected a Member of the London Group in 1979 and Member of the Royal West of England Academy in 1992. Whishaw has won many awards and his work has been exhibited in the UK, Spain, Brazil, Finland, Australia and the USA.
Whishaw says:'Within the various series one of my interests is the depiction of different kinds of space. Deep space; sky, receding perspectives – shallower space; forests, spinneys – shallower still; urban interiors, still lifes and finally micro space with little sense of scale, no top, bottom, or side, analogous to looking straight down at the soil or through a microscope. Other topics include movement of natural forces: river / sea meeting rock, wood, urban structures, tidal surges. The wind blowing: water surfaces, wheat fields, sand dunes, trees. Electro-chemical activity,fire, the eye tracking pin prick illusions of light over the surface of the canvas'.

Anthony Whishaw lives and works in London.
www.anthonywhishaw.com

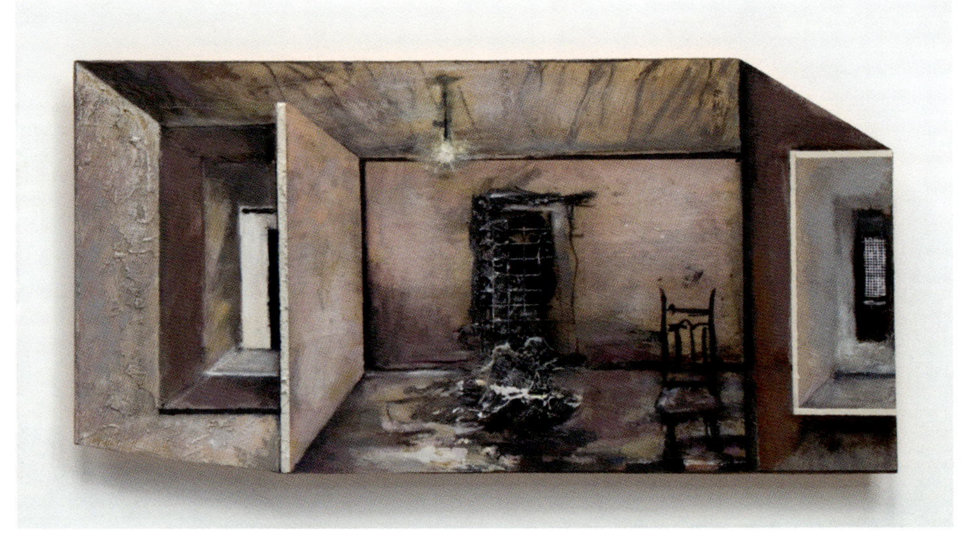

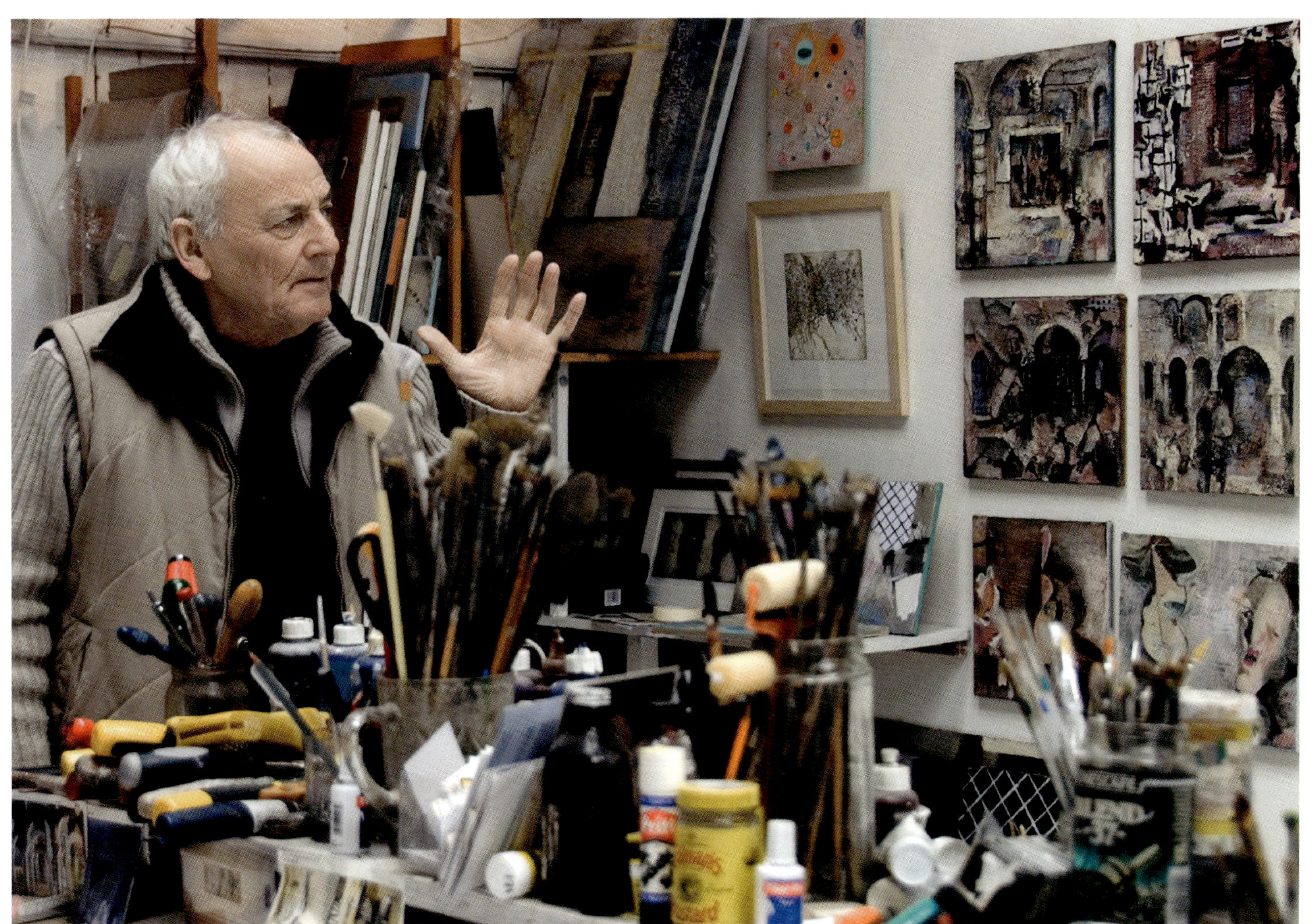

Dennis Toff (b 1926) trained at the School of Photography of the Regent Street Polytechnic (now University of Westminster) in 1942 and served in the photographic branch of the Fleet Air Arm during World War II. He left photography in 1950 to pursue a successful business career returning on retirement in 1993.

Since then his work has been exhibited in Australia, Austria, Denmark, France, Italy, Spain, USA and the UK including the Royal Photographic International Print Exhibition, The Association of Photographers Open, the London Salon of Photography, London Independent Photography Annual Exhibitions and the Mall Galleries. He has had solo exhibitions at Christchurch, Dorset and the Barbican Arts Library. In the USA his work can be seen in the Candace Dwan Gallery in New York.

Dennis Toff has work in the collections of The National Portrait Gallery, The London Jewish Museum and is a Fellow of the Royal Photographic Society.

The portraits in this book form a Limited Edition of 15 Original Archival Pigment Prints of 33 cm x 48 cm each.

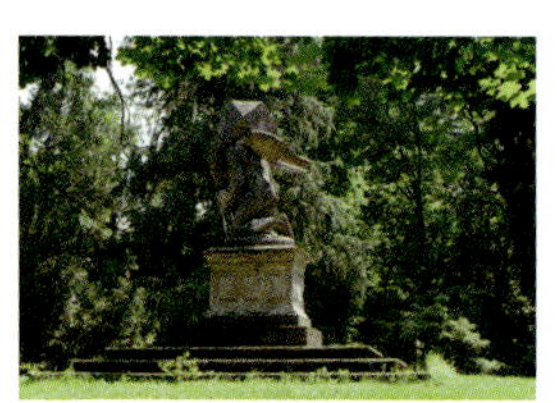

Jennifer Dickson RA
48-49

Bernard Dunstan RA
50-51

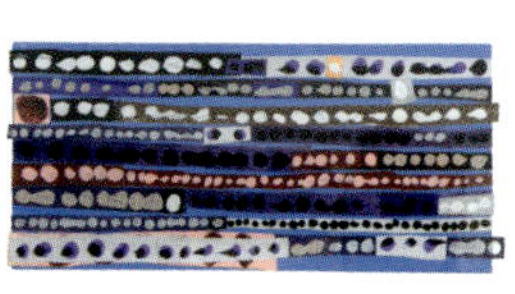

Jennifer Durrant RA
52-53

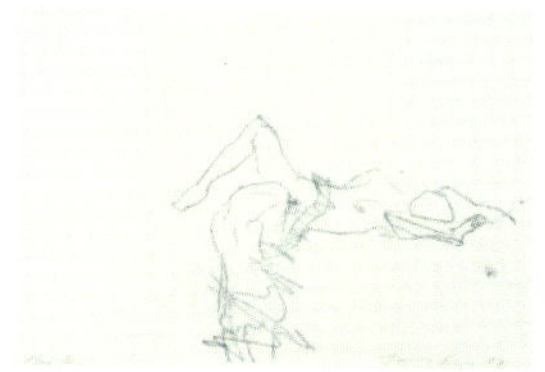

Tracey Emin RA
54-55

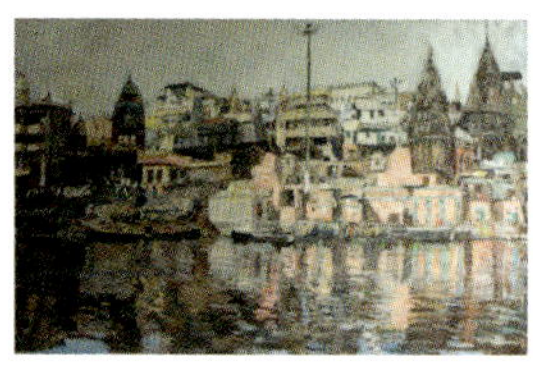

Anthony Eyton RA
56-57

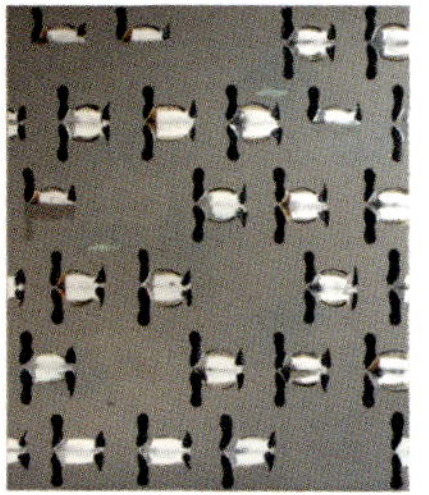

Stephen Farthing RA
58-59

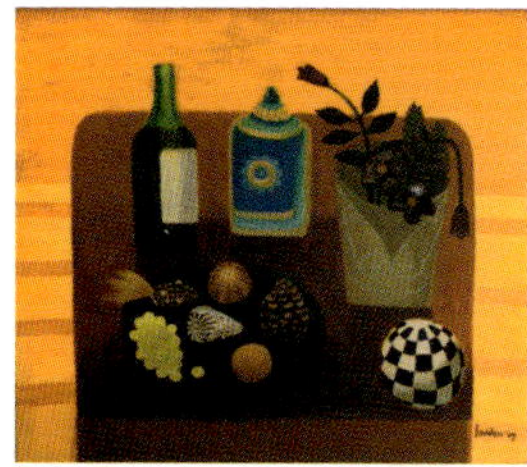

Mary Fedden OBE RA
60-61

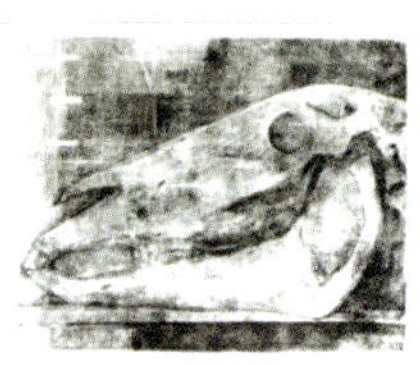

Peter Freeth RA
62-63

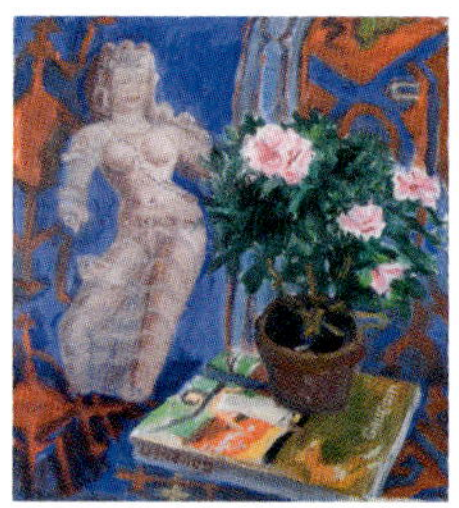

Frederick Gore CBE RA
64-65

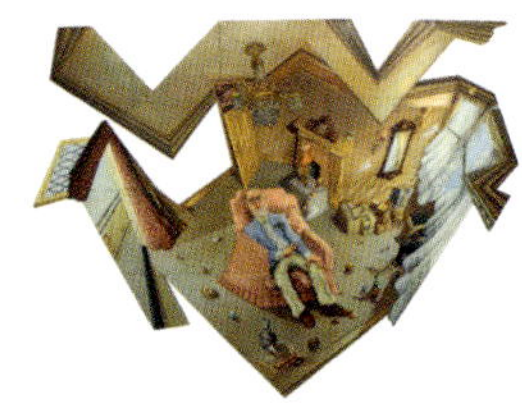

Anthony Green RA
66-67

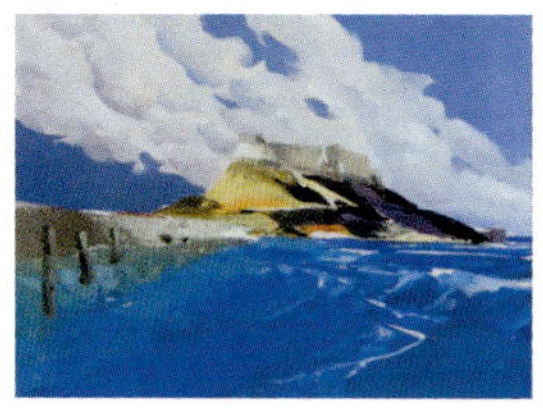

Donald Hamilton Fraser RA
68-69

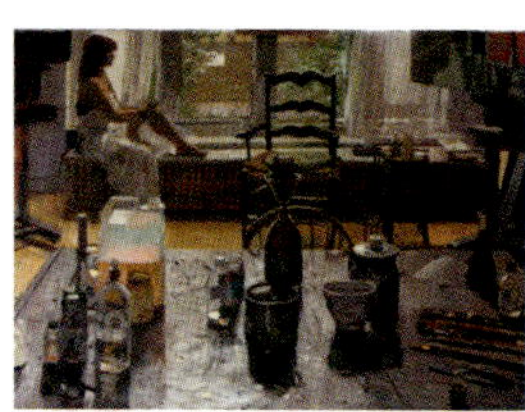

Ken Howard RA
70-71

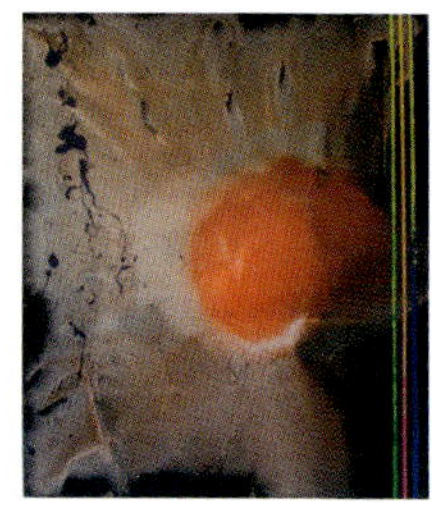

John Hoyland RA
72-73

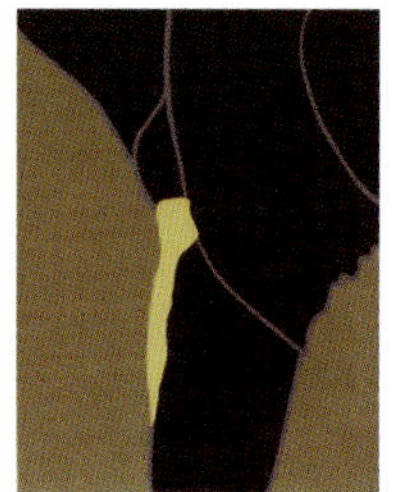

Gary Hume RA
74-75

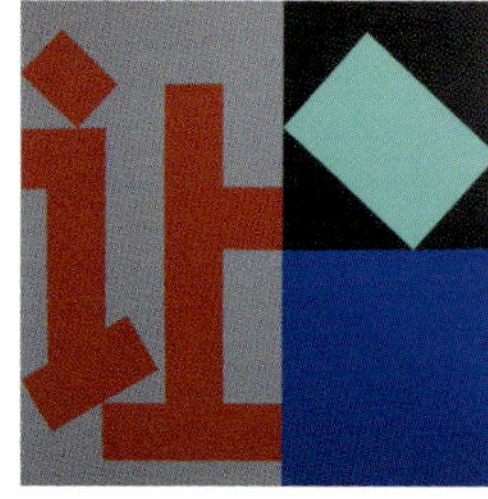

Paul Huxley RA
76-77

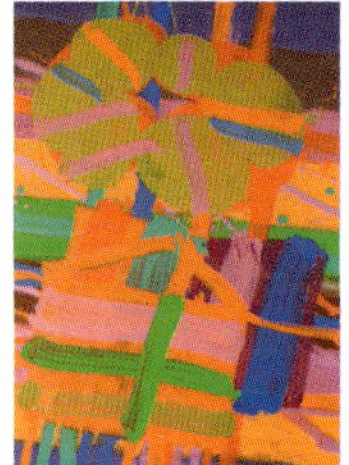

Albert Irvin RA
78-79

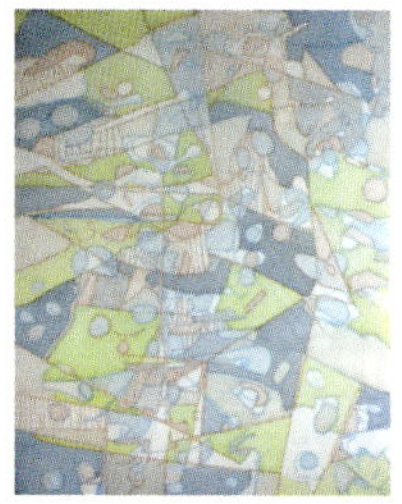

Flavia Irwin RA
80-81

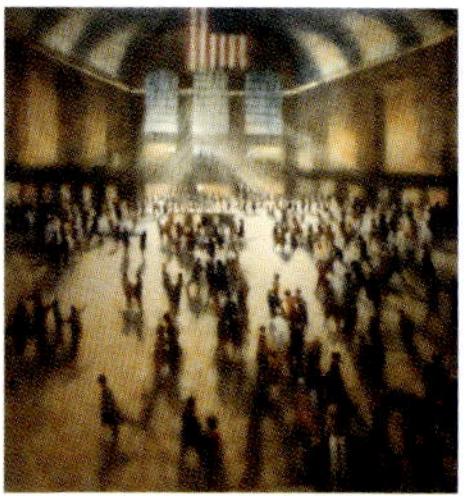

Bill Jacklin RA
82-83

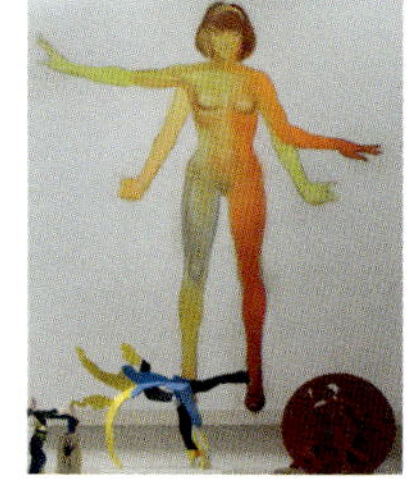

Allen Jones RA
84-85

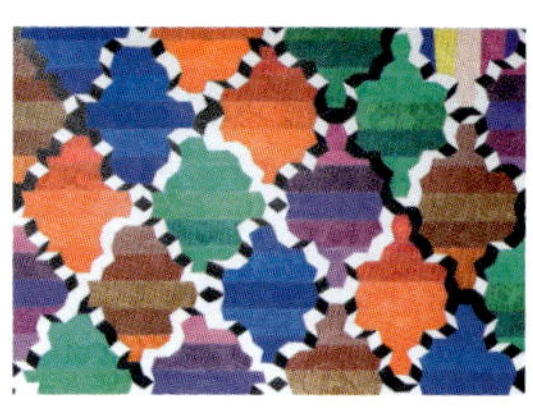

Michael Kidner RA
86-87